"The absorbing stories in *Maximum Leadership* go beyond inspiration to provide illuminating details about how and why the best CEOs add value to their organizations—yet do it in so many different ways. This useful book's global perspective and strategic approach can guide leaders anywhere in the world in their own quest for success."

—Rosabeth Moss Kanter, Harvard Business School,
Author of *World Class: Thriving Locally in the Global Economy*

"This book provides fascinating insights into how highly effective chief executives can impact stakeholder value. Transformation of a major corporation is an immense task. The lessons here are powerful and practical."

—Philip J. Quigley, Chairman of the Board,
President, and CEO, Pacific Telesis

"This book is a useful synthesis of broad management strategies. But it's also a revealing account of individual problems faced all over the world by people who find themselves CEOs of major corporations—candid, compelling, and very valuable."

—James E. Preston, Chairman and CEO, Avon

"An imaginative inside look at some of our leading corporations and the men and women who make them tick—insightful, intelligent, and usable."

—Gerry Roche, Chairman, Hendrick and Struggles

"The Bain directors offer 'maximum' insight into the challenges that all CEOs face, and how to deal with them. Whether you end up agreeing with them or not, their insights are important and stimulating."

—Albert R. Dowden, President/CEO,
Volvo North America Corporation

"Farkas and De Backer show us how some of the best and brightest CEOs excel at the job—vision, hard work, and the communication skills to make their objectives everyone's objectives. *Maximum Leadership* is right on."

—Peter G. Peterson, Chairman, The Blackstone Group

Maximum Leadership

LEADERSHIP

FIVE STRATEGIES FOR SUCCESS FROM THE WORLD'S LEADING CEOS

CHARLES M. FARKAS
AND
PHILIPPE De BACKER

DIRECTORS, BAIN & COMPANY, INC.

A Perigee Book

A Perigee Book
Published by The Berkley Publishing Group
A member of Penguin Putnam Inc.
200 Madison Avenue
New York, NY 10016

Henry Holt and Company hardcover edition: January 1996
First Perigee trade edition: March 1998

Reprinted by arrangement with Henry Holt and Company, Inc.

Published simultaneously in Canada.

The Penguin Putnam Inc. World Wide Web site address is
http://www.penguinputnam.com

Library of Congress Cataloging-in-Publication Data

Farkas, Charles M.
    Maximum leadership : five strategies for success from the world's leading
CEOs / Charles M. Farkas and Philippe De Backer. — 1st
Perigee trade paperback ed.
        p. cm.
    "A Perigee Book."
    Includes index.
    ISBN 0-399-52385-5
    1. Leadership.   2. Success in business.   3. Chief executive officers—
Attitudes.   I. Backer, Philippe de.   II. Title.   III. Title: Five strategies
for success from the world's leading CEOs.
HD57.7.F37   1998
658.4′092—DC21   97-28379
                                        CIP

Printed in the United States of America

1 2 3 4 5 6 7 8 9 10

To my wife, Lora, and my children—
Alexander, Cameron, Caroline, and Zachary—
for their love, support, and boundless enthusiasm.
—CMF

To my father, who gave me the opportunity
and support to pursue my goals
and to whom I owe so much.
—PdeB

CONTENTS

ACKNOWLEDGMENTS

This book would not have been possible without the contributions of the 161 chief executive officers, presidents, and chairpersons who invited us into their offices and homes and shared with us their thoughts and experiences on the challenge of leadership in their organizations. We would like to record our appreciation to those executives, in alphabetical order:

Raymond Ackerman, Chairman, Pick 'n Pay Ltd. (South Africa)

Krister Ahlström, President and CEO, A. Ahlström Corporation (Finland)

Heikki Allonen, Senior Vice President, Metra Oy (Finland)

Angelo Amoroso, CEO, Rinascente (Italy)

Rob Angel, CEO and Managing Director, Engen Ltd. (South Africa)

Christian Aubin, Deputy Managing Director, BNP (France)

Charles Baird, Managing Director, AEA Investors Inc. (U.S.)

Robert Baldridge, Vice Chairman, Transgenics (U.S.)

Percy Barnevik, President and CEO, ABB Asea Brown Boveri Ltd. (Switzerland/Sweden)

Claude Bébéar, President, AXA (France)

Charlotte Beers, Chairman of the Board and CEO, Ogilvy & Mather Worldwide Inc. (U.S.)

Jean-Louis Beffa, CEO, Saint-Gobain (France)

Carlo De Benedetti, Chairman and CEO, Olivetti (Italy)

Bo Berggren, Chairman, Stora Kopparbergs Bergslags A.B. (Sweden)

Michael Blackburn, Chief Executive, Halifax Building Society (U.K.)

J. P. Bolduc, Former President and CEO, W.R. Grace and Company (U.S.)

John Bond, Group Chief Executive, HSBC Holdings PLC (U.K.)

David Bradley, Chairman, The Advisory Board Company (U.S.)

Cedric Brown, Chief Executive, British Gas PLC (U.K.)

Dominic Cadbury, Executive Chairman, Cadbury Schweppes PLC (U.K.)

Wayne Calloway, Chairman and CEO, PepsiCo Inc. (U.S.)

Ronald Cambre, President, Vice Chairman, and CEO, Newmont Mining Corporation (U.S.)

Ferdinand Chaffart, CEO, Generale de Banque Belge (Belgium)

Ken Chenault, Vice Chairman, American Express (U.S.)

Robert Cizik, Chairman and CEO, Cooper Industries (U.S.)

Neil Rex (Nobby) Clark, Chairman, Foster's Brewing Group Ltd. (Australia), CEO, National Australia Bank Ltd. (Australia)

Warren Clewlow, Chairman, Barlows Ltd. (South Africa)

Marcel Cockaerts, Chairman, Kredietbank (Belgium)

Françoise Colloc'h, Director of Corporate Culture and Communications, AXA (France)

Timm Crull, former Chairman and CEO, Nestlé USA (U.S.)

Brian Davis, Chief Executive, Nationwide Building Society (U.K.)

Michael Dell, Chairman and CEO, Dell Computer Corporation (U.S.)

John F. Devaney, Chief Executive and Managing Director, Eastern Group PLC (U.K.)

Wim Dik, Chairman, Koninklijke PTT Nederland (Netherlands)

Michael Edwardes, Former CEO, British Leyland Motor Co. (U.K.)

Jan Ekberg, President and CEO, Pharmacia A.B. (Sweden)

Per-Olof Eriksson, Former President and CEO, Sandvik A.B. (Sweden)

Richard Evans, CBE, Chief Executive, British Aerospace PLC (U.K.)

Fritz Fahrni, President and CEO, Sulzer Ltd. (Switzerland)

Robert G. Faris, President and CEO, Polish American Enterprise Fund (Poland)

Paul Fentener van Vlissingen, Chairman, SHV Holdings (the Netherlands)

Emilio Fossati, CEO, Benetton/CSII (Italy)

Michel François-Poncet, Chairman of the Board, Paribas (France)

Jacques Friedman, CEO, UAP (France)

Stephen Friedman, Senior Chairman and Limited Partner, Goldman, Sachs & Co. (U.S.)

Paul Fulton, President (retired), Sara Lee (U.S.)

Dionisio Garza Medina, Chairman of the Board and CEO, Alpha S.A. de C.V. (Mexico)

Peter George, Group Chief Executive, Ladbroke Group PLC (U.K.)

Melvin R. Goodes, Chairman and CEO, Warner-Lambert Co. (U.S.)

Sir Alistair Grant, Chairman and Chief Executive, Argyll Group PLC (U.K.)

Sir Richard Greenbury, Chairman and Chief Executive, Marks & Spencer PLC (U.K.)

Anthony Greener, Chairman and Chief Executive, Guinness PLC (U.K.)

Rainer E. Gut, Chairman of the Board, Credit Suisse Holding and Credit Suisse (Switzerland)

Lars Halldén, CEO, Tetra Laval (Sweden)

John Hardiman, Vice President, Parts and Services (retired), Ford, Europe

Toru Hashimoto, President and CEO, Fuji Bank, Ltd. (Japan)

John Heine, CEO, Sola International (U.S.)

Lars-Åke Helgesson, President and CEO, Stora Kopparbergs Bergslags A.B. (Sweden)

Sir Christopher Hogg, Chairman, Courtaulds PLC (U.K.), Chairman, Reuters Holdings PLC (U.K.)

William R. Holland, Chairman and CEO, United Dominion Industries (U.S.)

Amos Hostetter, Chairman and CEO, Continental Cablevision (U.S.)

Patrick Houel, Financial Director, LVMH (France)

John Hunter, Principal Operating Officer, Coca-Cola Company (U.S.)

Norman Ireland, Chairman, BTR PLC (U.K.)

Georges Jacobs, CEO, UCB N.V. (Belgium)

Peter Jarvis, Chief Executive, Whitbread PLC (U.K.)

Robert A. Jeker, Managing Director, Anova, Nueva, and Unotec (Switzerland)

Edmund Jensen, President and CEO, Visa International (U.S.)

Peter Job, Chief Executive, Reuters Holdings PLC (U.K.)

Finn Johnsson, President and CEO, Euroc A.B. (Sweden)

Ryuzaburo Kaku, Chairman of the Board and CEO, Canon Inc. (Japan)

Stanley Kalms, Chairman, Dixons Group PLC (U.K.)

Xavier Karcher, Managing Director Citroen, Citroen/PSA (France)

Kazuhiko Kasai, Deputy President, Fuji Bank, Ltd. (Japan)

Herb Kelleher, CEO, Southwest Airlines (U.S.)

JA (Tony) Killen, Managing Director, National Mutual Life Association of Australasia Ltd. (Australia)

Hilmar Kopper, Chief Executive Officer, Deutsche Bank (Germany)

Naohiko Kumagai, President and CEO, Mitsui & Co., Ltd. (Japan)

Michael C. Kwee, Chairman and Chief Executive Officer, Prudential Asset Management Asia Ltd. (Hong Kong)

Steven G. Lamb, E.V.P. and COO, Case Corporation—Racine (U.S.)

Alan Langlands, Chief Executive, National Health Service (U.K.)

Pierre Lescure, CEO, Canal (France)

Daniel Cardon de Lichtbuer, President and CEO, Banque Brussels Lambert (Belgium)

Alfonso Limbruno, CEO, ENEL (Italy)

Jon Linen, Vice Chairman, American Express (U.S.)

Maurice Lippens, Chairman, Fortis AG (Belgium)

Brian Thorley Loton, AC, Chairman, Broken Hill Proprietary Company Ltd. (Australia)

Vernon R. Loucks, Jr., Chairman and CEO, Baxter International Inc. (U.S.)

Olof Lund, Chairman and CEO, Celsius Industries Corporation, (Sweden)

Patrick Lupo, Chairman and CEO, DHL Worldwide Express (U.K.)

K. Linn Macdonald, President and CEO, Noranda Forest Inc. (Canada)

Bernt Magnusson, Chairman, NCC A.B. (Sweden)

Minoru Makihara, President and CEO, Mitsubishi Corporation (Japan)

Robert H. Malott, Chairman of the Executive Committee, FMC Corporation (U.S.)

Marvin L. Mann, President, Lexmark International Inc. (U.S.)

Dr. John Maree, Chairman, Eskom (South Africa), Chairman, Nedcor Ltd. (South Africa), Chairman, Denel (South Africa)

Sir Colin Marshall, Chairman, British Airways PLC (U.K.)

Dr. George Mathewson, CBE, Chief Executive, Royal Bank of Scotland PLC (U.K.)

Helmut O. Maucher, Chairman of the Board of Directors and CEO, Nestlé (Switzerland)

John H. McArthur, Dean (retired), Harvard Business School (U.S.)

Dana G. Mead, President and CEO, Tenneco Inc. (U.S.)

Gérard Mestrallet, CEO, Banque IndoSuez (France)

Comte Diego du Monceau, CEO, GIB Group (Belgium)

Jérôme Monod, CEO, Lyonnaise des Eaux (France)

Dr. Anton Moolman, Managing Director, Transnet Ltd. (South Africa)

Sir Geoffrey Mulcahy, Chief Executive, Kingfisher PLC (U.K.)

Haruo Naito, President and CEO, Eisai Co. Ltd. (Japan)

John Neill, Group Chief Executive, Unipart Group of Companies (U.K.)

Dr. H. Richard Nesson, CEO, Partners HealthCare System Inc. (U.S.)

Eric Nicoli, Chief Executive, United Biscuits UK Limited (U.K.)

Kjell Nilsson, President and CEO, Trelleborg A.B. (Sweden)

Ed O'Hare, CEO, American Security Group (Fortis AG) (U.S.)

Georg Obermeier, Chief Executive Officer, VIAG (Germany)

Julian Ogilvie Thompson, Chairman, Anglo-American Corporation of South Africa Ltd. (South Africa)

Robert B. Palmer, Chairman of the Board, President, and CEO, Digital Equipment Corp. (U.S.)

George Paul, Chairman, Harrisons & Crosfield PLC (U.K.), Chairman, Norwich Union Insurance Group (U.K.)

Timo Peltola, President and CEO, Huhtamäki Oy (Finland)

Sir Brian Pitman, Chief Executive, Lloyd's Bank PLC (U.K.)

Sir David Plastow, Chairman, Inchcape PLC (U.K.)

Lewis E. Platt, Chairman, President, and CEO, Hewlett-Packard Company (U.S.)

Dr. Ian Preston, CBE, Chief Executive, Scottish Power PLC (U.K.)

William Price, Managing Director, Texas-Pacific Group (U.S.)

Philip J. Quigley, Chairman, President, and CEO, Pacific Telesis Group (U.S.)

Edzard Reuter, Chairman and CEO, Daimler-Benz (Germany)

Roberto Rocca, CEO, Techint (Italy)

Jim Rogers, former Managing Director, Specialty Coatings Inc. (AEA) (U.S.)

Cesare Romiti, CEO, Fiat (Italy)

W. Mitt Romney, Managing Director, Bain Capital (U.S.)

Richard M. Rosenberg, Chairman of the Board, BankAmerica (U.S.)

James Ross, Chief Executive, Cable & Wireless PLC (U.K.)

Jean-Pierre Rosso, CEO, Case Corporation (France)

Thierry De Rudder, CEO, GBL (Belgium)

Johann Rupert, Chairman, Rembrandt Group Ltd. (South Africa)

Tom Ruud, President and CEO, Aker A.S. (Norway)

Mauritz Sahlin, President and Group Chief Executive (Aktiebolaget SKF (Sweden)

Melker Schörling, President and Group Chief Executive, Skanska A.B. (Sweden)

Pierre Scohier, Chairman, Copeba (Belgium)

Ernest-Antoine Seilliere, CEO, CGIP (France)

Christopher Sekula, Managing Director, Polish American Enterprise Fund (Poland)

Allen Sheppard, Chairman, Grand Metropolitan PLC (U.K.)

Alan Smith, Group Managing Director, Anglian Water PLC (U.K.)

Hans Smith, Managing Director and CEO, Iscor Ltd. (South Africa)

Sven Söderberg, Chairman, Förvaltningsaktiebolet Ratos (Sweden)

Thomas G. Stemberg, Chairman and CEO, Staples Inc. (U.S.)

Jeffrey Stiefler, President, American Express (U.S.)

Martin Taylor, Chief Executive, Barclays PLC (U.K.)

Jan Timmer, Chairman, Philips International B.V. (Netherlands)

Geoff A. Tomlinson, Group Managing Director, National Mutual Holdings Ltd. (Australia)

Erik Tonseth, Group President and CEO, Kvaerner A.S. (Norway)

Morton Topfer, Vice Chairman, Dell Computer Corporation (U.S.)

Michael Treschow, President and CEO, Atlas Copco A.B. (Sweden)

Marco Tronchetti Provera, CEO, Pirelli (Italy)

Sir Iain Vallance, Chairman, British Telecommunications PLC (U.K.)

Derek Wanless, Group Chief Executive, NatWest Group (U.K.)

Gerhard Wendt, Former President, Kone Corporation (Finland)

James Will, Chairman and CEO, Armco Inc. (U.S.)

Mike Woodhouse, Chairman, Rexam PLC (U.K.)

Gérard Worms, CEO, Compagnie de Suez (France)

Hiroshi Yamauchi, President and CEO, Nintendo Co., Ltd. (Japan)

Alfred M. Zeien, Chairman and CEO, Gillette Company (U.S.)

Giordano Zucchi, Chairman and CEO, Zucchi (Italy)

The transcripts of the interviews with these men and women fill over 12,000 pages—enough material to have written this book four times over. We have included portions of many of those interviews, but unfortunately could not accommodate them all. Our choices were designed to demonstrate the universality of the ideas, spanning nationalities and industries.

The idea for this book was conceived nearly three years ago during a lively and thought-provoking conversation with Allen Sheppard, chairman of Grand Metropolitan. In the period since then Lord Sheppard has remained an engaged and enthusiastic participant in the complex process of bringing this project into being. His involvement opened doors for us around the world, and his challenging questions pushed us to new levels of insight. Similarly, GrandMet's commercial affairs director, Keith Holloway, worked closely with us every step of the way, contributing his intelligence and persistence.

We would like to thank especially Sir Michael Craig-Cooper, who not only encouraged us to undertake this project but also helped and guided us all along the way.

Bain & Company encouraged and supported us throughout the process of developing the ideas in the book. A few people at Bain deserve special mention. Tom Tierney and Orit Gadiesh provided the direction that encouraged us to explore new ways of thinking about the role of the leader.

Many of our colleagues at Bain played a significant role in developing, challenging, and advancing our ideas. Barry Harrington, Chris Zook, David Kenny, John Donahoe, and Steve Schaubert in the United States; Robin Buchanan, Mark Daniell, Louise Patten, Jean-Marie Pean, Jean-Pierre Felenbok, Peter Törnquist, Janet Voute-Allen, and Ulf Lindgren in Europe; and Hiroshi Uchida, Shintaro Hori, Shozo Uchida, Jim Hildebrandt, and Greg Hutchinson in Asia all made significant contributions.

Tom Stemberg, Bob Baldridge, David Bradley, and Robert Haft reacted to our thoughts from their perspectives as chief executives, pushing us to make the book useful to those in a position of leadership.

Julie Griffin, Julie Harding, Nick Lehman, and Mary Kroupa provided us with exceptional administrative and research support. Alice Martell, our book agent, worked miracles when we needed them. And our editor at Henry Holt and Company, Bill Strachan, provided thoughtful and creative guidance and polish throughout the editorial process.

Finally, there would be no book if it weren't for our writer, Suzy Wetlaufer. Suzy brought extraordinary energy, insight, wit, and wisdom to the entire process. Without missing a beat, Suzy had her fourth child in the middle of the project. We also thank Roscoe, Sissy, Marcus, and Zoë for sharing Suzy with us.

Charles M. Farkas, Boston
Philippe De Backer, Brussels
June 1995

MAXIMUM

LEADERSHIP

INTRODUCTION

"We're from Corporate,

and We're Here to Help You . . ."

Some forty years ago, a young man just out of college joined a Japanese company as a clerk in a small department. He did his job dutifully, he recalls, but he did something else as well. He frequently contacted corporate headquarters to point out flaws in the organization and suggest ways to correct them.

For ten years, his opinions were rarely acknowledged, if at all. Then one day, an executive from corporate headquarters tracked the man down as he was leaving work. Quickly, he was led to one elevator and another, and finally was ushered into the president's corner office. There he was told that one of his suggestions was about to be implemented. The president expected it to save an entire division from bankruptcy. A few months later, it had.

Today that young clerk is sixty-eight and chairman of the company that once ignored his phone calls from below. But because of his leadership, it is now a profoundly different organization, one in which individuals who challenge the status quo are encouraged, even celebrated. And Canon, the $19-billion maker of cameras, copiers, printers, and fax machines, is considered one of the most successful, enterprising companies in the world.

Similar accolades also go to Gillette, the worldwide manufacturer

3

of razors and blades and literally hundreds of other personal-care products. Its CEO didn't begin his career by needling top executives, and his approach to his job at the $6-billion concern, with 34,000 employees from Newfoundland to New Zealand, tells quite another story about managing success. Although he certainly encourages employees to speak out for change, the CEO of Gillette is characterized more by the way he champions people who share his values, who best replicate his business sense, who "live and breathe the Gillette way," as he puts it. He travels continuously to business units worldwide because "that's where the people are," he says, and to make sure decisions are being made with the same ground rules he would use. He personally conducts 800 performance reviews annually. No one in senior management is fired without his approval.

Two decidedly different approaches to management but one result—global market share and product leadership.

Business success stories like these, with all their contradictions and paradoxes, capture our imaginations—and prompt myriad explanations. Business success is a function of a great strategy, we are told, or reengineering, or customer insight, or world-class manufacturing facilities, or "game theory," or technological innovation . . . or all of these, plus more. Hearing why a company owns the top spot is a bit like hearing the speeches at the Academy Awards: there are so many people to thank for the winner's success. Or sometimes we are told they owe their victory to some miraculous "silver bullet"—the new and improved business "technique" of the moment.

Bain & Company's consulting practice has spent the past twenty-four years critically examining what makes companies succeed. The answer is neither a long list of random particulars nor a "silver bullet." Instead, the reason is as fundamental as a rigorous, systematic analysis of a company's capabilities, its context, and its key success factors. It is as disciplined as scenario and implementation planning. It often involves statistical and quantitative material, not easily adaptable to the style of many popular business books. The responsibility for success ultimately falls on the CEO, making his or her position among the most complex there are in business, its responsibilities unlimited, its demands without boundaries. The job is, in a sense, an infinite one.

But at the end of the day, the question most often posed by the

CEOs with whom we work is this: How should I spend my time to make a difference and add the most value to my business? We see this question as the challenge of maximum leadership—*the challenge to deliver consistently extraordinary results.* If this goal has been a constant of business since money first changed hands, it is only getting harder as we enter the twenty-first century. The geographical dimensions of competition are expanding. Technology is advancing. Time horizons for results are shrinking. Customers are demanding more, faster, and better.

Given these exigencies, what then is the role of the CEO and his or her top staff in the marketplace of today and tomorrow? Are there any overarching rules or guidelines for how CEOs and their corporate staffs can best add value? The work of our practice over the past twenty-four years has helped answer these questions for hundreds of companies, but two years ago we set out on a journey to hear what CEOs, chairmen, and presidents of major corporations around the world had to say *themselves* about the challenge of maximum leadership, as we have defined it. Bain partners on six continents interviewed 163 top executives in companies selected not because they were successful per se—although many of them are—but because of their companies' diversity in product and geography, their scope, and the length and richness of experience of their senior management. Our goal in this process was not to critically test what these top executives told us, but to exercise "innovative listening"—that is, to identify meaningful patterns, common themes, and recurrent insights.

We heard them, and they are the topic of this book. More specifically, in the coming pages we present five distinct approaches toward leadership that emerged from our interviews—the tactics and behaviors that these CEOs say they employ to move their organizations toward success. They are the *how* of getting a company to results. Put another way, if a company's strategy and its assets are its hardware, then its approach is its software. None of these approaches guarantees success. But what is remarkable, we believe, is that the CEOs, chairmen, and presidents of such a broad variety of companies worldwide display five distinct ways to respond to the challenge of leadership. To hear their stories, as told in the coming chapters, is to realize that this insight is relevant to every member of the organization. We report them to introduce a new vocabulary to the debate about organizational effectiveness, and to dispel the mystery of what some of the world's leading CEOs do all day and why.

The mystery—this, too, was a common theme in our interviews. Many of the executives we spoke to noted that if their positions in the inner sanctum often inspire awe and respect, they sometimes also seem to invite skepticism. They said they are aware that their performance is closely watched and rated, their results benchmarked against the competition, their compensation compared to value added.

We encountered this last phenomenon not too long ago during a conversation with an engineer who has worked for twenty years at an electric utility company. After telling him about the topic of this book, he exclaimed, "The CEO of my company made $6.4 million last year, and if you can explain what in God's name he did to deserve it, I'd be very surprised." His interest—bordering on indignation—is not uncommon. Every year, the highly publicized list of CEO salaries causes similar reactions. People wonder what Michael Eisner of Disney could have done in 1993 to earn $203 million. Even the CEO at number 700 on the list, Charles Stuzin of CSF Holdings, made $575,000—quite enough to give pause to working people everywhere.

Likewise, the sense that CEOs are disconnected from the *real* work of business also exists within virtually every company. The title of this chapter—"We're from Corporate, and We're Here to Help You . . ."—comes from Jeffrey Stiefler, president of American Express, who jokingly calls the line the third great lie, after "The check is in the mail" and "This won't hurt a bit."

"When you're running a business unit, and you're out in the markets, the corporate office just seems like a bunch of people who typically want information from you for some reason that isn't terribly important, and they want oversight in areas where you feel very competent, and they want to provide you with advice, the expectation being you will take it wholeheartedly," Stiefler says. "And then they make suggestions that they say they don't expect you to take, but they really do. And all that is against a backdrop of you working as hard as you possibly can.

"So," Stiefler says, "you don't really look forward to calls from the corporate center." Like many other executives interviewed for this book, Stiefler admits that when he was a line manager, he considered the corporate staff a bother, at best. All those demands for data, meaningless data—"They slowed us down," Stiefler recalls of his days before he was at the top, asking for data himself.

"Now," he says, laughing, "well now, I am in a position where I can clearly provide enormous amounts of help and insight to people in the businesses who are desperately in need of it. It all depends on where you sit, I guess."

Stanley Kalms, the founder and chairman of Dixon's, the British retail empire that includes photo equipment, electronics, and home appliance outlets as well as Currys and PC World, speaks less of the skepticism that he engenders than he does of the awe, which he considers equally unhealthy. He notes that when he wanders around the stores he controls, word quickly spreads: "The governor's been out—God!"

He recalls spotting a display at one store, turning to the young buyer in charge, and commenting, " 'I don't think much of that.' I was hoping he would say, 'It's terrific, here's why,' " Kalms explains. "Next thing I know he has withdrawn the product. I didn't mean him to *withdraw* the product. I just wanted to stimulate him to defend it. It's a pity that the boss's word does that, but that is how it happens."

The stories in this book, grouped within the framework of the five approaches, aim to demystify "the boss's word" by letting the bosses themselves explain the logic of what they do day-to-day, year-to-year—how they organize their time, where they choose to go, what they want from their employees, why they hire and fire whom they do. These are the voices of *practitioners*, explaining real decisions, real programs, real techniques, real mistakes, real achievements.

The book begins with the story of Allen Sheppard, chairman of Grand Metropolitan, the $12.5-billion (in sales) food-and-drink business that owns Burger King, Pillsbury, and J&B whisky, to name just a portion of its portfolio. As his two-decade career at GrandMet comes to a close this year, Lord Sheppard is a fascinating study of the approaches at work; moreover, he speaks for many of the executives in this book when he says what drives him is the belief that a CEO should "add value, or get out of the way for someone who will." He describes how he meets that challenge in his own version of the Ten Commandments, listed in chapter 1.

In chapters 2 through 6, we examine the five main management approaches that form the core of this book. In general, we found that most CEOs we talked with use all of these approaches in some measure, but by the same token, most focus on one or two as their primary vehicle of value addition. At the same time, some of the approaches overlap or blur into each other at the edges, and we do not intend to force them into rigid, nonintersecting "tunnels." But all told, we discovered there are at most a dozen permutations of the five approaches, because some contradict each other and others are complementary. We also discovered that most CEOs stick with one or two approaches over the long term, changing only when the business situation demands it, which usually is not more than twice in a decade. In other words, companies evolve and approaches do, too. As Edzard Reuter, managing director of international automotive maker Daimler-Benz, says: "A business is a living organism. There will always be a point where the environment changes, the competition changes, something critical changes, and you must realize this, and take the leading role in meeting change."

These approaches, we should note, do not seem to be a function of a CEO's personality. They are a function, rather, of the business *situation*, which includes the CEO's personality but also includes marketplace dynamics, a company's culture, its human and technical capabilities, its competitive position, its cost structure, its inheritance, and its future. If nothing else, the executives in this book illustrate how complicated effective leadership can be, but their stories also illustrate the following five ways to approach the challenge.

#1: THE STRATEGIC APPROACH, in which the chief executive says he manages for success by acting as the company's top strategist, systematically envisioning the future and specifically mapping out how to get there.

Not surprisingly, virtually every CEO we interviewed mentioned strategy formulation as one of his roles. But in fact a smaller group, only about 20 percent of the total, spoke of it as a *defining* role. Strategic CEOs, we found, focus the bulk of energies on determining how their companies can be the market leaders of tomorrow, and then structure their corporate centers and the rest of the organization to support this focus. They typically delegate day-to-day operations to others, and then spend their days asking big-picture questions—of managers, suppliers, analysts, shareholders, and especially customers. They travel to other companies and study new processes. They interview scientists and academics about fundamental research. They build time into their schedules to sit and think. "My secretary wonders, I'm sure, why I stare out the window so much," one CEO told us, "but if I don't schedule that time, the little stuff takes over."

Strategic CEOs, in other words, believe they add the most value by using long-term strategy formulation to inform every aspect of the company's business system—that is, its procedures, policies, values, communications, and incentive, training, and reward programs. In chapter 2, we look at the strategic approach as practiced by eight companies. One of them is **Dell Computer Corp.,** the upstart PC manufacturer, whose chairman says he focuses on the future because, "in my business, the life cycle of a product is six months, and so there are two types of people, the quick and the dead." Other companies featured in this chapter are **Coca-Cola,** owner of the world's most powerful brand; the phoenix-like British survivor **Unipart,** maker of world-class auto parts; gold purveyor **Newmont Mining; Staples,** the office-supply superstore chain; the French conglomerate **Lyonnaise des Eaux; Nestlé,** which employs a combination approach; and **Deutsche Bank.**

#2: THE HUMAN ASSETS APPROACH, in which the chief executive manages for success through people policies, programs, and principles.

In marked contrast to the executives who list strategy formulation as the primary way they drive the organization forward are those who say success all comes down to people. It's a popular notion—who hasn't heard a corporate executive describe himself as a "people person"? But this approach is more complicated than a CEO's knowing his employees by first name. It means he knows their capabilities, or lack thereof, and manages them in a systematic way. It means designing powerful training systems and coherent programs for measuring performance. It means monitoring relationships between people. It means explicitly teaching employees desired values and behaviors. It means empowering people to act as the CEO would, and then rewarding them when they do.

Human assets companies span industries from airlines to electronics, but the voices of the chief executives who use this approach to achieve organizational effectiveness are remarkably similar. They concur with Herb Kelleher of **Southwest Airlines,** who says, "We hire great attitudes, and teach them any functionality they need." At Southwest, that attitude means, in part, having a great sense of humor and humility. At **PepsiCo,** it means having integrity; at **Gillette,** it means commitment to corporate goals over personal ones. Other companies featured in chapter 3 are **Philips,** the electronics conglomerate based in the Netherlands; the U.K.'s **United Biscuits;** and international energy conglomerate **SHV Holdings,** where the CEO sometimes responds to memos asking for help with the missive, "You do indeed have a difficult problem. Good luck solving it!"

**#3: THE EXPERTISE APPROACH, in which
the chief executive manages for success by becoming
the champion of a specific, proprietary expertise,
and using it to focus the organization.**

At some companies, the CEO and his top staff identify the particular expertise that is their company's competitive advantage, and then focus their energies on guaranteeing that that expertise moves up, down, and between operating units. Put another way, the corporate office at an expertise-approach company designs programs and systems, and often promotes and supports a culture that actively disseminates critical knowledge about the products or processes that lead to market dominance.

One such company is **Cooper Industries.** Nearly thirty years ago, when CEO Bob Cizik joined Cooper, it had $60 million in sales and no competitive advantage to shout about. Today Cooper, with $4.5 billion in sales and 40,800 employees, is known as one of the nation's strongest manufacturing companies. "When I started out, manufacturing was being frowned upon in the United States; we were the Rust Bowl," Cizik recalls. "Everyone wanted to be market oriented, *that* was the future." Over the years, as he worked his way up to CEO, Cizik came up with a series of initiatives to train all Cooper managers and salespeople in cutting-edge manufacturing techniques and technologies and then *guarantee* this knowledge was consistently spread throughout the organization. Ironically, Cizik admits, "I'm not a manufacturing guy. I just knew it had to be done."

Chapter 4 also takes a look inside the British telecommunications concern **Cable & Wireless;** gold-mining giant **Anglo American,** which employs the expertise approach for complex socioeconomic and political reasons; **Ogilvy & Mather,** the advertising agency; **Motorola,** the telecommunications equipment leader; and **Eisai,** a Japanese pharmaceutical company where the CEO sent his middle managers into hospitals and rest homes to turn his staff into experts on the customer's "extraordinary" experience. The chapter concludes with brief profiles of two companies moving to the expertise approach for different reasons: the $5-billion Swedish drug company **Pharmacia,** and **Saint-Gobain,** a French company that first gained fame making the mirrors at the Palace of Versailles.

#4: THE BOX APPROACH, in which the chief executive manages by building a set of rules, systems, procedures, and values that essentially control behavior and outcomes within well-defined boundaries.

Without a doubt, every company has a "box"—that is, rules, procedures, systems, structures, and values that control what employees do day to day and over the long term. But not all companies have corporate centers that make that box—its creation and its maintenance—the primary focus of their time, consideration, and insight. In chapter 5, we look at companies in which the box *defines* how value is added. The top executives in this chapter concentrate their energies on control issues, both financial and cultural, as the best means to sustainable competitive advantage. Virtually every company has controls, but at some controls are background music; at the companies discussed in this chapter, controls are the main act.

Perhaps not surprisingly, given the heavily regulated nature of the industry, many of the banks we examined used this approach. But companies from several other industries did as well. The reason is that a box can be large or small, made of concrete or velvet. A "hard" box, as we call it, has walls made of numbers. Managers must hit certain financial goals or else, as one CEO puts it, "it can be damaging to your health." For other companies, the box appears to be built of more ephemeral material. Lewis Platt, the CEO of **Hewlett-Packard,** the worldwide maker of computer products with $25 billion in revenues, describes the H-P box, or in his words "the H-P way," as its values. As long as employees stay within those walls, he maintains, everything else follows: quality, cost control, customer satisfaction—and profits. His may be a soft box, but the result is the same: a company where employees at every level know the rules and the consequences of breaking them.

This chapter also examines **British Airways; HSBC Holdings,** owner of the HongKongBank; Japanese game maker **Nintendo,** which combines the box with the human assets approach; one of the United Kingdom's largest banks, **NatWest Group;** and **AXA,** the insurance giant that owns the Equitable Companies, where the box is reinforced by a "corporate language" with phrases such as "the valley of despair" and "the immobility trap." These terms mean the same thing to more than 50,000 AXA employees from Africa to North America.

#5: THE CHANGE-AGENT APPROACH, in which the chief executive says he manages for success by acting as an agent of radical change, transforming bureaucracies into organizations that embrace the new and different.

Change is thrilling; change is terrifying. All companies talk about the need for change; many fewer make building the business systems and values that encourage and integrate change the defining vehicle of value addition. Chapter 6 is about those companies in which executives focus on changing the *fundamental underpinnings* of their companies, from operating procedures to compensation programs to the way people talk to one another in the hallways. These firms are not necessarily in crisis, but their leaders still see the need for continuous and significant change, and the center as the place that will make it happen. At **Goldman, Sachs & Co.,** former managing partner Steven Friedman spent ten years implementing this approach, turning a venerable investment banking firm with a reputation for conservatism into an international concern known for competitiveness on Wall Street. "If you're not an agent of change, you're at best a steward of something which is going to erode," Friedman says, "and why would you want a job if all you're going to do is perpetuate what previously existed?"

This chapter also includes **Tenneco,** a leading American distributor of natural gas and automotive parts; and two Japanese companies, **Canon,** and the world's largest trading company, **Mitsui,** where the CEO's radical program of change "touched the sacred." It concludes with a discussion of **W.R. Grace,** where a former high-ranking government appointee named J. P. Bolduc moved boldly to install the change-agent approach at a staid, family-run conglomerate that had experienced slow growth and slim profitability for decades. It worked, but came to an abrupt halt when, citing "differences in personality and style," Grace's board of directors accepted Bolduc's resignation in early 1995.

NOT FAILED EXECUTIVES . . . FAILED APPROACHES

If business success is what the CEOs in this book are driving toward with the five approaches, what then do we make of business failures? Chapter 7 examines four companies that hit rock bottom, or nearly so. These cases indicate that failures seem to occur when the center either picks the wrong approach for the situation or applies it incorrectly. At **Wang Laboratories,** a booming company descended into bankruptcy because the center's brilliant strategic approach was never revisited. At **Digital Equipment Corp.,** the center promoted the expertise approach when change was urgently called for. At the international conglomerate **ITT,** the center was forced to fight off hostile raiders for five years because its box was too rigid; and at **British Leyland,** the once formidable car manufacturer, the center had no approach at all.

Chapter 8 includes several CEOs who managed to rebuild companies that veered very close to the fate of these four, examining the use of approaches in the process of "firefighting." The voices of this group are united by the exhaustion, and also by the excitement, of turning around an organization at the edge of bankruptcy. Many of them spoke of the awkward phone calls to disgruntled customers, the pain of laying off good employees, and the thrill of finally seeing their efforts pay off. They are linked also by how they managed their turn-arounds. All began by quickly erecting a box, introducing controls to an out-of-control environment. Once the crisis was past, each of these CEOs let the box recede and selected a new approach to add value.

In this chapter, we hear from Kjell Nilsson, of the Sweden-based rubber and mining giant **Trelleborg,** who considers it his primary responsibility as CEO to turn around troubled divisions in the cyclical industries in which his company competes. We also profile **Armco,** the American steel maker that nearly went out of business in the early 1980s. CEO Jim Will describes his efforts to prevent that as "declaring war." Other companies in this chapter are Canada's **Noranda Forest Inc.,** the conglomerate **United Dominion,** and **Fuji Bank** of Japan, one of the largest banks in the world.

THE FIVE APPROACHES—BEYOND BUSINESS

The great majority of our interviews addressed the challenge of maximum leadership in large, established, usually global, and publicly traded companies. But after the five approaches began to emerge, we wondered if they were universal to all organizations—small enterprises, family-owned ones, not-for-profit organizations, or even businesses in which the "center" is a leveraged buyout (LBO) or venture capital firm. The answer to this question appears to be yes. In chapter 9, we see the approaches at work in organizations that are not traditional businesses—for instance, in educational settings such as **Harvard Business School,** where John H. McArthur explains that he ran the institution for fifteen years using the human assets approach. They work at hospitals, such as **Massachusetts General** and **Brigham and Women's,** where Dr. H. Richard Nesson describes his management style in similar terms. And they work at firms where the classic CEO has been replaced by, or is overseen by, an LBO or venture capital firm. Typically, these types of firms have been seen as classic holding companies, buying and selling assets in complicated but highly lucrative paper transactions, but this is not always true. In this chapter we profile **AEA Investors** and **Bain Capital,** which use the approaches to create organizations with returns frequently exceeding 50 percent.

The last chapter of this book revisits the approaches described within these pages, and introduces a CEO who has just taken the helm at a large, world-renowned company. What lessons can he draw from the stories in this book as he considers how to manage his organization? How can he spend his time, day to day and year to year, to make sure that his organization consistently delivers extraordinary results?

This is the challenge of maximum leadership in the next century, one that many of the world's most interesting companies have already begun to tackle. The following stories show how.

1

ADD VALUE OR GET OUT:

THE LORD SHEPPARD IMPERATIVE

f you are to believe annual reports, the executive staff of virtually every company in corporate America is "adding value." Enormous value, these reports claim—even at companies losing money. Everyone is working better and faster. Products are more exciting than ever, processes more efficient. The future is bold, bright, and beautiful.

There are many real success stories in business—some of them are included in this book—but that still leaves open this question of "adding value." In the first place, what does it mean? Ask around and you'll hear all sorts of answers. Corporate leaders are adding value when stock prices rise, when dividends increase, or when they buy a profitable new business. According to others, CEOs add value when they meet the needs of all their "stakeholders," from organized labor to community groups to industry lobbies in Washington. A company's executives have added value when they pick the right time to close shop, expand internationally, invest in cutting-edge technology, or decisively beat a competitor in battle.

While all of these assertions have merit, we define value addition in broader terms: corporate staff adds value when it drives business units to achieve sustained, superlative levels of performance that they would not have achieved left to their own devices. The ultimate test of added value is this: If Corporate vanished, would business-unit performance founder? If the answer is no, then the chief executive and his corporate staff aren't earning their keep.

Business libraries are filled with books that measure value addition by the numbers. The tools they offer include cost-of-capital analysis, economic value analysis, market value analysis, and indexing of stock prices to market indices. No matter which one you use, however, the conclusion is always the same. Fewer than 20 percent of all companies consistently perform above average—that is, 80 percent of the time or more. Now, for the sake of argument let's look at a more basic concept—simple staying power. How many companies have managed to remain in the Fortune 100 since its inception in 1955? The answer, taking into account mergers, acquisitions, and name changes, is one third. It's even harder to stay on the magazine's list of "Most Admired Companies," which are selected by 10,000 financial analysts, senior managers, and outside directors based on quality of management and products, investment value, and use of corporate assets. Not a single company made it from the 1983 list to the 1993 list.

The reason, we would suggest, is this: most companies labor under what we call "the illusion of satisfactory performance." There is an enormous gap between their actual performance and their potential performance, but until a raider or a foreign competitor comes along, it is rarely realized. In America, this problem probably has its roots in the country's extraordinary postwar dominance in industry, when it possessed most of the raw materials, most of the educated people, most of the technology, and most of the pent-up demand. This period was glorious—and brief—yet it created an attitude of complacency that lingers. The problem, we should note, is not uniquely American. We find that in the majority of companies, overall financial targets are still pieced together from the bottom up, and the individual pieces tend to be set to provide maximum cushions for individual managers. These pieces are added up, and after a little of the cushion is squeezed out, top management try to leave some cushion for themselves, whether it is in their capital structure, the earnings they try to hold for future years, or the fat they save to cut later. The budgeting process in most companies consists of personal cushions being stacked on top of personal cushions throughout the system. People in these companies acknowledge that there are things that could be done in the next year that they are planning to do over the next three or five. They see no cost in this. On the other hand, if they do these things in one year, they may not get any more bonus than they would have anyway, plus they might have to work harder and they might be taking on greater career risk. So they actually *plan* to underperform, creating an environment diametrically opposed to the kind in which innovations and breakthroughs occur. Capable people who desperately need a breakthrough come up with them with impressive frequency. Capable people who don't need a breakthrough don't seem to be nearly as lucky, nor do the companies for which they work.

Thus satisfactory underperformance sneaks into an organization, with *sneaks* being the operative word. It often happens slowly and goes undetected for a long time because it represents a slow drift from being the absolute best to being something less than that. It can be seen as a decline in growth from 20 percent a year, to 18 percent, and then to 16 percent—increments small enough to be blamed on the "cycle" or an industry slowdown. Satisfactory underperformance frequently is gradual enough that it doesn't cause alarm until it is almost too late.

Such is the situation in more companies than one might expect, especially given the competitive environment of 1995, with markets wide open and fierce challengers in every industry. No company—no matter its size, resources, or formidable history—is invulnerable. But still, in our practice we constantly see companies in which one cushion is stacked upon another, where satisfactory underperformance goes unchecked. The statistics noted above, sadly, do not come as a surprise.

The good news is that companies are, as Edzard Reuter of Daimler-Benz said, "living organisms." They are made of people, ideas, and processes, all pliable in the best sense of the term. They can and should change; in fact, companies *must* reinvent themselves to close the gap between actual and potential performance. This reinvention must start at the top, and not just with a pronouncement. A company's executives do not add value simply by saying they do, no matter how noble their intentions. From our interviews throughout the world, and from our experiences counseling companies in crisis and in flux, we have seen that adding value is, in reality, a conscious decision by the CEO to take purposeful, well-planned action. It is a decision, coordinated with and supported by senior managers, to make other hard decisions and to make them every day. It means defining how to abolish a company's illusion of satisfactory performance, and then doing so with a determination that borders on the obsessive. Going to the office and attending to what is on your desk or calendar is not enough unless you only want to pay lip service to "adding value."

It would be dishonest to say that every CEO we interviewed fits the proactive mold we've just described, but the vast majority talked explicitly about the trust placed in them by employees, shareholders, customers, and communities to add as much value as humanly possible. It is a challenge, they said, that they take to heart.

But none, perhaps, said so with the gusto of Allen Sheppard, chairman of **Grand Metropolitan,** the company that sells products ranging from Burger King fries to Häagen-Dazs ice cream, Baileys Original Irish Cream to El Paso tacos. "The people running a company had better add value or they don't belong running it, they don't deserve it," Sheppard says. "I say: Add value or get out."

LORD SHEPPARD—LAYING DOWN THE GAUNTLET

Allen Sheppard's tenure at GrandMet is the stuff of corporate legend. When he joined the company in 1975, after spending the first eighteen years of his career as a manager with various car makers, GrandMet owned a miscellaneous collection of pubs and breweries, some dairies and several bingo and dance halls, and a poorly performing hotel chain. He took over the firm as CEO eleven years later and focused on marketing expertise in the food and drink industries. In what has been called the British financial deal of the decade, he sold off the hotel chain, Intercontinental, in 1989 for $2.8 billion. He then added Burger King, Pillsbury, and a dozen other food and drink companies, but perhaps most notably, he installed what he calls "The Challenge Culture." In real time, this means that Sheppard pushes himself and others to their limits of performance, and urges all to replace conventional thinking with something better. He sets the example with his own frenetic work schedule and ambitious personal and corporate goals. "People aren't stupid," he says. "I can't be telling them, 'Go out and give it your all,' and then not walk the talk myself. I'd rather kick myself out the door."

It would be a swift kick. In the British media, Sheppard has been called bold, brash, aggressive, and tough. He is frequently quoted as describing his style as "management by light grip on the throat."

In person, however, Sheppard is also funny and surprisingly self-effacing. Retiring, however, he is not. When he's thinking, he paces around his office in long strides. When he talks, he leans very close to the listener, his intense blue eyes focused like laser beams. His speech is a torrent of words. Sheppard, like all legends, seems to be a mixture of a larger-than-life image and this down-to-earth reality. Regardless, as a businessman, he embodies the "add value or get out" philosophy, pushing it through the organization with a combination of two approaches—expertise and human assets management. Sheppard himself has translated this dual approach into his Ten Commandments, which he uses to communicate his message throughout the company. They are as follows:

Commandment 1: Develop a culture that welcomes change.
Commandment 2: Delegate a capacity to succeed.
Commandment 3: Articulate a clear vision and strategy.
Commandment 4: Persevere.
Commandment 5: Keep the business simple.
Commandment 6: Aim for the impossible.
Commandment 7: Hire the very best people.
Commandment 8: Generate the challenge instinct.
Commandment 9: Overcommunicate to be on the safe side.
Commandment 10: Keep central staffs lean.

"We always say, 'Successful management is dead easy. Failure is complicated,'" Sheppard says. "The center has got to make sure successful management happens. It has to own the company, take full and complete responsibility for everything, really—the strategy, the people, the products, the values, the rules, everything. And then it has to orchestrate it all. I call what goes on around here 'orchestrated anarchy.' It keeps it interesting."

Interesting and demanding, because Sheppard requires three things from his managers. First, that they refuse to accept the inevitable. By this, he means he expects them to challenge conventional wisdom; capitalize on circumstances, even bad ones; and never use the word *impossible*. (The word *difficult* is permitted, he says without irony.) Second, he requires them to use "magic numbers" in setting goals. He explains: "People expect me, as an accountant, to use figures that add up, but I find it better to use figures that quantify a vision—to make the impossible seem possible." And third, Sheppard pushes responsibility for success down into the organization by allowing decisions to be made as close to the customer as possible. Responsibility for failure is pushed down, too. Everyone, he says, is accountable; managers who do not adhere to these three rules of the GrandMet game quickly become ex-employees.

"You have got to be willing to get rid of people who don't add value, who don't perform," he says. "Which means we have to talk to people openly and honestly, and tell them not only good news but also bad news about themselves or about the businesses. Which we do.

"It doesn't mean we're cruel," Sheppard adds, "but it must be done. You can't go around asking people to achieve magic numbers, for instance, and then look the other way while they don't. That's not tolerated here. Of course, we'll help them set those numbers, and we'll help them reach them. We have a center that says 'We helped you,' not 'We gotcha.'"

But if a manager gets that help and still does not contribute . . .

"*Everyone* contributes," Sheppard cuts off the question. "We expect every staff member to carry a rifle," he says. "Either you are making an input, or you are output."

Sheppard doesn't mention—he doesn't need to—that when he took over GrandMet, few managers were achieving his goals. He does, however, recall the day soon after he was appointed CEO that he traveled to New York to meet with the management of Intercontinental. The hotel chain's name had cachet, but excluding property profits, it had been underperforming.

"I was to meet with a group of managers and one of them introduced me as 'a representative of the shareholders,'" Sheppard recalls. "To which I told him, 'Thank you very much for welcoming me, but I am not representing the shareholders, I am your boss. And what's more, I think your profits are awful and it's about time we start running this business for the shareholders.'"

The following year, new GrandMet management doubled the chain's profits. Shortly thereafter, the chain was sold, and the same week GrandMet purchased for $5.8 billion the American food conglomerate Pillsbury, maker of frozen dough, Green Giant vegetables, and Häagen-Dazs ice cream, to name just a few of its products, as well as the owner of Burger King, the fast-food chain. At the time, the acquisition was considered risky because of Burger King's market position. "If it was a mistake, my career was over," Sheppard says matter-of-factly, "but I believed it was the right thing to do for the shareholders, if we were to become one of the world's premier food and drink companies."

So far, his belief has been confirmed. Pillsbury and Burger King have both posted increasing profits and cash generation since the GrandMet takeover. Since then, GrandMet has added many other food and drink makers, including Cinzano vermouth and Glen Ellen wines, and divested others—some for underperformance, others because they didn't fit with corporate strategy.

But the buying and selling of companies isn't the main source of GrandMet's added value. Rather, it is what the company's business-unit managers do every day. Their actions (and results) show that the center's approach is now so ingrained that it drives itself—and the organization—forward. Here are some examples of refusing to accept the inevitable:

• In 1993, managers at Häagen-Dazs were told by Japanese customs officials that the company's ice cream had to go through the ten-day inspection procedure at Tokyo's docks, just as all other imported dairy-based products. Those ten days practically ruined the quality of the "super premium" product, which was formulated from better-tasting but quick-spoiling ingredients.

Häagen-Dazs managers immediately set about finding a way to change the rules. At first they appealed to the U.S. Department of Agriculture and the Japanese Ministry of Health for help. None was forthcoming, so in short order the company volunteered to serve as a test case to help the Japanese Ministry of Health develop a new ice-cream clearance procedure, *at Häagen-Dazs's expense*. This the Japanese Ministry accepted, and it worked closely with GrandMet managers to resolve the problem.

The test is in its final stages today, and it seems assured that in a matter of months, Häagen-Dazs will clear Japanese customs in three days. In the meantime, Häagen-Dazs has become the market-share leader in that country's premium ice cream category.

• In 1994, Heublein, a North American GrandMet division that sells tequila, was hit with an unexpected marketing assault by two major competitors, Seagram's and Gallo. Both advertised products as "margaritas," even though they contained no tequila, and sold them for less than Heublein's product.

Heublein, based in Connecticut, responded with a three-pronged attack. First, it petitioned the federal bureau that oversees the sale of alcohol to amend regulations so that products could not be labeled "margaritas" unless they contained tequila. Second, it filed lawsuits against its competitors, claiming false and misleading advertising and promotion of unfair competition. And third, it launched an "education campaign" targeted toward the retail outlets that sold the drinks.

"We were quick to react, but this is a slow process, since there is nothing fast about lawsuits and government petitions," says Heublein manager Peter Seremet. "What's important, though, isn't the speed of getting it resolved, but the fact that we are intent on bending the environment in our favor, rather than letting it bend us in ways that hurt us competitively."

As for setting "magic numbers":

• In 1993, managers at GrandMet's IDV division, which makes and distributes its alcoholic beverages, decided to establish a beachhead in India. At the time, three other competitors were on the same track, and the race for market dominance was on. Since the Indian government forbids the importation of alcoholic beverages in bottles, IDV had to start its operations from scratch, finding raw-material suppliers, building or buying factories, hiring local managers to run them, setting up a distribution network, and stimulating demand. For all intents and purposes, IDV India was a startup, but that didn't stop Corporate from giving it one year to be first on the shelves and number one in market share.

It happened. Within nine months of the project launch, Smirnoff vodka was being made and sold in the country, and IDV India was producing a new brand called Kellys Original Cream Liqueur made from local ingredients. Not only was the group first to hit the market, but by the end of the year 100,000 cases of IDV brands had been sold.

"Many factors contributed to the India effort," says Deepak Roy, managing director of IDV India, "but I'd think most vital and important was the teamwork between all involved. The goals were very high, but they motivated everyone from marketing to finance, people in legal and human resources, people in India and in London, to push hard to reach them."

In terms of delegating to succeed:

• Six years ago, a twenty-six-year-old junior brand manager named Mark Teasdale got an idea for a new product: a cinnamon schnapps drink filled with flecks of (edible) twenty-four-karat gold.

"I was just a young brand manager," Teasdale recalls now. "And I guess I should have just felt lucky that I was already managing a brand with 22 percent growth. But the feeling in the company was, 'Hey, what else have you got going?' So I had this idea, and they told me to run with it."

Within nine months, Teasdale had created Goldschlager. "I went to them the first time and said I needed $20,000," he remembers. "Then I went back and said I needed another $25,000, and each time, they said okay. I still laugh when I say it, but it had to be the most exciting time in my life."

Goldschlager hit the market with a splash. Teasdale and his supervisors had been hoping to sell 7,000 cases in the first year, but they sold 200,000, and by 1994 Goldschlager was responsible for $100 million in revenues. Today, Teasdale has a new job—he runs seven brands.

"We talk a lot about having an entrepreneurial environment here, and I know it sounds like a cliché," he says, "but now that I have other people working with me, I try to do for them exactly what was done for me. That's the GrandMet way."

• GrandMet also owns the American eyeglass chain Pearle Vision. In the early 1990s, the company struggled financially, but it has rebounded with a successful turnaround program. Part of the company's challenge had been industrywide price wars, a challenge top management met with the policy of "delegate to succeed."

"In the past, local marketing decisions had really been controlled from Dallas," explains Karen O'Neil, Pearle Vision's director of public relations. "But the big buzz words here are *field focus*, which means giving the responsibility to the stores. That's what we did with local marketing." Specifically, headquarters told the stores, grouped into market "co-ops," that they could design their own advertising, pricing, and promotional programs. "That meant instead of Dallas telling everyone, 'This product is going to be 50 percent off in June,' that local co-ops could say, 'No, children are really important in my market, so I'm going to promote kid specials,' or, 'I've got to compete with the Wal-Mart down the street, and that means I'm promoting my lens products.' There was just much more autonomy and authority passed down," she explains.

"Our senior management emphasizes that our business should be run by the people who talk to the customers every day, which is part of the GrandMet philosophy as I understand it. And I think it works."

AT GRANDMET: ONE CEO WHO SPEAKS FOR MANY

The intent of this chapter is not to aggrandize Allen Sheppard as an individual, but to listen to him as a manager, as a business leader. During his tenure as CEO, GrandMet went from being a scattershot collection of unspectacular businesses to one of the world's largest and most successful international food, liquor, and retailing concerns. By focusing on Allen Sheppard at the outset our intent was to illuminate—with real words and with real stories about a management philosophy in action—one CEO's own relentless focus on creating an organization that delivers consistently extraordinary results. Sheppard represents the vast majority of the chief executives with whom we spoke in one key way: his day-to-day activities are all about making the whole greater than the sum of its parts. They are all about adding value.

What sets these leaders apart from one another is the *how*—the approach to reaching that singular objective. In the next five chapters, we take an in-depth look at each strategy.

2

THE QUICK AND THE DEAD:
THE STRATEGIC APPROACH

Ask most businesspeople what single issue most concerns their CEO, and they would probably answer "the future." It's an assumption that makes sense. In most large global companies, other corporate concerns—advertising campaigns, manufacturing programs, distribution channels—are delegated to any number of skilled and focused senior managers and their executives in the field. The CEO has both the room and the time to look at competitive challenges arising in the months and years ahead.

But in reality many of the CEOs we interviewed felt entirely comfortable saying they believed the days of top-down strategy formulation are past, because decentralization and globalization mean strategy should (and must) be made in the business units close to the markets. Instead of creating a corporate vision, the CEO becomes a strategy "guardian," making sure the plan pushed upward by one business unit is realistic given the firm's financial resources and that it doesn't contradict the plan pushed upward by any other division. The center, rather than creating strategy, *coordinates* strategies. It reviews them, sometimes refines them, and finally, makes sure they are executed by analyzing results. As Peter George, CEO of the British company **Ladbroke,** puts it, "I think there are really two main pillars of the corporate center, the finance function and the human resource function. They are both concerned with resources, not with

27

strategy per se. Strategy is the domain of the business units because the people running them are closest to the markets.

"I only get involved when I have to, and I don't like that very much," says George, who has spent his career at Ladbroke, which owns Hilton International, with hotels in forty-seven countries, as well as operating the world's largest commercial offtrack betting organization. The company posted revenues of $4 billion in 1994 and employs some 78,000 people. "I prefer to be there for the business units, to be the place they feel they can go for help or advice or guidance or to bounce an idea off someone," George explains. "That's where I can add value."

George's opinion represents that of many of the CEOs who fall into the other chapters of this book—CEOs who have rejected strategy as their dominant role and picked other management approaches. But in the coming pages we will look at six executives who assert that what the CEO does best is contribute to the organization by acting as its chief strategist. It is a role they have embraced, they say, because they believe no one else can, or should.

What does it mean, though, to be a visionary? To be a strategist?

Not surprisingly, there is a wealth of material in business literature that addresses these questions. One of the most recent responses comes from Gary Hamel and C. K. Prahalad, in their book *Competing for the Future.* The authors, both professors of business, say their research indicates that top managers spend only 3 percent of their time actually thinking about the future. They spend the rest of the time "acting instead of imagining." And this, say the authors, is a mistake of major strategic importance. In order to succeed, top managers must "create the future"—not by the popular routes of restructuring or reengineering, which are short-term solutions, but by focusing on the *fundamentals,* asking, "What does the future hold for my industry? What does that mean for my company?"

A true strategist, the authors maintain, then answers these questions with careful analysis of business economics, shifts in sources of customer value, government regulations, new technology, and any number of other relevant issues concerning customers and competition. He does not make decisions based on sudden flashes of brilliance, but on the knowledge gained by painstaking analysis. He is a strategist not because he has supernatural insight, but because he has extraordinary foresight.

We agree. In fact, our research into dozens of large companies since 1983 indicates that while most CEOs claim to focus on market issues, in practice they spend only 20 percent of their time on external matters, such as economic trends, customer needs, or competitor technology. The rest of their time is devoted to internal issues, all of them pressing, but very few with direct impact on the future direction of the company. True strategists, the kind examined in this chapter, seem to have the ratio reversed—80 percent of their time looking outward, 20 percent looking in.

In addition, strategists start with a clear framework of what they want done and of where they want to be in the future. Of course, for every company the future means something different. In high-tech companies, the future is six months off, while in capital-intensive industries such as forestry or mining, the future might mean the year 2015. Regardless, as a colleague of ours says, "These CEOs know their point of departure, and their point of arrival."

Point of departure—in other words, these CEOs know exactly where they are today. They understand their customers intimately, what they want, how they behave, what really matters to them in terms of price, quality, and speed of delivery. This goes beyond talking to customers and getting a "feel" for their concerns. It means getting inside the customer's needs, forming partnerships and interdependencies based on hard research and real data. At **Whitbread,** the $5.6-billion British company that counts the T.G.I. Fridays restaurant chain and numerous beer pubs in the United Kingdom among its holdings, senior management administers a questionnaire four times a year, asking internal and external customers to rate the services they receive from many of the company's 65,000 employees. The information is then fed back into the system, and in some cases determines bonuses. "I know it may sound trite, but we are in the hospitality business," explains chief executive Peter Jarvis. "At the end of the day, a piece of steak is just a piece of steak, and our competitor has the same piece of steak as we do. What actually matters in our business is that the customer is well cared for. We take that very seriously."

And understanding customers means understanding that all customers are not created equal. Customers fall into segments, some large and others tiny, with different needs and behaviors. They should be treated accordingly.

Another point of departure is a company's competitors. A strategic CEO has full command of this topic, including as much knowledge as possible of every competitor's strengths, costs, technologies, and key customers. And she not only knows who the competition is, but recognizes that competitors innovate; that they can and will attack any vulnerabilities they see; that they learn and study. A strategic CEO looks at competitors and asks, "How can I advance my firm in a way that they cannot match or imitate?"

But being a strategic CEO goes beyond analysis of the competition's strengths and weaknesses. It often means embracing an attitude that Oscar Wilde once expressed: "It isn't enough that I succeed, my enemies must also fail." A strategic CEO strives to defeat his company's competitors by a wide margin—in a rout. His goal, simply stated, is defining a strategy that puts the other company at permanent disadvantage. A great strategy is great only if it is sustainable.

Finally, a strategic CEO knows his firm's point of departure in terms of its capabilities. This means knowing what an organization can and cannot do, how well it delivers against any strategy. What are the organization's costs? How good is its best quality? How fast can it get products to market? How talented are its managers? The answers to these questions are not guesses, but honest, thorough assessments.

Knowing his point of departure, the strategic CEO then picks his *point of arrival* through the kind of rigorous analysis of fundamental questions prescribed by Hamel and Prahalad. A point of arrival can be as simple as a single number. For Helmut Maucher of **Nestlé,** for instance, the point of arrival is $80 billion in sales by the year 2000. Or it can be a more broadly put "mission." For Charlotte Beers of the international advertising agency **Ogilvy & Mather,** for instance, it is to be "the agency most valued by those who most value brands." Moreover, picking a point of arrival also means designing the culture, values, incentives, and corporate structure that will lead to that goal. Strategic CEOs do so, all the while communicating what is happening over and over (and over) again to every stakeholder, inside and outside the company.

And after that, the strategic CEO *acts*, because a great strategy is pointless without execution. Usually he acts quickly, simply because exhaustive analysis creates conviction. In fact, we found that the CEOs in this chapter took the biggest risks compared to their colleagues. They were less afraid of change because they had calculated what it cost to make change and what it cost not to. And finally, a strategic CEO *revisits* his strategy regularly, making sure it is fresh and relevant.

If it is not, he begins the process once again.

COCA-COLA: THE REAL—REINVENTED—THING

CAPE CANAVERAL, Fla.—The next time astronauts fly in the space shuttle, they plan to spend 18 hours proving they have the right stuff to test the Real Thing.

So began a news item announcing a mission planned for 1995 in which three astronauts were scheduled to dispense Coke and diet Coke in space, then evaluate the drink three times over eight days, rating it for carbonation, sweetness, and tartness. The company invested $750,000 in the experiment, it said, in order to test how its products might perform in the markets of the distant future.

The way the newspaper article on the mission was written, there was no doubt it was intended to raise a laugh, but having spoken with the company's top executives, we knew what a NASA spokesman meant when he said, "It's serious enough I'm not going to make fun of it."

Coca-Cola, owner of the world's most famous brand, embraces the role of positioning and promoting that brand every day with a fervor perhaps unmatched in the history of consumer products. Its corporate office is the crucible of the strategic approach relentlessly focused and rigorously applied.

"If you can't be different," CEO Roberto Goizueta has said, "you might as well be damned." By "different," he means better than the competition, and that imperative translates into a company in which powerful systems, programs, and practices launched by Corporate essentially require managers at every level to focus on the company's future.

■　■　■

"You can't sell today's consumers yesterday's product," explains John Hunter, the frank-speaking Australian who runs Coke's international operations. "So we spend our time here thinking about that very carefully, about reinventing our brand for every new generation. We look into the future every day, figuring out ways to make Coca-Cola more relevant to today's generation. We discuss it, debate it, then we act on it."

The success of Coca-Cola's approach is hard to dispute. The company's flagship product is sold in more than 195 countries and territories and consumed 773 million times in a single day. Combined, all of Coca-Cola's drink products, which include Fanta and Sprite, brought in revenues in 1994 of $16 billion and net income of $2.5 billion. These figures are all the more remarkable when you consider that Coke is, at its essence, simply a mixture of sugar, water, lime juice, nutmeg oil, and glycerin, plus a few other ingredients. But the drink has always been more than the sum of its parts. It was concocted in 1886 by a man named John Pemberton, a patent medicine inventor who had an inkling that Prohibition would be good for soda sales. Pemberton marketed his beverage as a relief for thirst, headache, hangover, exhaustion, and depression. Over the years, Coke dropped its medicinal claims, but its salesmen ascribed to it almost greater powers—those of bringing people together and making them happy. Needless to say, everyone knows a drink is only a drink, and even Coke devotees scoff at some of the company's feel-good pitches, but no one can argue that Coke hasn't made one particular group very happy. In 1994, the company's return on capital was in excess of 32 percent, or three times its cost of capital. For the company's shareholders, 195,000 in number, things do indeed go better with Coca-Cola.

These financial results were one reason we initially expected our conversations with Coke's top executives to be about management's responsibility to *maintain* success. We hypothesized that Coke might be what we called a "box" company, in which the CEO and his staff focus on implementing rules and procedures that keep the status quo just that. After all, part of Coke's appeal is that Coke is Coke in Argentina and Zimbabwe—and Ottumwa, Iowa. Across the globe, despite cultural differences, Coke deliverymen wear the same uniforms, Coke trucks are painted the same colors, Coke bottling plants operate under the same quality standards, Coke advertising signs off with the same message: Always Coca-Cola.

But it turns out that these matters of standards and consistency are almost on autopilot at Coke, the company has been at them for so long. Our meetings with Coke were hardly about Corporate's role in maintaining anything, but instead about creating everything anew, and about winning a war. In fact, a visit to Coke's corporate offices—atop the glass and pink marble Coca-Cola Plaza headquarters building in Atlanta—is a visit to what feels like a war room. Though the place has the look of calm about it, with its elegant colonial furniture in pristine white and deep red, soaring ceilings, and plush rugs, John Hunter's office is a place where there is one forbidden word: *complacency*. On his desk sits a photograph of a grandchild, no older than six months, gazing up from his crib, a Coke can (unopened) at his side. The battle starts young.

Hunter describes his job—he is officially the company's executive vice president and principal operating officer with responsibility for international operations outside of Europe—as continually "reinventing" Coke so that it is always relevant, new, and irresistible to consumers around the world. His vision, he says, is every thirsty person everywhere reaching for a Coke more than once a day. To achieve that vision, he and other top Coke executives spend their time figuring out what the future holds for Coke, and what Coke holds for it. This means understanding all of Coke's markets, and *potential* markets—their people and their culture, as well as the passability of their roads and the quality of their water supply. It means meeting consumer needs, be it with new flavors or bottle sizes or sales outlets. It means anticipating the competition, and then destroying it. Coke executives do, of course, think about the other approaches discussed in this book, such as the management of human resources. But mainly, we learned, they think about the future and how to get there, very quickly and with no prisoners.

For Hunter, this imperative translates into a schedule that has him traveling 60 percent of the time, circling the globe in an intensive effort to create Coke's strategy for the next year and beyond. The first step of this process is meetings with country managers and their staffs, on their home turf. The meetings can last up to three days per market because, as Hunter explains, "we have found that no two markets are alike. Every market is a little different. We can never underestimate the importance of that." In these detail-laden sessions, "We debate what we are doing right, what is working, and what we are doing wrong," says Hunter, who has worked around the world for Coke since 1960. "We talk about strategies for the next year, and three years. We ask, 'What's going to change in terms of our consumer, our market, the marketplace environment, the competitors, our bottler system?' We run down and review all these things, and then say, 'Where do we need to be three years from now, and what do we need to do to get there?'

"We aren't just batting around ideas, either," Hunter adds, "we are talking about action. Fast action. Focused, flexible, and fast."

Several months after Hunter's visits, the same country managers are flown to Atlanta to present their formal one- and three-year strategic plans and operating budgets. These sessions are attended by the top ten executives in the organization, who question every assumption, every number, every proposal, every request for capital. Hunter describes these discussions as "lively." (Country managers themselves describe them as "terrifying" and "brutal," as well as "amazingly productive" and even "fun.") Once budgets are set, the country managers fly home and try to beat them.

In addition to this planning process, there is another forum for strategy formulation that takes center stage at Coke, a set of off-site senior management meetings. These sessions are attended by the company's top forty-five executives, and can sometimes become quite emotional, Hunter says, because they are supposed to.

"Titles are checked at the door," he elaborates. "Everyone says what he or she is thinking. The point is talk about Coca-Cola as a corporate entity—what are we doing right and wrong. How do we need to change our corporate culture to be a better company for the future?"

The meetings begin, Hunter says, when he and M. Douglas Ivester, Coke's president and chief operating officer, as well as other senior managers, present a topic to the group for debate. One previous year, for example, it was "people skills"—in other words, whether Coke had in its ranks the management talent to pull off its worldwide goals for growth and market penetration.

"We determined that as we head to the future we need to be more critical in terms of defining the skills that we have, and defining the skills that we need to grow our business in the future," Hunter says of the meeting. "We looked at the cadre of people we have, and talked about ways to determine what we have to do to train them, or else find people who can perform those roles."

As a result of the dialogue at these off-site sessions, Coke has markedly changed its top-level hiring practices. "I can tell you we spend a lot more time today interviewing people for key jobs than we ever did before," Hunter says. "And we have a more standardized process for doing it, so we can all be sure that we're judging people from the same set of criteria."

In addition to overseeing business planning, Hunter also has another job at Coke—investigating what he calls "strategic opportunities" but what an outsider might call "hot spots." He examines places where Coke's market share is not as strong as the company would like it to be, where a new market is suddenly opening, or where disaster, either natural or political, has just struck. "Every day, I don't know if the issue is going to be a coup d'état in a certain country—do we need to evacuate people? Or maybe there's a typhoon in the Philippines," Hunter says. "Or Taiwan is under water. Or Norway is taking a vote on the economic union. And I have the role of asking, 'What will that mean for Coke?'"

Take East Germany as the Berlin Wall came down in 1989.

"We had to decide right away how we were going to go to market," Hunter recalls. "Would we look for new bottlers in the eastern part of Germany? Would the West German bottlers be the ones that went in there? We went through the debate in Atlanta, and we said, 'We've got to move today. We've got to look at the situation immediately and determine our level of investment and commitment.'"

A few hours later, a team of senior managers was on a plane to Berlin, and for the next two weeks the group trekked around the country, figuring out how to get Coke's infrastructure up and running. They looked at plant sites, they talked to potential bottlers, they listened to consumers, they met with political leaders. It was, he says, an unforgettable experience, one wrought with hope, fear, and confrontation.

"It was a period of time when a lot of people were saying, 'Hey, the Wall has come down, but East Germany is in a terrible economic situation,'" Hunter relates, "'and people who go rushing in to invest with large amounts of money could get their fingers burned.'

"But we said to our people in Germany, 'What is the opportunity and what is your recommendation?' And they came to us with a plan that involved an investment of half a billion dollars. That's an awful lot of money to invest, particularly in a market that has a big question mark around it.

"But at the end of the two weeks, having seen it firsthand, we knew it was an opportunity we had to seize because we could move faster than anyone else. And so our plan was put into motion."

Perhaps this doesn't sound particularly like the "blue-sky thinking" some other CEOs in this chapter describe, but we would suggest that it is just that—on fast-forward. Hunter describes a company obsessed with the future, a future that is *tomorrow.* His is blue-sky thinking on the fly. And what makes it work is the upfront talk and debate about markets, consumers, and resources that Hunter and other colleagues manage in meetings from Atlanta to Australia.

It also requires upfront work on corporate values—ground rules for all the action, if you will. Doug Ivester, the company's COO, spoke to this issue at an industry convention in 1994. Using the keynote speech as his platform, Ivester openly castigated the makers of un-branded "generic" soft drinks for being "sheep" and "parasites," threatening to destroy the industry with their behavior.

"Sheep are only comfortable when they are standing right up against each other, and when one moves, they all move," Ivester said. "Secondly, sheep are only capable of looking a few inches ahead of their noses. And thirdly, when sheep are troubled, their natural instinct is to start crying loudly and backing into each other."

Soft-drink makers suffer by the comparison, he said. Competitors routinely copy each other's products. They surrender to short-term financial pressures by slashing prices. And like sheep whining and shuffling backward at the first sniff of a fox in the woods, they complain about the economy's impact on their bottom line, and "more embarrassingly," Ivester noted, "they complain about the weather.

"For sure those things are factors," Ivester went on. "But let's be perfectly blunt about it. With all the talk you hear in our industry about the weather, you'd think our business was suntan lotion."

Ivester then turned his attention to parasites. They suck the life-blood out of their host, he said. They transmit diseases. They weed out the weaker members of the species on which they feast.

Parasites abound in the soft-drink business, he continued. Specifically, they are private-label brands—commonly called store brands—that never introduce new products or packages. Worse, they sell their product to supermarkets and consumers claiming it is just as good as Coke. Simply put, they are insulting the world's most powerful brand, he told the crowd, and it's a lie.

The parasite "cannibalizes decades of goodwill built into the public consciousness," Ivester asserted. They are claiming Coke Is It, but So Are We. They will not, however, get away with it, Ivester said, and that's because Coca-Cola is a company with an explicit set of values that infuses its strategic approach. He repeated Goizueta's command to be different or be damned.

Does this jibe with Hunter's description of the center? Exactly, although Hunter talks about making the credo happen in tactical terms. Ivester's slant is philosophical. Coke's corporate office focuses on the future, he says, and that means its top executives act . . . like a pack of wolves.

"I kind of like wolves," Ivester said. "They're one of the most misunderstood species in our world." Wolves, he explained, are independent yet extremely loyal to the pack. They are both nomadic and territorial. Yet as they move to follow their prey, "they are downright militant" in defending their turf from other packs of wolves. "And, oh yeah," Ivester added, "wolves like to eat sheep."

In the silence that followed this remark at the convention, Ivester played a tape recording of wolves howling. "That's just a friendly pack of competitors over at Coca-Cola Company having a good time," he said.

Laughter filled the hall, and some of it was very nervous. Everyone seemed to get the point: a well-executed strategic approach, with systems, practices, and values aligned, can be as powerful as Coca-Cola makes it.

AT DELL COMPUTER: LIVE FAST OR DIE

If executives at Coca-Cola are preparing for a future so far off that it involves consuming soft drinks in space, Michael Dell, founder and CEO of **Dell Computer Corp.,** is bracing for a future so imminent that it's practically here.

"In our business, the product cycle is six months, and if you miss the product cycle, you've missed the opportunity," he explains in a voice a little more weary than you might expect from a thirty-year-old, especially a thirty-year-old multimillionaire. "If you stop, you're dead, basically. In this business, there are two kinds of people, really, the quick and the dead."

And, Dell adds, his job as a strategic CEO—although he is so self-effacing these days that he would undoubtedly be reluctant to describe himself that way—is to make sure the $3.5 billion personal computer company he runs stays quick. How? By devoting himself to the task of keeping his organization focused on its "point of arrival."

"We are, and will always be, a personal computer manufacturer who has a *direct* relationship with the customer," Dell says. "The key to our success is making sure we don't lose that relationship, that this remains a company built on listening to the customer and responding."

Dell leans back in the chair of his Austin, Texas, office, a rather understated but modern chrome-and-glass room decorated with photographs of his wife and daughters. "We're different from the rest of the industry," he reflects. "Other companies have generally been led by an engineering mindset and a 'technology is the answer' mindset. Our business was created from the customer's viewpoint. When we created it that way, it seemed in many ways to be backwards. Starting with the customer's input was a fairly unheard of idea. But that's what's driven this company, and will continue to do so into the future."

To that end, Dell spends most of his time creating organizational systems and reinforcing a culture that puts the customer at the top of the corporate pyramid—systems that make sure managers hear 50,000 customer calls a day, for example. Systems that guarantee dissatisfied Dell PC users get special attention in weekly "customer advocate" sessions.

"It's like if you wake up at four A.M. every day and do one hundred push-ups, then you're going to get a strong, healthy body because you are always exercising," Dell explains. His job, along with seven other top executives, is to make sure the corporation's 6,500 employees gladly drop to the floor, so to speak, each daybreak.

Dell wasn't, of course, always in a position to oversee armies of employees. He started his company at age nineteen with $1,000 in savings, and in the beginning he did everything an entrepreneur has to do, and he did it alone. By night, he slept on a cot in his office; by day, he answered phones. He designed advertising, bargained with truck drivers, negotiated warehouse rental contracts. He was, however, not alone for long, for although his story may have started as a David slaying Goliath, today Dell is Goliath himself. With sales approaching $3.5 billion, earnings in 1994 reached $149 million, reflecting a 78 percent compound annual growth rate over five years. The company's stock price, with a high in 1989 of 7$\frac{1}{8}$, climbed as high as 93$\frac{7}{8}$ in 1995.

This is not to say that Dell has been without its troubles. In 1993, apparently struggling to manage its rapid growth, the company lost $35 million. Some thought it might be the beginning of the end for the brash young entrepreneur, but his company quickly came back swinging. Today, Dell is considered by most to be a genius with staying power. In addition, time seems to have mellowed him. He now seems thoughtful, even soft-spoken. He laughed wryly when he noted that one of his jobs is teaching new employees "some of the lessons that have been learned through some of the cycles. We have to teach them the wisdom of experience. That probably sounds strange coming from a thirty-year-old," he conceded.

What Dell focused on in our interview is his role in designing and maintaining the organizational programs that will keep his company on track for the future it wants to own. As an example of one of these initiatives he points to the weekly "customer advocate meetings" throughout the firm. "We have these every Friday," he says. "You go to Dell offices all over the world, and we have a version of this. They might call it something different, but it's got the same purpose."

The meetings gather employees from several different functions—marketing, manufacturing, human resources—with the agenda of discussing "whether we're keeping customers happy," Dell says. This means listening closely to what customers say they want, in terms of products or services, and figuring out how to provide it. It was through this process that Dell ended up making a 100-megahertz notebook computer. "We knew from all the calls we got asking if we sold a small, powerful notebook computer that there was enough demand to commit to manufacturing one," Dell explains. "We didn't make one at the time, but there were enough calls for us to know we should." The company was among the first to market with the product.

The agenda at "customer advocate meetings" also includes an examination of recent failures: Where did something go wrong, and why? Who's going to fix it? By what date?

These meetings also include a time in which an unhappy customer is put on the speakerphone to explain the source of his dissatisfaction. "The point is to sensitize the entire organization to the customer," Dell says. "We want to make sure everyone *literally* hears the voice of the customer, to hear the frustration when we do something that makes it difficult to use our products, like we forgot to ship a part or a manual or something.

"We want everyone to hear this guy's voice on the other end of the line, to hear how upsetting it is to him that he's spending his hard-earned paycheck, and we didn't deliver."

Dell names several other examples of his efforts to keep the company focused on its core strategy of being customer driven. He spends several hours each week reading the bulletin boards on CompuServe and Prodigy, looking for comments by avid PC users about product performance and reliability. "It's sort of like an on-line focus group where consumers are discussing their likes and dislikes, and different brands and attributes and why one company is doing well versus another, and what's really going on in the market. I find those discussions extremely helpful in understanding the perception of our consumers," he says. Moreover, from a wide range of employees with direct customer contact, Dell regularly seeks out what he calls "anecdotal feedback" about customer satisfaction, explaining, "Certainly the aggregated statistics are very important, and we do structured customer surveys, as most companies do. But I also go out of my way to get the odd feedback from wherever it might come. It's another window on what the customer is thinking."

Finally, Dell says he allots a portion of his time to roaming around the company's buildings. "I go to salespeople and ask them how demand is, ask them what the customers are saying, ask them how they like our products. I roam around the factory. And I spend a reasonable amount of time amongst our employees, ensuring they have a good sense of what our strategy is and where the company is headed—where we're going." Specifically, this means Dell has a brown-bag lunch once a week with twenty-five or so randomly selected employees who, as he says, "don't manage anybody." The point, he says, is to spread the Dell customer gospel from the top, as well as to keep an ear cocked for what's being whispered in the pews.

The even bigger aim, Dell adds, is making sure everyone is fixed on the same goals, the same values, the same future. If they are, then he can take what the organization is telling him and set what he calls performance and growth objectives.

The feedback systems "allow us to do a bit more planning," Dell says, "as opposed to a few years ago, when we had to fix the car while it was in motion." Some of that planning freedom, for example, has allowed Dell and his team to design new products that will push the company into the area of PC systems customized for individual accounts. But mainly it has put Dell in a position he welcomes: designing the company's road map, by which he means a map of where the company is going in terms of products, markets, and technologies. For a man who was answering all the little questions about his company as recently as five years ago, it is a pleasure, and a relief, to address only the biggest ones today.

AT NESTLÉ: GLOBAL THINKING, LOCAL COMMITMENT

Ten years ago, when Timm Crull ran the Carnation Company, a major subsidiary of **Nestlé,** the largest branded food company in the world, he had a brief but revealing encounter with CEO Helmut Maucher in the firm's Swiss headquarters in Vevey, on Lake Geneva. The occasion was a meeting to review Crull's new TV advertising campaign for Mighty Dog pet food.

"It was the commercial that showed the little dog flying around in a cape," Crull recalls, "which over in America we had all judged to be pretty hilarious. We loved it."

The reaction in Vevey was less enthusiastic. A group of Maucher's top marketing executives immediately denounced the spot. "It's fair to say they hated it," Crull says. "They didn't see the humor in it at all. They asked me, 'Who would spend money on a product based on this advertisement?' People will think it's ridiculous; they'll be insulted."

Crull fought his case. "I told them, 'Trust me, Americans will find this funny.' But they didn't buy that argument."

Deadlocked, Crull and the Nestlé marketing executives turned to Maucher for his reaction.

"There was a minute of silence while he was thinking," Crull remembers, "and then he said, 'Let it go. Let it run.' It was just as he had always told us—every market is different and should be treated that way."

The commercial went on to become one of the brand's most successful advertising efforts, and as such, it underlines the thesis of

Maucher's strategy as he steers Nestlé into the twenty-first century: global growth can be best achieved by intimately knowing local markets and tailoring products (plus their advertising, promotion, and distribution) to each one. He says he sees his primary role as CEO as keeping Nestlé focused on this strategy, making sure managers understand, respect, and respond to the differences in each country—differences in culture, taste preferences, shopping behaviors, even, as in the case of Mighty Dog, what people find amusing. It is a strategy that also embraces emerging markets such as China, Vietnam, Latin America, and India, where profits may be large in the long term but long in coming. It is a strategy that requires patience, aggressiveness, and enormous logistical complexity in execution; Nestlé owns 8,000 brands in 100 countries. But as a vision, it is simple, for as Maucher says, "The markets are unique, and they are the essential thing. We have never mixed that up." And it is through these "essential" markets that he says he intends to make Nestlé, which posted $46 billion in sales in 1994, an $80-billion company by the year 2000.

As a strategist CEO, Maucher readily admits he does not get involved in the details. Structurally, the company is very decentralized; zone directors and country managers enjoy a large measure of autonomy overseeing the company's 210,000 employees and 489 factories, as well as a huge stable of brands that include Taster's Choice, Nescafé, Kit Kat, Contadina, Friskies, Fancy Feast, Quik, and Lean Cuisine. (Nestlé also has a strategic participation in L'Oréal, the world's largest cosmetics company.)

Instead, Maucher spends most of his time on decisions of major impact—that is, decisions that affect the performance of the entire company. He considers himself the ultimate guardian of Nestlé's brand name, which is why he says he was present at the Mighty Dog advertising review. He also picks what markets to enter, and often chooses which products to pursue and which to drop. As an example, he cites (surprisingly) chocolate. "When I took over this company, my predecessor was about to give up chocolate," Maucher recalls. "But I believed the Nestlé brand was intimately connected to chocolate, and that chocolate is a basic taste the whole world enjoys." Maucher expanded Nestlé's chocolate holdings globally, most notably with the acquisition of Rowntree. It was the same kind of role he played in deciding to put Nestlé into the pasta and cereal businesses. "You have to feed the world more from plants than animals," Maucher says, "because it is healthier and far more cost-effective." The same broad economic and demographic analysis of world markets was at work in 1989, when Maucher came to the conclusion that drinking water would be a scarce commodity in the next century. Over the following five years, Nestlé bought eight bottled-water companies around the world, including Perrier, Arrowhead, and Deer Park in the United States, and San Pellegrino in Italy.

Crull describes Maucher's management style as "the invisible hand," and the CEO himself concurs with this assessment. Even as a zone manager—one of Nestlé's top executive positions—Crull says his contact with the CEO was infrequent. But Maucher's strategic imperatives permeated many daily decisions, Crull notes. Maucher, for example, encouraged country managers to aggressively seek out acquisitions, which Crull did. (Overall, Nestlé has spent $10 billion on acquisitions since Maucher took over.)

But the CEO's focus on strategy formulation and implementation can perhaps be best seen in action in the emerging markets he has identified as so critical to Nestlé's future. From them examples abound of managers working to tailor Nestlé products to local preferences. In Thailand, for instance, the brand managers for Nescafé abandoned the hot drink's flavor and aroma (as it is sold in the West) and turned it into a cold "shake" beverage more suited to the country's climate. They repackaged the product with a plastic container for mixing and promoted it with a song and a dance-talent contest. Sales jumped from $25 million to $100 million in six years, and market share rose to 80 percent.

In China, Nestlé executives, led by Maucher, negotiated for more than six years to be allowed to set up a powdered milk and baby cereal factory. When at last the government allowed Nestlé to go forward in 1990, local managers had to figure out how to deal with a less-than-modern network of trains and roads. Maucher's clearly communicated strategy—use local resources, respect local customs, and take the long-term approach in emerging markets—laid the groundwork for what happened next. The country managers built an expensive network of gravel-covered "milk roads" between twenty-seven Chinese villages that allowed local farmers to get their product to Nestlé chilling centers, where it was analyzed for quality and sanitation. The Nestlé managers also hired retired government workers and teachers to serve as farm agents, and assigned them to the villages producing milk for Nestlé. The workers and teachers were trained by Nestlé hygiene specialists from Switzerland. But the goal was not to make the Chinese more Swiss; rather, it was to make sure the Swiss managers working in China completely understood the farmers who supplied the raw materials—their culture, needs, expectations, and abilities. "My philosophy is to let the Chinese be Chinese, but to bring to their markets Nestlé's expertise and corporate values," Maucher says. "That is what is meant by global thinking, local commitment."

Like many of the other CEOs in this chapter, Maucher says he didn't come up with his strategy in a sudden burst of insight. In his case, in fact, it was years in incubation. He joined the company in 1948, apprenticing in the same German factory where his father had worked. Over the years, he ascended to the head of Nestlé's operations in that country, and he was named to the company's top position in 1981. His selection was no surprise. Maucher, six foot four and regal in bearing, has a commanding presence. He picks his words carefully and is known more as a leader than as a manager. Certainly, one reason is his top-down style. "I listen a lot," he says, "but I make the final decisions." Then, in German, he repeats the saying, *Ich bin für ein Team mit Spitze und nicht ein Team als Spitze.* It means, "I want a team with a leader, but not a team as the leader."

Maucher says he developed his strategy for Nestlé based on decades of experience, and his own feeling for global trends in the way people think, act, move, and eat. Once he makes a decision, he says, he then tests it at one of his three-day senior management meetings. The input from these meetings influences him, but he ultimately acts based on an attitude reflected by many strategic CEOs we interviewed.

"I am all in favor of shareholder value," he says, "but not to achieve six-month results. I take the global view. I take the long view. When thinking of stock price, I am thinking about fifteen years from today, not tomorrow."

AT UNIPART: CAPITALISM, TAKE TWO

In 1977 John Neill was selected to run the small, moribund automotive parts division of British Leyland, a car manufacturer with its own set of serious problems. He was twenty-nine years old, and brash enough to tell a reporter he wanted "Lord Stokes's job"—that is, he wanted to run the whole organization, albeit in twenty years' time.

Neill didn't get his wish; he surpassed it. While British Leyland nearly collapsed and had to be bailed out by the government, today Neill is considered one of Britain's leading business visionaries. **Unipart** is no longer small or moribund but an independent company with sales of $1.3 billion and one of the world's most respected auto parts suppliers, selling exhaust systems, air conditioners, and fuel tanks to Honda and Toyota, among other car makers, and earning the accolade of running Britain's best factory.

Neill says he transformed Unipart using the tools of many of the strategists in this chapter. Like them, he says he has been a navigator, determining Unipart's point of departure, picking its point of arrival, and mapping the best route between the two. Like them, he says his role has been a systematic analysis of customers, competitors, and capabilities. Like them, he steps back from day-to-day operations in order to keep his eye on the big picture. But Neill's "big picture" is not an industry; it is the world economy at large, and his vision concerns how companies in developed nations should—and must—compete in the new market of emerging nations. His vision outlines Unipart's future, but goes beyond it to propose a new brand of capitalism for the twenty-first century.

"Communism and socialism have destroyed the dreams of millions of people," says Neill. "Now we are in a global market economy with the traditional wealthy but uncompetitive Western markets as the targets for the products and services of the high-performing Asian economies. Work can now be done by almost anyone, almost anywhere.

"Couple this with the traditional Western focus on short-term profits," he adds, "and is it any wonder that the 'go-go' companies of the eighties became the 'gone' companies of the nineties?"

The new and virulent competition, never before seen on a worldwide scale, will only grow more intense over the next several decades, Neill says. The urgency of his message underscores his belief that in this era of change, every CEO must turn his or her attention to rigorous strategic analysis and the imperatives that arise from it.

"How can we even grasp the magnitude of the supply onslaught from emerging world economies, such as China and the Pacific Rim, with a collective population of three billion people?" he asks. "They've got low pay, no welfare costs, and a population hungry for a Western lifestyle. Many of their workers are well educated, many are ambitious."

Europe and the United States face this challenge with high labor costs, expensive welfare systems, long holidays, and short working hours—none of which are likely to be altered by politicians anytime soon, Neill asserts.

So instead, capitalism itself must change, he says, into a system of long-term "shared destiny" relationships between stakeholders—suppliers and manufacturers, employees and management, companies and customers. These relationships must be based on mutual survival and growth, each partner helping the other to succeed, all working together to bring down cost and increase quality. Adversaries, he insists, must become allies, or both will lose.

"Look at what happened in Britain between trade unions and so many companies in our [auto] industry," he remarks. "Every year, a knock-down-drag-out fight, always utterly unproductive. Every time a company posted profits, the unions demanded more pay with shorter hours and enhanced benefits. The outcome crippled our industry. Labor won their short-term, power-based struggle. But what has been the price? Tens of thousands of jobs lost in the Western auto industry, and there is more to come."

Neill's vision of a shared-destiny relationship puts all employees together, working as a team to eliminate waste, improve processes and technology, and lower costs, all in a joint effort to increase profitability, increase market share, and increase quality—and thus ensure job security and job growth, and provide long-term, enduring results to shareholders.

Although Neill is well known in Britain for this philosophy of business, he says he primarily considers himself a practitioner. The facts bear him out: he has implemented dozens of shared-destiny relationships between Unipart and its stakeholders. For instance, the company works closely with employees (who are no longer unionized) on efficiency and productivity programs, as well as granting a stock-owning opportunity to virtually everyone who works for the company. "This goes right to the heart of our philosophy," Neill explains. "It inspires our employees to have long-term relationships with us."

The same goes for customers. Using a complex computer system, Unipart segregates each customer's business, and each month gives the customer audit accounts and performance information that he doesn't have himself. At the same time, working with suppliers on quality, Unipart has been able to decrease rejected components from 1 in 50 to 1 in 5,000. The point, Neill says, is for both sides of the equation to make money in the long run.

"There is no point in our making huge profits and our dealers losing money, because they will die," Neill says. "And there is no point in our being soft on them and letting them become fat, dumb, and happy, because we will die. We are not talking about cozy, relaxed relationships, but relationships in which everyone is striving to bring down costs to the final consumer, so the whole demand chain will survive."

To spread this message, Neill spends about a quarter of his time as a spokesman for the cause, addressing employees as well as politicians, businesspeople, and the media across the United Kingdom. But on a day-to-day basis, his schedule indicates his energies are focused primarily on putting his vision into action at Unipart. He lectures six hours a week at Unipart University in Oxford, set up to teach the how and why of his new system of shared-destiny relationships. He frequently travels to Unipart's plants and warehouses, and spends weeks each year meeting with suppliers and customers, further developing partnerships. Once a month he presents "Mark in Action" awards to employees who deliver outstanding customer service, in a ceremony he likens to the Oscars for their large turnout and prestige within the company. Every four weeks, he oversees the production of a videotape about Unipart's strategy, highlighting new manufacturing techniques, competitive data, or examples of shared-destiny values in action.

"The center is there to share the vision and lead the vision," Neill says. "You have to lead, and create vitality."

Both would seem to come naturally to Neill. Now forty-seven, he is charismatic—an engaging speaker and an engaging personality, witty and honest, as well as forceful in his opinions. But Unipart's fortunes didn't turn around on charisma alone. Neill came to the company with what he calls a mission, a mission to redefine the firm's competitive strategy. At the time, not only was Unipart rapidly losing market share due to poor relationships with its dealer network, but it also operated some of the worst factories in the United Kingdom in terms of quality and speed to market. As merchandising manager, Neill first focused on marketing problems. He devised a new advertising campaign with the slogan "The answer is yes. Now, what's the question?" and fortified relationships with both suppliers and dealers. The goal was to build a strong brand and consumer loyalty; it was a goal greeted with a great deal of skepticism within the organization. Unipart was considered too much a "skunk" to succeed.

Undaunted, Neill says he approached the company's managing director and asked for a $2.8-million marketing budget. After some haggling and persuasion, he got it.

"We launched a completely new brand identity—new packaging, new signing and identification programs, new motivation programs, all of them thought through," Neill says. "All of this by a bunch of managers who were considered the dregs of the industry—not by us, but by the industry and by themselves."

Results changed that. Unipart's sales on the first product to get the marketing treatment skyrocketed 400 percent in eight weeks.

"It was like being at the bottom on the third-division football team, but actually having great players who don't know they are good, and training them and putting them through the pain barrier to the point where they don't like you and don't understand and are upset," Neill recalls. "But they go through the pain barrier and see themselves playing at the top of the third division, and they get a nice surprise and say, 'Isn't this amazing we can do this?' And then they move into the second division, and suddenly they are realizing that nothing stops them from being first division except themselves."

During this period, Neill says he kept himself relentlessly focused on Unipart's point of arrival: a company in tune with its critical success factors that had a lifetime relationship with its customers.

"During the early days, I spent many evenings thinking, 'What is the philosophy? What is the strategy? What are we going to do?'" Neill says. "The philosophy was to understand the real and perceived needs of the customer better than anyone else and serve them better than anyone else.

"We talked for hours about what this really meant," Neill adds, "and today, it is still our philosophy."

It is a philosophy that has been tested.

In 1980, Neill and a few other executives began talking about taking Unipart private in a management buyout, but as British Leyland foundered, so did their plan. He describes the period until 1987 as one filled with "hope and despair" as many good employees left the company and Unipart tried to keep afloat as its parent drowned.

The management buyout did finally succeed in 1987, with senior executives and employees taking 22 percent ownership. Today, they own almost 50 percent of the company, Rover owns 20 percent, and institutional investors own the rest.

Neill says his first order of business as head of the new, independent Unipart was to take manufacturing to the same place he had driven marketing.

"It was mission impossible when you look at what we started with," he recalls. "We had British Leyland's worst factory and we were a marketing company. Could we make it the best factory in Britain? It seemed an impossible dream. I didn't grow up in manufacturing, but I knew our country had to be successful in manufacturing. We couldn't just be a nation of consumers. The world was changing and the economy was changing. We had to inspire people to step up to the challenge, and ignite amongst our people a spirit to win."

Over the next several years, Neill says, he and his top executives closely studied business operations in Japan, where Neill saw the success of shared-destiny relationships in action. His management team, as well as many employees, traveled to the country and spent weeks at a time observing management and manufacturing practices at Honda plants. They spoke with Japanese managers about the logistics of setting up shared-destiny relationships with suppliers, as well as waste elimination techniques and Japanese business philosophies and operating procedures. The goal was not to replicate the Japanese model but interpret it for Unipart.

"If you copy someone else, the only thing for sure is that you will always be behind, and if you've got it wrong, you will be even worse," Neill explains. "So I always said, 'Let's learn, let's observe, but let's work it out our own way.' I told people to talk about Unipart, our company, our stakeholders. We could see what others were doing, but we had to find our own way."

Today, Unipart's own way is well enough defined and operating successfully enough for the company to run its own university. Opened in 1993 at a cost of $3.8 million, the university includes a state-of-the-art business library, a computer technology showroom, and dozens of classrooms. Its professors are Unipart managing directors (as well as Neill), and at any given time, three quarters of the company's 4,000 employees take courses. Already, satellite campuses have been opened in Unipart factories and warehouses around Britain, and suppliers and other Unipart stakeholders participate in classes.

"There is nothing like Unipart U. anywhere in the world," Neill says. "Our people designed it. All sorts of people in the company own it, run it, and improve it all the time. They understand what the mission for the company is. They understand the mission and the vision of the university, which connect it completely to the mission for the company."

In the long run, Neill proposes, everyone who attends the university will be thoroughly versed in why shared-destiny relationships are necessary, as well as how to make them happen. His vision of a new model for capitalism might occur without this, but not nearly as quickly. And speed, he maintains, is essential.

"Change is happening ten times faster in the nineties than in the eighties," he says, echoing a common theme of the strategists examined in this chapter. "And at the end of the day, I know the only prospect of this company competing successfully in the year 2000 is to have, throughout it, individuals who share the vision, and can bring it to life."

AT STAPLES: STAYING FAR AHEAD OF THE CONVOY

On the long Fourth of July weekend in 1985, Tom Stemberg needed a typewriter ribbon, but he couldn't find a single store open to sell him one. "This is crazy," he remembers thinking at the time, "there's no place to buy this stuff from a Thursday to a Monday."

It wasn't just a passing frustration to Stemberg. At the time he was a supermarket chain executive, and he had been watching closely as the industry shifted toward superstores offering deep discounts and convenient shopping hours. A few years earlier, while at Jewel's Star Market chain, he himself had promoted the first unbranded, generic goods, such as store-labeled cookies and paper towels. Initially, many industry insiders dismissed the idea, arguing that customers would never abandon brand loyalty built over many years and through millions of dollars of advertising, even if it meant saving money. They were wrong, and unbranded products quickly spread up and down aisles in supermarkets everywhere.

These experiences came together as a new vision for Stemberg: superstores for office products, offering low prices and convenient hours, targeting small businesses, students, and households. Again, his idea was initially doubted, this time by several venture capital firms who questioned the size of the potential market for such a concept. But Stemberg did find backers, and again his forward-thinking insight into customer behavior was right. **Staples,** as he called the chain he founded, will have 443 stores in North America by the end of 1995, and 45 others in joint ventures in the United Kingdom and Germany. Its revenue and profit growth has been explosive—from $219 million in sales in 1989 to roughly $3 billion this year, with earnings increasing from $1.8 million to an estimated $60 million in the same period. Staples, as a concept, has also expanded dramatically from mainly suburban retail outlets. It now includes smaller Staples Express stores located in urban centers, a large mail-order business, and a contract stationer division that focuses on sales to businesses with more than 100 employees. Staples's success, not surprisingly, has spawned many competitors, such as OfficeMax and Office Depot, but it was Stemberg's vision that invented an industry that is expected to keep growing at double-digit rates for at least another five years.

But having a vision doesn't necessarily make a CEO a strategic CEO as we have defined it, and in fact, many entrepreneurs don't make the transition from one to the other, as they remain deeply involved in day-to-day operational details. Stemberg appears to have made the transition, delegating most operational duties to senior executives and keeping himself focused on his company's point of departure and its point of arrival. He says he continually analyzes and assesses the market, its customers, and its competitors, and examines every critical aspect of Staples's product line, distribution system, location plans, and organizational structure to position the company for the future. Stemberg says his role is so defined by "big picture" analysis that he is even able to ask, less than ten years out of the starting gate, whether Staples should even *have* retail stores, given the promise of its catalog business. This is not to suggest that the company plans to stop opening new retail outlets—just the opposite is true—but it indicates the extent of Stemberg's rigorous, systematic strategic thinking. Every scenario of the future competitive situation is scrutinized with an open mind—an open mind toward changing strategy and direction because of it.

"Oftentimes the analysts ask you, 'Gee, what do you do when you hit a bump in the road?' " Stemberg explains. "And the right answer to that is, 'My job is to do enough surveying work and be far enough ahead of the convoy so that we've reengineered and fixed the road long before we hit the pothole.' "

In the past few years, staying ahead of the convoy has meant that Stemberg has aggressively put Staples into businesses he hadn't originally conceived as part of his plan. Back in 1986, he sought to replace the fragmented market that served small businesses with less than twenty employees, students, teachers, and families shopping for paper, pens, report covers, packaging materials, and small office equipment such as calculators. Shopping at stationery stores or at mass merchants with small office-supply departments, these consumers typically had to pay close to list price, and Stemberg thought offering them up to 50 percent off would build a successful enterprise. Staples would open stores roughly 18,000 square feet in size, offering 5,600 items. What Stemberg quickly found, however, was that his target market was bigger than he predicted. Businesses with twenty to one hundred employees were taking advantage of Staples's discounts—a case of copy paper that once sold for $75 was offered for as low as $20 at Staples—as were larger national and regional companies with dozens (or hundreds) of small offices. In addition, many customers wanted the convenience of not shopping retail at all; they wanted to buy direct, through a catalog or through contract services with a seller as close to the manufacturer as Staples. Many customers wanted Staples to expand into selling a wider variety of computer hardware and office furniture. With Stemberg and his executive team keeping their vision long term and constantly updating their analysis of market trends, the response was swift. The company made heavy investments in marketing programs directed at midsize businesses, built a contract stationery business, and began a major direct-sales operation, with several telemarketing centers and next-day delivery service for most orders. It has also doubled the floor space devoted to computers and business machines.

"You've got to keep looking around and saying, 'Where are we not as good as we need to be?'" Stemberg says. That means watching great companies in other industries and emulating them, as well as studying data about your own market's customers, competitors, and trends. In addition, it means encouraging managers to "live reality, but dream the dream," Stemberg adds. "And then you have to be very careful that you don't punish people for taking chances. We just don't. You make it very clear that the people who go out there and are the pioneers, who try things, shouldn't be punished if it fails. Nobody wants to be the guy out on the point when something doesn't work, but you have to let them know that's okay. It's hard, but it has to be done."

What's even harder when it comes to being a strategic CEO, Stemberg says, is making those decisions about the future that can't be fully confirmed through careful analysis—the soft decisions, as he calls them, that are part and parcel of a rapidly changing business environment. Not all questions about the future can be answered with systematic data crunching. Sometimes they require judgment calls—based on real experience, but leaps of faith nevertheless. Stemberg mentions Staples's jump to the West Coast as an example of this aspect of his role.

"Now, how do you address what we should do in California?" he asks. "This is where you, the CEO, have to put your opinion on the line and say, 'We are going to try this.' It's an executive decision. We're just going to try this—my sense was that California was going to be very successful for us. There was no getting around the ambiguity of it, but that was my sense."

By the same token, Stemberg says, a strategic-approach CEO must then take responsibility for the near-term pain his long-term decisions may cause, such as deflated income or otherwise slowed growth. "It's absolutely essential you don't let Wall Street run your business," he says. "Not that what a lot of analysts say isn't true, it's just that most of them do not have the kind of time horizon a CEO should or does." Listening too closely to analysts, investors, or even the board of directors can discourage you from taking the kind of bold risks that can pay off in bold terms. A strategist must put his reputation on the line for that reason, he says, because usually no one else in the organization will.

Stemberg also talks about another major challenge at a fast-growing company and one of his major goals: implementing a human assets focus to complement his strategy approach. The problem, he notes, is that given the pace of change in the industry and within Staples, jobs can quickly outgrow the people in them. "Of all the challenges you face," he says, "this is as difficult an issue as it gets." He tries to overcome it, he says, by actively seeking people with the desire and capability to mature and change with their jobs.

Given Stemberg's track record for shaking up industries, you might wonder where he has set his sights next, when the day comes that Staples's growth slows from 40 percent a year to a more pedestrian 20 percent. He first jokingly answers that he'll be headed for a beach, to get some rest. But then he talks about not letting that happen, by continuing to press his organization to take risks, to scrutinize every competitor, to anticipate the needs of every consumer, and to remain focused on the company's next point of arrival.

OTHER VISIONS, OTHER VOICES

It may be five years or five months off, but the future is where the CEOs in this chapter focus their sights. It is their point of arrival, and reaching it, that informs virtually every activity, every meeting, every trip, every decision of the corporate office. For John Hunter, it determines how many hours he spends on a plane. For Helmut Maucher, it means watching TV commercials from around the world. For Michael Dell, it even affects where he eats lunch.

But the future, and how to get there, is not the only role of the strategist. Several of the CEOs we interviewed spoke of an additional responsibility they see for themselves as guardians of the long term: protecting divisions, projects, or products that the rest of the organization would either dismiss or disregard as too experimental, financially draining, or strategically incorrect. These strategic CEOs say that it is by virtue of their bird's-eye perspective that only they can know which trees should be cultivated and which should be cut down for the benefit of the entire forest. Being a strategist, therefore, is not just a matter of assessing the future of the company but of advocating, and even championing, the sometimes unpopular decisions that arise from the process.

One CEO who describes his job in these terms is Jérôme Monod of

Lyonnaise des Eaux, the giant French service and construction firm. In 1994, the company had revenues of $20 billion and earnings of $206 million from building projects such as the "Chunnel" between Britain and France and the nine-mile bridge linking Canada's Prince Edward Island to New Brunswick. It also supplies water to 40 million people in cities from Buenos Aires to Sydney to Macao, China. Monod says that the corporate center at Lyonnaise concerns itself with creating synergies between its business units as well as mapping their long-term strategic pathways; but he identifies its primary role as "protective," and he points to the example of the Degrémont company as an example.

In 1975, Degrémont, an international engineering subsidiary of Lyonnaise, almost fell into bankruptcy, mainly due to the oil crisis. Many members of the board of directors wanted to sell or liquidate the company, but one (the former president of Lyonnaise) mentioned to Monod that Degrémont perhaps had valuable experience in water treatment. "Others said, 'You lived through more than a century of water distribution without water treatment, so really why take the trouble to straighten it out and why put any money into it?'" Monod recalls. "I realized that without one person who had an interest in saving it, Degrémont would be dead."

Monod decided to be that person. He restructured the organization and sold some of its divisions and some of its assets, including its headquarters in the United States. At the same time, he established operations in Japan, installed CAD/CAM systems in the R&D divisions, and changed top management. "By making an extremely drastic effort, we succeeded in creating a company that today has not only repaid the majority of its returns at a better rate than we signed up for in the subsidies that we capitalized then but has paid dividends, too," he says. Degrémont's sales and profits have been growing at 15 percent a year for seven years, and Monod adds, "As a business unit, it is essential to Lyonnaise today."

Because of the Degrémont story, and others like it, Monod concludes, "I think that the first role of the headquarters of a holding company such as ours is to know whether to keep a company alive, whether or not to keep a company present, and whether or not to protect a company in the group."

Ron Cambre, CEO of the Denver-based **Newmont Mining Corp.,** said something similar about projects, in his case a vast time- and money-draining gold and copper mine in Indonesia, and an experimental technology called bioleaching. He has championed both in an effort, he says, to protect the company's investors long after he has retired.

Many CEOs, of course, share Cambre's goal, but few have a time horizon as long as his. The mine in Indonesia, for instance, might not show a profit until the next century. Still, the mine, called Batu Hijau, requires a more than $1 billion investment to open, and that's money Cambre decided to spend.

"I'm doing my successor a huge favor," he comments. "I mean, I'd be better off, selfishly, to just let this pass. Sell it to someone else. Capitalize on it. But is that fair? Hell, no." Once it starts producing, Batu Hijau will have an enormous impact on Newmont's income and cash flow for thirty years, Cambre says.

He hopes to see quicker results from bioleaching, a potential extracting process that had foundered at Newmont for several years before Cambre was named CEO in 1994, because many perceived it as too speculative. The process involves tiny bacteria called *Thiobacillus ferrooxidans*, which researchers believe have the potential to "eat" the sulfur in iron and gold ore, turning waste into a profitable, albeit low-grade, product. If bioleaching works, it could increase Newmont's gold reserves by as much as 8 million ounces, about 30 percent. That's critical for the company; its main source of growth and competitive advantage is exactly what bioleaching promises: increased output at low cost. While profitable overall—it had an income of $85 million from $664 million in sales in 1994—Newmont has not excited Wall Street for many years. In fact, the company is considered the antithesis of a growth stock, based on Newmont's steady and predictable output of 1.5 million ounces of gold a year since 1900. Cambre is determined to get that number up to 2.5 million by 1997. Bioleaching is still an unproven technology—and unpopular with some within the company, he acknowledges—but as CEO, he is the one to take the risk. He put $11 million into the demonstration project.

"I spend a lot of time abroad, a lot of time meeting with foreign governments about old mines and new ones," Cambre says, "and I spend a good portion of my time with our exploration people, and all of this is necessary work for me as CEO.

"But I also think it is very, very important to leave this company in a very strong position for the future," Cambre adds, "so that the next person stepping into my shoes will say, 'Look, I've got not only a good strong operation position today but I can see five or ten or fifteen years into the future and I'm still okay, thanks to some risks they made back before my time.'"

Finally, at **Deutsche Bank,** Germany's largest bank with $350 billion of assets under management and one of the world's most powerful institutions, CEO Hilmar Kopper says part of his role is to protect strategically critical products that the organization itself resists for any number of reasons—cultural bias, fear of change, lack of expertise. As an example, he mentions derivatives, the business of creating and trading contracts in which the value of the contracts is derived from future prices of stocks, bonds, or currencies. Although widely traded in the United States, derivatives can be volatile, and therefore are considered risky. Throughout the 1980s, Deutsche Bank traded derivatives only internally, among its own divisions and subsidiaries, and never for external customers. But in 1991, Kopper decided that policy had to change.

"Three or four years ago, despite all the talk about innovation, no one wanted to do [externally traded] derivatives in this company," Kopper recalls. "They were not liked very much in Europe, and not at all in this country."

But for Deutsche Bank to become a universal bank—Kopper's top strategic goal—external derivatives could not be ignored. By "universal," he means international in geography and highly diversified in the financial instruments it offers. The institution currently has more than 1,500 offices in Germany and 405 in foreign locales, but Kopper has been expanding operations since he took over in 1989, buying banks and insurance companies from the United States to Australia to bring Deutsche Bank into sixteen countries.

"I said this is something we must do," he recalls. "There is no way around it." Today, Deutsche Bank is becoming a major player in the derivatives market, particularly out of its New York operations, competing with the likes of Wall Street powerhouses Morgan Stanley and Goldman Sachs.

Kopper had to exercise the same kind of decision making when Deutsche Bank agreed to purchase ITT's consumer finance operations in the United States in late 1994. "That was part of our bigger strategy again," Kopper says. "You know, the people over in the mortgage banking business, they were saying, 'What are we doing that for?' But that's the test of value for the center—that is our part, to make those cumbersome decisions that no one else can make, for the good of the overall group."

THE STRATEGIC APPROACH: VISION AND BEYOND

Virtually all business leaders have vision, at least as the term is used in today's jargon. They intuit what customers want next, they anticipate a competitor's next maneuver, they know which managers to promote and which to let go. In this chapter, however, we have laid out another, more complex definition of vision, as a *management approach*. This approach, as we have seen in the nine examples presented here, certainly draws on business acumen—a second sense, as it were—derived from years of experience and education. But the strategic approach as described by the CEOs and presidents we spoke with is more of a process than a state of being, with senior management making long-term strategy formulation and its execution the major vehicle for value addition. The strategic approach, these executives assert, is not management by gut, or intuition, or the kind of imaginative thinking associated with business visionaries such as Henry Ford or Walt Disney. It is instead systematic, dispassionate, and structured analysis of what we have called a company's point of departure and its point of arrival, and it is carefully forging the path between them. It is the rigorous and continuous examination of an organization's capabilities and its market context. It is, ultimately, a determination of where and what a company must be to compete in the future, and how to get there better and faster than anyone else.

The voices in this chapter tell different stories, but they all speak to this one theme. At Coke, the focus is on continually reinventing the brand to make it "new and relevant" for soft-drink consumers—not just now but so far in the future they may even drink the Real Thing in space. Michael Dell similarly faces the challenge of positioning his personal computer company for tomorrow, but in his case, "tomorrow" is to be taken almost literally. Unipart's John Neill talks not of reinventing a brand as management's overarching concern but of reinventing an entire nation's manufacturing policy. Senior management in every organization in this chapter says it is relentlessly focused on what comes next and making it happen.

Their means to these ends are varied: Coke and Nestlé engage in long, demanding strategic planning processes, and Nestlé, like Unipart, trains its managers at state-of-the-art corporate universities. At Staples, Tom Stemberg says he pores over market data about purchasing patterns, studies competitors to see what his office superstore chain can do better, and frequently meets with major customers to ask the same question. Managers at Dell listen to 50,000 customer phone calls a week. Ron Cambre at Newmont Mining says he devotes his energy, and corporate resources, to an experimental new leaching technology that could change the way his company has done business for the past hundred years.

But if their tools are different, these strategic CEOs say they do share one trait, and that is to delegate day-to-day operations to the business units or among their senior staff. Without exception, these CEOs say they must be free from detail to keep their attention on the big picture. They do, however, step into the midst of operations in crisis or investigate when they need to know more about customers, products, or other business issues in order to plan for the future. But then they step back, and look forward again.

When does a CEO choose the strategic approach? In and of itself, industry type doesn't seem to matter. Strategic organizations make coffee and car parts, they mine gold and trade currencies. What is important is complexity, in terms of technology, geography, or functions. Volume and pace of change seem to matter, too. The less stable the situation, the more senior management says it needs to play the role of both navigator and pioneer. And to play that role well, it needs all the information and insight this particular management approach generates. Strategic organizations, it seems, take the biggest risks, because senior management has made it a priority to know what those risks entail. They have done the work. Sometimes, the work fails them. But more often, it pays off by an order of magnitude: Nestlé's Asian expansion, for example; Deutsche Bank's move into derivatives; Staples's geographic expansion.

The companies in this chapter, and strategic companies worldwide, seek to add extraordinary value by grasping what the future means, and grabbing its rewards. It is a job that takes more than vision. It takes the strategic approach and the leadership to drive it through an entire organization.

3

"I ALWAYS GET BACK TO THE PEOPLE": THE HUMAN ASSETS APPROACH

The markets are the most essential thing. We have never mixed that up," **Nestlé**'s Helmut Maucher declared, explaining why he has selected the strategic approach to guide his organization into the next century. But Maucher also employs, with nearly equal emphasis, the approach that is the focus of this chapter: human assets management. In this approach, the center of the corporation works to add extraordinary value through the policies, procedures, programs, and systems surrounding the hiring, retention, and development of people at every level in the organization. An underlying belief of these executives is that the corporate center cannot and should not try to add value through the day-to-day management of operations. "The people in charge of the operating companies must do that; we at the center should not be trying to oversee or monitor the day-to-day management of the businesses," asserts Anthony Greener, CEO of **Guinness,** one of the world's leading alcoholic beverage companies, maker of Johnnie Walker Scotch whisky and Gordon's gin. Instead, Greener says, Corporate's "natural role" is managing money and, more important, "the key asset we have—people." To that end, many of the CEOs in this chapter often know hundreds of their employees, but the human assets approach goes many steps further. It involves career planning, mentoring, face-to-face discussions about values, decision making, and performance. Human assets executives travel continuously, manage the relationships between individuals, and define the values—often personality traits—that they believe will yield strong financial results.

The executives in this chapter say they have selected people management because they find it the most effective way to respond to business situations involving complexity, in terms of both products and geography. In addition, these executives are united in their belief that day-to-day, block-and-tackle management is more important than long-term strategy in creating a competitive advantage in their industries. And many of them also believe, on a philosophical plane, that empowering individuals is the right thing to do.

Two other themes run through these interviews. First, the human assets approach is, simply put, good fun. Its proponents enjoy the work of it. But at the same time, it is perhaps the hardest of the five approaches to implement. The following stories illuminate why.

AT NESTLÉ: BRINGING A GLOBAL CULTURE, RESPECTING LOCAL ONES

Helmut Maucher is as direct and systematic about his approach to people as he is about his approach to strategy. He believes that as CEO it is his responsibility not only to lead but to build a team. To that end, he says he spends much of his time dealing with people, "and more time is spent thinking about them." Those close to his office estimate Maucher and his top lieutenants meet with nearly 5,000 **Nestlé** employees of varying rank throughout the year, resulting in nearly nonstop travel. Of these trips to Nestlé divisions, Maucher says, "I do my homework beforehand. I look at their numbers, I know what they are doing, what questions to ask. And when I get there, I want to meet with the management, see the products, the advertising, see the shops, and from time to time, see the factories." At the same time, Maucher himself hand-picks the top twenty-five market heads as well as the top three or four managers in the ten largest markets. He also picks about forty-five staffers to work with him in Nestlé's headquarters.

"Values are very important," Maucher explains. "To be decentralized and to give power to the market managers, we have to keep people on the same wavelength. We have to remind them they are part of the Nestlé world. So, in order to make sure we have shared values, we have to know our people. We do know our people." Pressed further, Maucher adds, "I know more people than anyone in this company. I've been here for forty years. No one knows more people than I do."

How? Maucher brings country heads and other top managers into the company headquarters for days at a time. Most of these men and women are invited to top management meetings, where Maucher watches them closely and later, in the privacy of his office, discusses their performance and their thoughts about Nestlé strategy. In addition, Maucher keeps Nestlé's zone managers, a key group of people in terms of shaping performance, in Vevey with him. Many have offices on the same floor. Maucher also attends a two-day off-site meeting once a year where top managers discuss Nestlé's strategy but also socialize. The same kind of interaction occurs twice a year at a "senate" meeting with the heads of the most important dozen markets, plus the general managers in Vevey. But Maucher doesn't just focus on the company's senior executives. Hundreds of managers three or four levels below the top ranks—men and women typically in their thirties, often with the company only five or six years—also are invited to the company's training center for interactive sessions on manufacturing innovations, advertising, and technical skills. But as Timm Crull, the former North American zone head, notes, "These meetings aren't just about knowledge, they are about the cross-fertilization of ideas. They are about the Nestlé way and Nestlé values."

Maucher concurs. His strategic vision of local market expertise requires that Nestlé managers stay in one country for as long as possible, so a global culture—a *Nestlé* culture—can be built only by bringing managers to Switzerland as often as possible to talk explicitly about corporate values.

"We are very careful about the type of people we have," Maucher says. "They must share our values of hard work, honesty, and commitment to the company. They must be modest. They must have style, class, and quality, but not show it off. They must be pragmatic and not dogmatic."

If Nestlé employees veer from this model of behavior, Maucher is not reluctant to let them know.

He tells a story of a recent visit to France, where he spotted a Nestlé billboard he didn't like. In fact, it violated several rules in the advertising bible he had written for the organization. The billboard had hard-to-read brown lettering on a dark background, it contained more than two messages about the product, and it couldn't be easily read from more than forty yards away. In short, it was too cluttered to be effective.

"I do delegate," Maucher says, "but when I see something that is not the Nestlé way, I will question it immediately." A few days later, Maucher called the country manager and told him the billboard was "crazy" and had to be changed.

It was, by the next day.

GILLETTE: 800 PERFORMANCE REVIEWS, FOR THE BOTTOM LINE'S SAKE

Al Zeien's touch may be lighter than Maucher's—it's impossible not to warm up to this CEO, with his easy humor and irrepressible personality—but its reach is just as great. Zeien also knows an astounding number of his company's 34,000 employees, traveling almost constantly to meet with them in groups and alone, even in new, small operations in Russia and the Far East. He doesn't miss a product group, from **Gillette**'s stalwart blade business, which makes up 70 percent of profits, to its Paper Mate and Waterman pens and Liquid Paper operations, to the divisions that make products such as Right Guard deodorant, Braun electric shavers, and Oral-B toothbrushes. Traveling around the globe, he personally conducts 800 performance reviews annually. ("When the personnel department told me that, I said it wasn't possible," Zeien says, "but then they walked me through the paperwork from Argentina and Pakistan and so forth, and I realized they were right.") In addition, Zeien makes it his business to carefully monitor and guide the careers of literally dozens of managers, such as the New Zealander who was working for Gillette in Australia until Zeien spotted a good opportunity for him within the corporation in Redwood City, California. The man's boss in Australia assured Zeien the New Zealander would never move, so Zeien caught up with him on a plane and asked him himself. In fact, Zeien's involvement with the people in his company is so deep-rooted that he was once heard to remark, "Now, we have a manager in India who is originally from Japan, trained in Boston, spent two years in Houston for us, then back to Japan, before a stint in France, and then after that . . ." And at the end of this career history, Zeien was able to comment, in his typical rapid-fire way, that the employee had recently had a baby boy.

But you can't misread Zeien's devotion to the people approach as simply a big heart and a terrific memory for details. It is, fundamentally, the function of strategic imperatives, born in the tension-filled period in the late 1980s when Gillette was the target of four unsuccessful hostile takeover attempts. Coming out of that experience, the company was determined to make itself as invulnerable as possible. It aggressively refocused its strategy on global growth—specifically, on being the number one player in every product and market in which it plays. ("Not number one or number two in each *individual* market, like GE," Zeien states emphatically, "we have to be number one worldwide with the product, or we won't make it and won't sell it.") Gillette also took the takeover attempts as a message that the company had to improve its technologies and how they were shared across borders, making the company so strong (and so profitable) that it was raider-proof. Zeien explains that on a given day, the lowest cost way to get razor blade cartridges to the Australian market might start at a steel plant on the west coast of Japan, move next to a processing plant in Rio de Janeiro, to Singapore for packaging, and then to Melbourne for distribution. "But that might change tomorrow," Zeien says, "so we have to be on top of it. Everyone in this company has to know what everyone else knows; they have to be thinking alike, sharing information, really working as one person."

Zeien describes the takeover fight as "very troubled times." He says, "Those times changed the culture quite dramatically. You know, two companies, one of them growing 10 percent a year and the other growing 20 percent, will both end up at the same place eventually, but the 20 percent company gets there faster. We realized we had to be that 20 percent company."

To be that company, Zeien sees one determinant—Gillette's ability to expand its corps of experienced international managers—and hence his focus on personnel development and training. Seventy percent of Gillette's $6 billion in revenues is derived outside the United States, and hundreds of employees manage those revenues. Yet only 350 of them are what Zeien calls "expatriates," men and women who willingly move around the world for the corporation. The others remain in their native country.

"More than any other factor, our growth rate in the future will be controlled by our ability to increase that number of expatriates from 350 to 700," Zeien says. "It won't be finances that make us grow. It won't be capital. We could try to *hire* the best and the brightest, but it's the *experience* with Gillette that we need. About half of our expats are now on their fourth country. *That* kind of experience. It takes ten years to make the kind of Gillette manager I'm talking about—ten years at the base."

Along with the experience of its global workforce, Gillette's success will be based on those managers (and all employees, in fact) sharing the same values, values that put the company's earnings before those of a single country or product line. "I like to say: there's a right way, a wrong way, and a Gillette way," Zeien reflects with a wry smile. "The Gillette way isn't always the right way, but it is consistent, and that's what we have to live by."

To illustrate his point, he tells the story of a manager in Sweden.

"I don't know if you know much about Sweden, but its population is located in the southern half of the country," Zeien begins. "The guy there has to decide if he's going to increase his sales force in northern Sweden—if he should put on six more salesmen up north.

"Now, how do you want him to make the decision? If you don't work at it—if someone like me doesn't get involved in shaping this guy—he might say, 'Well, if I put six more salesmen up north, I can sell a certain amount more, and it pays for the new employees. I think I'll do it.'

"But, you see, we don't want him to decide that," Zeien says, his voice gathering momentum. "We want him to think, 'How much extra money does the *entire Gillette world* make as a result of adding those six salesmen in northern Sweden?'"

A good accounting system will help him make that choice, Zeien says, as will a performance rating system that rewards him for thinking about the company's worldwide profitability. But the best guarantee that there won't be too many salesmen in northern

Sweden, Zeien says, is for the CEO to visit southern Sweden and spend a few hours chatting with the manager in charge. And to that end, Zeien travels almost continually. He is often out of the United States two weeks a month, and sometimes more. And when he is in the United States, he frequently spends another week a month on the road.

"People have asked me time and again, 'Why do you spend all that time traveling?' And the answer to that is really kind of simple," Zeien says. "I travel because that's where the people are. I travel because I want to be sure that people who are making the decisions in, say, Argentina have the same reference base as I do for the company. I want to make sure they are all using the same ground rules I would use. I want to see if they have the same objectives. I travel because you can only find these things out on the home ground."

Additionally, he says, travel helps keep him connected with what he calls "special situations."

"We fire general managers from time to time," Zeien says. "I personally want to be involved. I'm always suspicious of those kind of decisions when they don't involve the chief executive." But Zeien doesn't make a case for the underdog.

"I hate the word *fair*," he remarks instead, his voice unapologetic. "Everybody says, 'Yeah, I want to be treated fairly.' I say, 'The world is not fair.' I use the word *appropriate*. I think it's important that the company treat people appropriately."

Does Zeien actually veto many firings? The answer is no.

At the same time, he does protect and reward employees who, as he puts it, "are carrying a torch for something."

"Lots of times, I will make a trip or a phone call or whatever to support a guy who is carrying a torch, and carrying it right off a cliff," he says, laughing. "But most of those times, we have asked him to jump off the edge of a cliff. People need to know what failure means, and they need to know that the organization stands behind them. That's a role I play."

But for all this emphasis on people management, Zeien says he still spends 50 percent of his time on Gillette's products, explaining that good people in an organization are critical, but they don't guarantee good products.

"Our lifeblood is new products, ever improving products," Zeien says. "We are a technology-driven company, and we figure it takes about fifteen projects in research for every three that go into development. And for every three that go into development, we only get one to market. And that one has to be great. I'm not talking modification. I'm talking a great new product. It takes a lot of support from senior management to get through that process. A lot of focus on picking the winners."

For Zeien, that translates into a trip to Germany, during which he spends two days doing nothing but listening to product reviews in the Braun business. Not too overwhelming. But then multiply the trip to Germany three times, since he visits that often to review products, and then multiply that by all the other countries he visits, and by the six other business units.

That's a lot of days listening to engineers and marketing specialists. And he's not just listening. Take the case of a new line of toiletries— that is, its deodorants, shaving creams, hair-care products, and cosmetics—that Gillette intended to label with its own corporate name, a first. The line was supposed to be launched in 1991. Zeien personally delayed it eighteen months.

"I stopped the launch," he says, "I stopped it three times. They had everything ready to go, but I read the [consumer] test results, and I said, 'Hey, they're not winners.' They told me, 'Well, ten out of fourteen are, what's wrong with that?' "

Zeien shakes his head, as if the answer is obvious.

"A lot of people, a lot of our investors and a lot of security analysts, thought we were crazy," Zeien adds, "but we had spent a lot of money on that line, and we had to get it right."

Once you get Zeien talking about products, he is as unrestrained on the topic as he is about managing people. But if you listen to him long enough, you begin to sense that there really isn't a line between the two areas. He says good people don't guarantee good products, but when you push him, his stories attest that the two are intertwined.

He talks, for instance, about a new shaver in Japan, and how it became a success.

"About two years ago, I sat through a presentation on the product, and I said, 'This product is absolutely fantastic,' " he recalls, "but I also said, 'You're not spending enough to get it to market. Now, what would happen if we doubled the rate of expenditures?' "

Zeien did just that—a process he calls "endorsement"—and the shaver arrived on Japanese shelves a year ahead of schedule, and promptly sold off them.

"I believe in individual rewards," Zeien says. "When I left that meeting, that guy felt like I had given him a blank check. Individuals are individuals, and this guy deserved the reward, even if it wasn't monetary. It's psychological—people like to win, and people have to be rewarded as winners. It's not just passing out a bonus check at the end of the year. It's my job, my role, to let them feel that way."

Zeien tells another story about products, but again it ends up being about people.

There is a high-speed camera Gillette has developed, he says, a camera so tiny that company engineers have placed it between the blades of a Sensor razor to photograph a man's face as it is being shaved. (The camera takes pictures 100 times faster than a normal movie camera.) Gillette engineers have also placed this camera inside toothbrushes to study the best bristle length for Oral-B products. Zeien can barely contain his enthusiasm when he describes the miniature device. But after a moment discussing the remarkable technology of it, he ends up talking about the importance of giving researchers the freedom and rewards they need. And finally, he talks about the managers who must judge how many of those things are enough, and how many are too little.

"I happen to have a vice president in charge of R&D who I hired from General Electric who is really a super scientist, who really knows how to call them. . . ." Zeien begins, and he is off on a tangent that concludes, "Well, that's people management, I suppose."

If it is, Zeien need not be reluctant to admit it. While he says Gillette, like all consumer products companies, is ever vulnerable to intense competition on every front, the company has been unstoppable recently, with net income soaring nearly 20 percent every year since 1990. The profitability figures bolster Zeien's conviction that he's running the corporation the right way, starting with its people and following them straight to the bottom line.

AT SARA LEE: CREATING CORPORATE ENTREPRENEURS

Paul Fulton is the former president of **Sara Lee,** the company that sells the world frozen cheesecake as well as Hanes stockings and underwear, Ball Park frankfurters, Coach leather products, Kiwi shoe polish, Playtex brassieres, and Jimmy Dean sausage, to name just a few of the products and brands that make up the company's $17 billion in annual sales. (In Europe, Sara Lee sells the popular Douwe Egberts coffee and Dim stockings.) Fulton, who served as Sara Lee's president from 1988 to 1993 and is now dean of the Kenan-Flagler Business School at the University of North Carolina in Chapel Hill, shares Maucher's and Zeien's belief that local managers must be empowered to operate alone, and therefore must be well versed in the company's values and culture.

"We can't worry about local decisions," Fulton says, "but what we can do is really create people who understand how to think about and make those decisions for us." What does this mean in real time? Fulton replies, "We teach them [Sara Lee managers] how to think about and understand brands and consumers. We give them a reasonable portfolio of products and brands to deal with. We visit them. We listen. We coach. We suggest. We move them around some, between countries and across divisions and functions, to expose them to new ideas and processes.

"But," he adds, "we cannot tell them how to sell it in their country. They've got to figure that out, and we have to create the structure that allows it."

Fulton feels this must be a structure that does not "churn" managers. "That doesn't generate the strongest kind of company for the long run," he says. In other words, managers have to be allowed to fail, then pick up and try again. "You've got to let people get a little bit of history with the company," he explains. "If you fire them after one mistake, you end up creating managers who don't take risks. You end up with managers who lack confidence to act alone and make tough decisions."

Risk and confidence—these two characteristics, Fulton says, are what make ordinary managers into "corporate entrepreneurs," which is exactly what Sara Lee needs to thrive in tomorrow's global marketplace.

"It's really worked for Sara Lee in general," Fulton says, but then he shifts in his seat and his face gets a rueful look. He remembers a time when the company had to push harder than usual to create corporate entrepreneurs. In 1990, the company sent a group of managers to

Taiwan, hoping to create a strong presence there to establish credibility for expansion into Japan and China.

"Next thing we know, we're getting calls at headquarters asking us for several million to start an aggressive upfront advertising program." Fulton laughs. "And so these people had to be . . . well, re-educated. You know, we had to turn their heads around and remind them, that's not how entrepreneurs behave. Entrepreneurs don't have anyone to call for money."

Fulton pauses for a moment. "What we really wanted," he says when he continues, "was for people to act as if they were desperate to succeed and grow; we wanted them to act as if there were no safety net. We wanted them to learn the lay of the land, talk to the customers, talk to the suppliers, find their way around, and think of how to build the business—sort of bootstrap it up in as aggressive and entrepreneurial way as possible.

"The idea was not to get them to think, 'Gee, Sara Lee has a lot of money to bring to the table,' but to get them to think, 'We've got to build this business *for* Sara Lee.' So we talked to them about that. We made a trip over there. It was a coaching thing, really. We talked to them about exploring new horizons, expanding their concepts of what it meant to work for Sara Lee. And after that, they started the process again."

SHV HOLDINGS: SHREDDING PAPER, SETTING MANAGERS FREE

If the previous three corporate executives manage people in the service of a corporation's greater goals—read: profitability—Paul Fentener van Vlissingen of **SHV Holdings** manages them in the service of human happiness and fulfillment. He wants his employees to feel free, he says, to slam doors and swear when the spirit moves them, and especially to laugh.

This sentiment has been voiced before in business, but usually by an ambitious young entrepreneur seeking to re-create the status quo in his own image. Van Vlissingen wants none of that. He is fifty-three, soft-spoken to the point of being shy, and reflective in nature, one legacy of a battle with cancer ten years ago. As for being an upstart businessman, van Vlissingen is quite the opposite. He is perhaps one of Europe's wealthiest men, part of the family that owns SHV, a company that sells energy and consumer goods, with sales last year of $11 billion and income of $315 million. In the past ten years, under van Vlissingen's unconventional people-focused stewardship, those figures have increased ninefold. As a result, the value of the company is estimated to be $3 billion.

With headquarters in the industrial Dutch city of Utrecht, SHV was formed in 1896 through the merger of Holland's eight main coal-merchanting families. Today SHV employs 65,000 people in more than twenty countries in the trade of liquid gas and dozens of Makro self-service stores. (These stores are typically in joint ventures with local partners, such as Kmart.)

Analysts say SHV is a force to be reckoned with in its businesses, owing to its bulk purchasing power, its low operating and distribution costs, and its cutthroat pricing. But these details seem of little concern to van Vlissingen. In fact, instead of talking about the nuts and bolts of markets, procedures, and strategies, van Vlissingen talks about how his company has achieved its success precisely because of its human assets approach. It's a topic on which he has been asked to lecture more than once.

"I go, because I always think that these things should never stay secret so I talk about them and about our organization," van Vlissingen says. "I tell people we succeed because we have a whole different system of looking at people, a whole different approach, a philosophy of looking at people."

It is a philosophy that comes down to the adage that people rise to the occasion. Give a little responsibility, get a little back; give a lot, and people soar. It's management by letting go.

"When I became CEO in 1984, I saw there was a whole new generation of managers coming in who were different from those people born in World War II or before, as I was. And the difference is they were much better educated, much more individualistic, less corporate minded," van Vlissingen says. "And to give those people a better chance you had to build an organization where they could have much more responsibility, because we didn't believe we could get anybody to do the best they can unless you really make them responsible."

In his first seven months, van Vlissingen decentralized SHV, pushing every possible decision to the field. "Total change, yes. But if you want to do something, do it fast," is how he explains the speed of the transformation. In the past, every decision involving more than $500,000 had to come through the head office. Van Vlissingen announced that he didn't want to hear about any decision involving less than $15 million after it had been approved in a yearly budget. He closed a corporate headquarters in Rotterdam, and decreased corporate staff from 380 to 50 people. But in keeping with van Vlissingen's concern for people's happiness, this didn't mean layoffs. Everyone got a new job—in the field. "I was there," he recalls of the day the change in assignments was announced. "If you want to have change, it's you, the chief executive, who has to be seen to do it himself. You have to expose yourself. I think that is the only reason you get paid very well."

After the decentralization, van Vlissingen took steps to push his approach to people management—his beliefs about personal responsibility—throughout the corporation. First, he abolished all reports and meetings with slide presentations. The goal was to promote face-to-face discussion of issues, not numbers. Second, he changed the rules at board meetings. No decisions were to be made until all sides of the issue were aired, and board members had literally slept on what they had heard, thereby "humanizing" the process by letting people adjust their reactions with time.

In general, however, van Vlissingen is most happy when decisions don't even reach the boardroom.

"It's very important all the time to tell people to do it themselves," he says. "We have very talented people. You don't have to stimulate an athlete who is running the thousand meters. You don't have to tell them that they have to win. They know that. But you can ask them, 'Have you checked your diet? Have you got the best trainer?' That you can do. But I don't believe in telling people too much because they're the whole young generation and those are the ones who are really making money now. You can ask them questions, but they find out themselves."

To this end, van Vlissingen says that sometimes when he receives a letter or memo from a manager in the field asking for advice, he writes his answer on the same sheet and sends it back. The reply reads, "I agree it's a difficult problem. I wish you success!"

Van Vlissingen so deeply believes in pushing responsibility away from the corporate center that, upon taking over as CEO, he personally supervised the shredding of 1 million pieces of correspondence per year between the divisions and his office. "We eliminated about 75 percent of all paper between the head office and the subsidiaries," he recalls happily. "We had everyone around the table, and I would hold up a paper and say, 'Who needs this? Why? Explain it to me.' If the answers weren't sharp, into the shredder!" Today, all reports to the head office are limited to one sheet of paper per company, and they are to arrive just once a month. The paper contains key numbers and a short narrative by the CEO of the company reporting.

Another part of SHV's people-management system is hiring the right people, getting them to collaborate, and letting them fail, even encouraging them to.

"I choose people with my nose . . . what else is there?" van Vlissingen asks. "I don't read psychological reports. I sit down at the table with them, and sometimes I have an hour interview, and I make life very difficult for them because I want to see how people perform under pressure.

"In the business units, we tell people to look for young people who do the unusual. You need an office where you hear the door slam from time to time, you need somebody who will burst in the door and say 'Dammit!' or something. You need excitement. They can't be too snooty or stiff. And you need people who like change. The most important ingredient for happiness is, after all, the ability to change."

Once people join SHV, van Vlissingen thinks it is critical that they enjoy their work and each other, so that they will collaborate. He invited 120 managers and their spouses for an all-expenses-paid three-day ride aboard the Orient Express across Europe. The trip, van Vlissingen says, created an "informal glue" between the participants, so that when they went home to Argentina or Singapore or wherever, they could call each other and ask, "How did you solve that problem? I have one like it."

"We had a lot of fun, a lot of laughter on that trip," van Vlissingen says, "and afterwards they put together a little cabaret making fun of me. Wonderful! Very funny."

Van Vlissingen also encourages the business units to let their people fail. "The failure will give you new ideas," he explains simply. "You know, I always say, 'The most stupid farmer has the biggest potato.'

"To sum it up," van Vlissingen says, "we put 90 percent of the responsibility of innovation, entrepreneurship, and success in the hands of the team that leads the business and there is 10 percent left in the central office."

And what does the central office do with that 10 percent?

"The center of the company should have lots of fantasies," van Vlissingen answers. "It should be a man or a woman with impossible dreams and incredible visions that he or she cannot rationalize and can't get out of computers. He should have this idea that something can be done somewhere, somehow." If the divisions have all the real responsibility of running the business, van Vlissingen says, that allows him to daydream about, say, expanding into Vietnam.

But expanding into Vietnam is not something van Vlissingen will be overseeing in the near future. He recently resigned as SHV's CEO. "I was getting too much power," he explains with a shrug. "Read your classic literature. Read the plays of Sophocles, Euripides, and Shakespeare, and you'll see it's an age-old problem. In power too long, and you lose your sense of reality. Too much power and a man or woman will create their own downfall.

"I think if I could create a golden rule of CEOs, it would be 'Out after ten years.'"

Van Vlissingen isn't yet sure what fingerprint his successor will leave; he only hopes it will be different from his—people should be free to be themselves.

UNITED BISCUITS: GETTING GOOD PEOPLE— AND KEEPING THEM

Eric Nicoli of the U.K.'s **United Biscuits** is another CEO who manages people from his heart, but instead of giving them the kind of ultimate freedom allowed at SHV, he has installed the most detailed human resource management system we encountered in our interviews. It includes frequent performance reviews, feedback sessions, and a people-management "godfather," among other initiatives.

Nicoli, the gregarious son of Italian immigrants, is remarkably open when it comes to why he focuses his attention on people instead of on strategy.

"Ultimately, I think the performance of a business is a function of strategic choices that are made years before," he says, "and no one should underestimate the importance of good fortune in all this.

"Basically, when it comes to strategy, you make your choices based on insufficient information, and you make them when you have to make them. We have chosen some categories, and we've chosen some geographies. Five years from now, some will look like great choices, some will look like fantastic choices, and some . . ." Nicoli smiles in the silence of what is left unsaid. "Sometimes circumstances change completely," he adds after a moment passes, "for reasons beyond your control, and your choices turn out to be bad. Some of the things that most influence our business aren't predictable—economic trends, the value of the pound. These things make a huge difference, and yet we have no control over them. That's the nature of our business."

Nicoli's business is food—in large part, cookies and snacks such as McVitie's biscuits, Keebler cookies, and KP snacks. The company has a presence throughout Europe and in the United States, as well as in Australia and China. Nicoli, forty-four, took over in 1991, after a career with another food company—an unlikely path for a man with an advanced degree in nuclear physics. (He switched to food marketing as a young man, after deciding that academia was too obscure for him. "I knew I was only a sports fanatic who happened to be good at taking exams," he admitted once in a newspaper interview.) Today, Nicoli is happy to be running a company with 40,000 employees, and he wants his employees to feel the same way about working for him. He calls his approach "structured informality." Its goals are manifold, including planning and budgeting and other traditional controls; but in the final analysis, Nicoli believes his best shot at success is to get talented people working at United Biscuits, and then keep them there.

"There are lots of companies that spend a lot of time recruiting excellent people and very little time worrying about how to retain them," he says. "The truth is, it's an awful lot harder to retain and motivate people than it is to hire them. The hardest thing is to keep good people, because the better they are, the more likely you are to lose them if you don't make an effort."

United Biscuits' effort on this front is expansive. Nicoli and his top staffers know the top hundred managers "all fairly intimately," he says, and spend "quite a lot of time" thinking about their careers. But, he adds, it doesn't stop with them. "It goes a long, long way down. We have a three-zone grading system that covers hundreds of managers, and we review zones one and two regularly, and the high flyers in zone three.

"We spend most of our time discussing the people with potential, rather than the people without it, although when it comes to those people, we do spend time discussing their needs."

The content of these meetings is quite specific, Nicoli says. "We have a well-honed appraisal system that is the basis of our assessment of all these people. We don't discuss things like, 'The problem with old Stan here is that he's pretty bright, but he's intellectually arrogant and a bit of a jerk.' There is no point in having that kind of conversation. Instead we have a full-year appraisal and a half-year appraisal that has on it your personal objectives, and your business objectives, and how you perform against them. We have an assessment of your potential year after year, and we see how that is developing, and we know what your aspirations are, and whether you have the qualities to be a general manager, or a manager across functions if not a complete general manager, or we will know if the best thing is for you to stay in a function and become a function specialist. We would know if you were mobile or not, and we would discuss you in those terms, and we would identify potential roles for you." This system also includes input from a senior executive that Nicoli calls a "godfather—not surprising, I suppose, given my Italian heritage." This executive is assigned to knowing all there is to know about United Biscuits employees, from how satisfied they are in their jobs to what additional training they might need. This information is fed into the formal appraisal system.

"The important thing," Nicoli adds, "is to keep an open mind in this process. I am constantly surprised at how people change and improve, and sometimes we find people were simply in the wrong job or improperly motivated."

Motivation, in fact, is another topic of importance to Nicoli in his role as a human assets CEO.

"There are a lot of companies where they attempt to motivate people by paying them a lot," he says. Nicoli doesn't dismiss this method's efficacy, but he asserts that people are likewise motivated when they enjoy coming to work, when they like the people they work with, when they can have a good laugh at the office, and when they are part of a caring environment.

"You can fire people in a caring way, or you can just fire people," Nicoli says. "I think one of the attractive characteristics of our company is genuine concern. There is a price for that, of course. It's cheaper not to care—in the short term. But that is one of the reasons, I suspect, why we don't lose good people."

And besides keeping good people, caring about them has another positive impact on the organization, Nicoli says; it creates "synergy" between divisions, the kind of cooperation that gets people to talk, share information, and cooperate in difficult situations.

But ultimately, Nicoli makes people his top priority because he wants to enjoy every day of his working life, not every tenth day. And the way he sees it, his cheerfulness begets cheerfulness in everyone around him. "It's chemistry," he explains, "and chemistry makes a hell of a difference when it comes to success in our business. I truly believe that."

AT PHILIPS ELECTRONICS: MANAGING RELATIONSHIPS, NOT JUST INDIVIDUALS

Jan Timmer is also a believer in chemistry, but for him it is managing the chemistry between employees. In fact, Timmer, the blunt-talking, high-energy son of a baker, has been using this approach to pull his company, the Holland-based electronics giant **Philips,** out of a crisis that has dogged it for several years. Philips is back on top now, with $34 billion in sales and $1.1 billion in net earnings in 1994, and Timmer is widely held responsible for the turnaround. But change did not come easily, or without cost. In the early 1990s, the company posted millions of dollars in losses and laid off some 45,000 employees. The root of the problem? The recession in Europe was one factor, but many Philips observers also blame the company's own bureaucracy, complacency, and a seeming inability to capitalize on its technical innovations. Analysts have said the company lagged behind the Japanese in getting products to market. And at the same time, they noted, Philips misjudged consumer demand with its compact disc interactive products, and again with pricey digital cassette technology. And yet, through this trouble, Philips managed to hang on to what is undeniably a strong identity over a variety of products, from lamps to TVs to kitchen appliances: Magnavox, Marantz, Norelco, and Grundig are among its consumer brands. The company also sells industrial products such as medical X-ray equipment, ultrasound machines, communication systems, and component placement machines, and has also been a leading global supplier of electronic components and semiconductors.

Timmer took over as CEO of the company in 1990, in the midst of its crisis. A career Philips man, he wasted no time distancing himself from his predecessors' business-as-usual approach by implementing a total restructuring of the company, which he named Operation Centurion. His first steps were to cut thousands of jobs—bringing the Philips workforce to 241,000—and sell off nonperforming businesses.

He announced that people had to change the way they communicated with one another within Philips or else nothing would improve and everyone would pay the price. Only people working together in new ways, he said, could put Philips back on the path to profitable growth.

"People are our core value, not so much money," Timmer states. If people are properly managed, then creativity follows, and from that—success. But it's not just managing people, he asserts, it's managing the relationships between them.

"When I go into a factory, no matter where in the world, I can sense the atmosphere if I walk around for a half hour with the factory manager," Timmer says. His presence is commanding, and his voice matches it. "I can tell you whether that factory works or not; I can tell it from the body language of the employees and the way the people react to the foreman and the answers people give to him and the managers, and how unafraid they are. And I can walk out without looking at the figures, and I can tell you if that factory makes money or not."

Timmer says he designed Operation Centurion to change the way people related to one another at Philips, with the intent of simply increasing honesty and sharing of information.

The program brings together several times a year employees of all ranks, products, functions, and countries for discussion and debate of strategic plans, products, and processes. At these meetings, the message from the top is clear: Every voice is to be heard with equal attention. Hierarchy is to be disregarded. There are to be no personal attacks, but all other comments and questions are welcome. Disagreement is encouraged, even with senior management. No power games or battles are allowed because, as Timmer says, "power games kill an organization."

Two years into Operation Centurion, Timmer sees the radical effect on how people communicate. "The relationships are different now," he says. "If you sit for three days, through sometimes very emotional discussions on very difficult issues, then you get to know each other, you get to respect each other. That is the most important fact that has contributed to our success."

Operation Centurion, Timmer says, is no longer a program—it's a way of life. It has expanded from the free-ranging discussions described above to "town meetings" held at plants, where managers must stand before the employees and answer questions—any questions posed—and to the posting of blank pieces of paper throughout offices and factories for people to write their comments and criticisms. "They stay up as long as they are not answered," Timmer says of the sheets. "This was really tough stuff. But the best of the managers went through it very well, and the advantage was, we really began to get the best out of people. Managers began to listen to the shop floor, where there is so much knowledge. It took the managers deflating themselves a little—deflating their importance—but it had to be done."

Timmer does not deny that Philips has traveled a rough road, and that more rocky terrain may still lie ahead. But he believes that with the change in attitudes—with the correct management of people's relationships with each other—Philips will become a winning company in the long term.

"What I have learned with the Centurion process is that in the end it's always people," he says. "Now this sounds like the greatest platitude to management, but forty-two years with this company makes me still say it. Always when I see problems, always when I see bad comments, I always get back to the people.

"I still believe," Timmer says, "in getting things done with people." And with Philips's turnaround as evidence, you can understand why.

AT PEPSICO: STEERING THE PEOPLE WHEEL

Not long ago, **PepsiCo** CEO Wayne Calloway was honored—although *roasted* is probably a better word—at a Harvard Business School alumni banquet, where his colleagues presented the Top Ten Reasons why Calloway is perfect to lead the $30 billion food and drink company. "Thrives on contradictions," one item stated. Among the others were: "Handles a Harley-Davidson like a Hell's Angel." "Attends church like a Southern Baptist." "Absorbs self-help books like a Rhodes Scholar."

The jibes sparked laughter and cheers. Those who know Calloway know he is a CEO with a firm but unconventional take on his job. While archrival Coca-Cola is waging strategic war, hunkered down in detail-laden five-year planning sessions around the world, Calloway is comfortable leaving strategy to the operating units, explaining, "You don't need to be an MIT rocket scientist to know what is important in our businesses." While other CEOs in the same industry, such as Allen Sheppard at GrandMet, relentlessly demand "magic numbers," new products, and breakthrough marketing expertise from managers, Calloway admits he doesn't "jump up and down, pound the table, or yell" about business imperatives. "That wouldn't be me," he says with a shrug. "People would see through it in five minutes." And while still other CEOs focus on creating change, or fighting fires, or erecting corporate boxes, Calloway dismisses these approaches as beside the point.

The point is people. Making sure they are learning. Making sure they are happy. Making sure they are proud. Those ends, he asserts, create PepsiCo's most powerful competitive advantage.

"Our competitors are in trouble if everybody around here has had a learning experience and feels better about themselves," Calloway says. "I wouldn't want to be competing against that kind of machine."

He would, however, want to *build* that kind of machine ever larger and more potent, which is why he spends, by his estimate, at least 50 percent of his time on human assets management—in his words, "making sure we've got the right environment, and our people are feeling good about themselves and everyone is having a good time, enjoying himself, making something happen, and feels a part of something he's proud of.

"That takes the majority of my time," Calloway remarks. "It's the single most important thing I do."

On a day-to-day basis, Calloway's schedule looks a lot like Al Zeien's at Gillette. Zeien travels virtually nonstop and conducts 800 performance reviews a year. No one in the upper management ranks is fired without his involvement. Calloway travels frequently as well and conducts 600 performance reviews a year. No one in upper or middle management is hired without his approval, and sometimes he even makes his opinions known during the M.B.A. recruiting process. Both CEOs see the human assets approach as the best, most effective way to oversee a dispersed, decentralized organization where country or operating unit managers must be able to make the right decisions quickly.

But Zeien and Calloway are hardly carbon copies.

Zeien sees the people approach as a way to move information quickly across borders, to grow the company internationally, to ensure that employees think of corporate goals before personal ones.

Calloway would probably endorse all these objectives, but he manages people first and foremost in order to create a virtuous circle of behaviors that lead to "continuous improvement," and thus extraordinary financial results. Even as CEO, he doesn't need to be more specific than that, he maintains. PepsiCo people—roughly 400,000 around the world—understand what he is driving at, and they agree.

The numbers bear him out. While Coke still outsells Pepsi and its margins are twice as high, Pepsi's strength is that it is more than a soft-drink company, with strong and in some cases unassailable market shares in the restaurant and snack-food markets. Its revenues and profits have been growing at a compounded annual rate of around 13 percent for the past half-decade, despite stagnation in the domestic food and drink markets, where Pepsi derives more than 70 percent of its business. Each day, PepsiCo dispenses $30 million of Ruffles potato chips, Doritos, and other snack foods such as Chee-tos, Rold Gold pretzels, and Tostitos. Through its fast-food subsidiaries of Taco Bell, KFC, Pizza Hut, and the California Pizza Kitchen, the daily sales figures are $43 million. And consumption of Pepsi, Mountain Dew, and Lipton Ice Tea register near $77 million a day. Pepsi has doubled revenues every five years since 1965, and intends to continue to do so through the year 2000. If this were to happen, the number of employees would reach 1 million in the same time frame, making Pepsi the largest employer in the world.

The prospect is attainable, Calloway says, but he doesn't cite new markets or new products as the reason. It will happen, he says, if PepsiCo's virtuous circle keeps spinning.

It is a circle that starts with a value that makes everything else happen: integrity. Integrity begets an environment of honesty, in which people feel confident and trust one another. This environment promotes risk taking, problem solving, and creativity, which results in employees who work hard and stay with the company a long time. These employees, experienced and motivated, naturally improve the company's operations and create, in a word, success. Success leads to happiness, which leads back to integrity.

But exactly what is this "integrity" Calloway speaks of?

"We're talking about the big sense of the word," he replies. "Not just 'Don't cook the books,' and 'Don't steal.' Obviously we don't let you do that. The integrity I'm talking about is an openness, an honesty, a willingness to put yourself on the line and say, 'Here's what I think,' and not to have any hidden agendas."

In companies without integrity as the core value, Calloway says, politics and manipulation thrive, and risk and creativity evaporate. And without risk and creativity in play, what good are complex marketing plans that blue-sky a distant future? The question is at the heart of why Calloway focuses on people and leaves marketing strategy to the operating units.

"Our planning process is just the normal thing, typical," Calloway notes. "We have meaningful discussions, but they are informal. It's not a lot of books and big binders which we study, and that kind of stuff. Besides, it is fairly simple, the businesses we're in. Complex in that we have 24,000 restaurants around the world, but it's not rocket science to get your mind around most of the issues that make any difference."

Moreover, Calloway says, because of the company's environment, its top managers have been around long enough to understand whatever competitive issues do exist, and know them well.

"We're not a bunch of ivory tower folks dreaming up silly things the divisions ought to do," he says. "We talk the shorthand, and so it becomes a question of the division president of Frito-Lay calling up and saying, 'Hey, Wayne, we said last October we were going to spend a lot of money in the Northeast because we thought Wise was going to do this, but the whole thing is changed with Borden now, and so what I want to do is take that money and put it in California.' And so then we will say, in a fifteen-minute conversation, 'Go ahead.' End of subject. In some places, you have to send in a thirty-eight-page report about your change in strategy."

He shakes his head in amazement. "We're blessed with having a different kind of environment," he says.

How, in concrete terms, is that environment created?

To Calloway, the answer is that the CEO must "walk the talk." He must prove to the company how much integrity matters. That is why he conducts the compensation reviews of the company's top 600 employees. In addition, he meets once or twice annually with every division head to discuss the careers of the top 300 people in each unit. In these sessions, Calloway learns about individual performance and potential, and says he always makes a point of asking, "What is it they want to do? What would make them happy?" Of course, not all needs and wants can be met, but Calloway says his concern represents the company's trust and openness, its desire to help employees grow and improve. He also uses these meetings with division heads to pinpoint those employees who best display the same kinds of quality—all part of integrity—so that they can be rewarded with promotions or salary upgrades. It also means identifying those who don't, so they can be removed.

"We have publicly executed a couple of people who were big on getting results but not so big on how they treated their people, and word gets around," Calloway says. "We have celebrated occasions where people have failed very publicly, and said, 'That's OK.' We wanted them to take the risk, and we promoted them."

In addition, Calloway endorses leapfrogging promising employees as another way to spread his message.

"Early on, you can tell some people are different from others," Calloway notes. "I want to hear about those folks. Who are they? How many do you have? Do you know them? What do you know about them? Because the fact is, in an organization as big as ours, without some intervention, the organization will just squash them and hold them back and take a little of that fire out of them, and stop them, and that's the last thing I want to happen.

"So we start to talk about those people early on, and then the real challenge is to treat them differently." What that means is sometimes handing someone a three- or four-level promotion.

"Pow—well, that makes a lot of people mad who were in line for that job," Calloway admits. "But you've got to do some of that. It helps if I am visibly, openly, energetically supporting that, because if it fails, they'll still go ahead and do it again."

Along with his involvement with performance reviews, firings, and promotions, Calloway gets involved in the Pepsi hiring process. Again, it's a matter of guaranteeing that core value of integrity, the value that spins the wheel.

"Nobody gets hired unless they sit right here in this office and I get to talk to them," he says, referring to the top 600 hires of the year (again, in terms of salary). "It doesn't matter if they're going to work in Pakistan or Philadelphia, they come here. We have to get a chance to get to know each other and make sure we have the same values and objectives and standards in mind.

"That way," Calloway adds, "when they're back in Pakistan and somebody wants to do something, they will say, 'Well, I don't know. That's not what I heard and I heard it straight from Calloway himself, so I think that's not what we ought to be doing.' It's mighty easy, you know, to sometimes do the no-fault thing, but this kind of face-to-face meeting makes it harder."

Calloway sometimes also participates in the hiring of new M.B.A.'s—"just for the heck of it," he says, "just to see the new crop that's coming." But his interest is less casual than it sounds. He's not just looking, he's scrutinizing.

"Sometimes what happens is the personnel department in Wichita, Kansas, will say, 'Jeez, I got two Harvard M.B.A.'s coming!' And he can be as happy as hell, and then when I see them, I may not be quite as happy as he is. Not that this is a dumb person or anything else, but he just doesn't quite have the experience I do setting up standards.

"So I just stick my nose in there every once in a while to make sure."

As one last component of "walking the talk," Calloway also makes it his business to know the human beings behind human assets management. He is not only interested in careers but in families, personal problems, and personalities. The more he knows, he says, the more he can help people achieve the happiness and motivation that keeps the circle spinning.

"Sometimes we have a person who has the right values, and it is still not working," Calloway says, meaning the employee's performance is falling short. "Then it is time to ask, 'What can we do to help you?'

"Sometimes you find out that his wife has had cancer for six months and he hasn't been able to sleep at night, and a three-month leave of absence gets things back on track.

"Then there are other times when they say, 'This job is not what I thought it was going to be, and it's not what I wanted to do, but I've got a lot of bills to pay and I just can't quit.' And we say, 'Maybe we'll pay your bills for a year. You go out and figure out how to make this more fun.'"

Both responses are "part of building trust," Calloway reflects, "of not saying, 'Screw them. They're not performing. Get them out of here.' That doesn't work."

It might at another company, but not at the one Calloway is running. Managing by the human assets approach, he says, is the best way to get what every corporation wants—financial success—and it has an added benefit of no small import. People are happy—the employees and the CEO.

"My job is fun," Calloway offers, not a surprising career objective from a man who spends his leisure time on a Harley-Davidson 883, one of the American motorcycle manufacturer's most gutsy models. Fun, he adds, but not easy.

"If it were easy, everyone would do it this way," he notes. And then PepsiCo might have to build a different kind of machine. Calloway, it seems, won't let that happen while he's behind the wheel.

AT SOUTHWEST AIRLINES: PEOPLE, PRACTICAL JOKES, AND PROFITS (IN THAT ORDER)

He's been called a zealot, a heretic, and a radical, but not by his enemies—by himself. Funny, honest, and offbeat, Herb Kelleher, CEO of **Southwest Airlines,** doesn't seem to engender enemies. Instead, he produces devoted employees, satisfied customers, delighted shareholders, and frustrated competitors. His twenty-three-year-old airline, with upwards of $2.6 billion in sales and $179 million in income, is the only consistently profitable carrier in the industry. Month after month, it wins the Department of Transportation's coveted Triple Crown for best customer service, on-time flights, and superior baggage handling. In 1994—the year in which Kelleher was named best American CEO by *Fortune* magazine—nearly 125,000 people applied for 3,000 job openings with Southwest. Continental Airlines, which had launched a direct attack on Southwest's no-frills short-haul strategy with its Lite service, began to retreat. *Condé Nast Traveler* magazine, one of the leading watchdogs of the travel industry, named Southwest the safest airline in the world over the last twenty years. And the company's stock rose to record highs.

But ask Kelleher the secret of his success, and he'll peer at you in amazement, as if the answer should be obvious. "You can duplicate the airplanes," he says after a pause. "You can duplicate the gate facilities. You can duplicate all the hard things, the tangible things you can put your hands on. But it's the *intangibles* that determine success. They're the hardest to duplicate, if you can do it at all. We've got the right intangibles."

At Southwest Airlines the intangibles mean the employees. Kelleher's approach is human assets management such as we've seen earlier in this chapter, but with his own distinct imprint, modeled on the kind of dynamics that make good families or friendships work. Simply put, he "cherishes and respects" his 18,000 employees, and his "love" is returned in what he calls "a spontaneous, voluntary overflowing of emotion." This tack of people management isn't nearly as impalpable as it sounds—it is, rather, a coherent and consistent system of clearly defined policies and practices and based on values that haven't changed since Kelleher co-founded the Dallas-based airline in 1967. These values—of humor, independence, and respect—inform every aspect of how Southwest is run, from the way people are hired, to who cleans up the trash in the terminal, to how people talk to each other in elevators, to who attends the company Christmas party. In fact, Kelleher's approach is so prevailing that when he became concerned that its impact was lessening as the company grew, he appointed several dozen "ambassadors" to monitor and reinforce it, and established a Culture Committee with the same mandate. He calls the committee "the most important in the whole company."

Of all the CEOs in this chapter, Kelleher is perhaps closest philosophically to Paul Fentener van Vlissingen of SHV Holdings. Like him, Kelleher talks about "liberating" his employees, and calls it "the moral thing to do." But Kelleher is hardly one to cast himself as a corporate missionary. (He chain-smokes and keeps a bottle of Wild Turkey on his desk.) He does call himself a zealot about his human assets approach, but he also talks about why it makes business sense. That doesn't make it any less moral, Kelleher says, just smarter.

"We think—and I believe we were the first to think this, by the way—that the airline industry is tactical, not strategic. Traditional long-range planning is absolutely inapplicable to what we do, to being successful," he explains. "In 1985 you can't be thinking, should we go to Baltimore in 1987? By 1987, there might be eighteen more airlines formed, some of them going to Baltimore, some of them not, some of them bankrupt.

"This is an industry where things happen very quickly—I mean, almost instantaneously," Kelleher adds. "Fares are changing all the time. Schedules are changing all the time. Destinations are changing all the time. Airlines are changing all the time.

"So my theory is that you have to remain loose and unconfined to deal with this. You have to remain limber and fast. It's better to make an erroneous decision than to be deprived of the opportunity to make any decision at all."

In other words, according to Kelleher, a sustainable competitive advantage in the airline industry is the result of a committed corps of employees willing, able, and highly motivated to act fast, without having to clear their decisions first with Corporate. Southwest Airlines is filled with that kind of person, Kelleher says, which is why it was ready when Midway Airlines went out of business in 1991.

"Midway announced it was ceasing operations on a Friday afternoon. By the end of that same day, our people out of Dallas had physically taken over every Midway gate at the Chicago airport," Kelleher remembers. "And when the press asked me about it, I told them, 'If you were from Texas, I'd call it homesteading.' We wound up with all those gates. We didn't wait around for long negotiations and all the hassles and applications to the bankruptcy court and that sort of thing. We went up and took physical possession of the gates.

"The next morning, a representative from Northwest came over. It was funny," Kelleher recalls. "And he said, 'Would you mind telling me how far your forces advanced during the night?' and we said, 'Everywhere.'"

But Kelleher doesn't tell this story as much to show his employees' aggressiveness as he does to illustrate the kind of independence of action his approach creates and the success it leads to in the marketplace.

"I didn't even know they were going to Chicago when they left. They didn't call me first," he says. "They came in later and said, 'Hey, Chief, we just did something, we thought you might like to know about it.'" They never doubted his approval, Kelleher says, because "we have such a great congruency among our people."

And on a day-to-day basis, Kelleher says, his role is creating and maintaining that congruency.

It is a role that begins with hiring, a subject on which Kelleher is a self-described fanatic. To explain his attitude, he tells a story of Southwest's operation in Amarillo, a small West Texas town.

"We were looking for a ramp agent in Amarillo, and our people department came to me and said, 'Herb, we're getting a little concerned because we've interviewed thirty-four people'—the implication being that they'd spent a lot of money in terms of time.

"My response was, 'If you have to interview 184 people to get the right ramp agent in Amarillo, do it.' Because that's where it starts. That's the freshet at the head of the river, and if you pollute that, then you gradually pollute everything downstream. And so, we don't want you to skimp or save or spend less time or have less people when it comes to hiring.

"You know, Tom Landry was coach of the Cowboys, and he said, 'We hire great athletes. We teach them to play any position.' I converted that at Southwest Airlines to be: We hire great attitudes, and we'll teach them any functionality that they need."

Great attitudes, Kelleher says, are people who want to improve, who treat others with respect, and who like to laugh, especially at themselves. Plenty of applicants claim to have these qualities, he adds, but Southwest has its own ways of making sure they do. It conducts group interviews to see how prospective employees interact. It watches how applicants treat the receptionist who greets them.

If they act self-important, and demand that she stop what she is doing, "they will not be hired," Kelleher says. Moreover, people looking for jobs, from pilots to mechanics, are routinely asked, "Tell us how you used humor to get out of an embarrassing scrape," and "What is the funniest thing that ever happened to you?" And on at least one occasion, applicants were tested to see how well they responded to a practical joke.

"You know pilots, right, they're pretty serious guys about employment," Kelleher begins the anecdote with a grin. "They've worked years and years to get hired by a commercial airline, and there's ten for every one that's hired. Well, we had some openings, we had them all come in. They've all shaved twice and gotten their hair cut, two haircuts in two days. They all have their suits on.

"So Ann Rhoades, our vice president of people, comes out to the waiting room and she says, 'We don't hire people in suits at Southwest Airlines. Take off your goddam pants. Go down and get some shorts from administrative purchasing. We only interview people who wear shorts while they're interviewed.'

"They all had to take their pants off and put on Southwest Airlines shorts with their jackets and ties to be interviewed. And one of them wrote me the funniest letter. He said, 'Kelleher, you son of a bitch! That was the first suit I ever owned and I never got to wear it.'" He was hired.

"What we're trying to find out is what people are really like," Kelleher says of the joke. "What are their flaws, foibles, prejudices, and biases? We want to know whether they are altruistic or not, whether they're selfish people. That's more important to us than where they worked for the past three years and all those stupid résumés people send in now. I think there's one person who writes them all, anyway. We don't pay attention to that stuff."

In addition to hiring, Kelleher also oversees another key aspect of his people approach: development. This means talking to and coaching as many employees as possible, not just managers. Kelleher says the real test of any CEO claiming to use the people approach is to check his calendar for how many nonmanagement workers he had in his office over the previous six months. The more the better, Kelleher maintains, because a company's real potential lies in unleashing the talents of its rank and file.

"We don't believe in labels, and we don't believe in credentials,"

Kelleher says. "You can have wonderful ideas and be an immensely productive person even if you didn't graduate from high school, because high school doesn't necessarily encourage imagination or creativity."

A case in point is a woman who joined Southwest as a secretary after raising her two children. After two years, Kelleher promoted her to director of marketing. "I just knew from dealing with her that she had the capabilities," he says. "She was imaginative, she was effervescent, she was intelligent, she was pragmatic. And she did a fabulous job."

Development also means keeping track of employees, getting their input on Southwest programs and practices. After six months with the company, representative employees meet personally with the corporate officer group to talk about their progress and perceptions of Southwest. The same session is held with representative employees who have been with the company for ten years. Between the two meetings, Kelleher and other top managers meet frequently with employees to discuss performance and career goals.

If someone is not doing well, Kelleher says, "it is our policy to give them a lot of instruction and a lot of support and a lot of help and a lot of advice as to what they need to do better and how to do it better. And we sit down with them. We actually put what we are saying in writing, and they sign it. We don't do it for legal reasons. We do it so we can come back to them in sixty days and say, 'Here's this document. Here's the conversation we had. This is what was agreed upon as your weaknesses. This is what was agreed upon as to your rectifying them. Have you?' " If they haven't, Kelleher says, they are let go, but that doesn't happen very often.

Instead, the much more common situation is employees who flourish at Southwest—flourish because they finally can.

"It's interesting to see people come here from other companies, and they start off by saying, 'Can these people really mean it?' And about six months later, they suddenly say, 'It's for real!' And they say, 'Hallelujah!' because their basic personality has been restricted and confined by the bureaucracies and hierarchies of where they used to work. But now they can say, 'I want to tell you something, Kelleher. You had the worst damn idea that I've ever heard in my life! Were you drunk?' And they really enjoy it, and they are liberated as a consequence of it. We tell them, 'Go ahead and be inconsistent. You're not a windup toy.' If they are consistent in values, which they are, then we have nothing to worry about."

Kelleher's attitude about employee empowerment extends to his relationship with unions. (Southwest is the most heavily unionized airline in the industry.) Instead of seeing organized labor as an adversary, he sees it as an ally, creating a relationship not unlike the "shared destiny" partnership advocated by John Neill of Unipart in chapter 2. "We don't go into union negotiations asking, 'Gee, what's the skinniest contract we can get away with?' We go in saying, 'How much can we give them without imperiling the future economics of Southwest Airlines? What's the maximum increases we can pay? If we're doing well, shouldn't they get a bigger slice of the profits?' Now that's not where we may start bargaining from, but everybody knows that's where we're headed."

Kelleher does admit that negotiations between the airline and its unions have sometimes been fractious, but he likens them to a family argument.

"Sure we fight, but the difference is we don't hold grudges and make a vendetta out of it," he says. "I fought with my brothers all the time. But we didn't go after each other on a permanent basis, and we didn't regard each other as enemies. With our union negotiations, there may be short tempers, there may be red faces and pounding on the table and glaring eyes, but when the contract talks are over, they're over. Everybody says, that was just negotiations. And off we go." To reinforce this point, Kelleher notes that Southwest invites its unions' national and international representatives to the company Christmas party.

Kelleher sees the third part of his role, after hiring and development, as maintaining Southwest's values—its employee-focused approach—as the company grows. "It used to be easier," he concedes, "we all used to be at Love Field. Everybody was here. You knew everyone. But now we're in forty-one cities with 18,000 people. And I think what can happen as you get bigger is that it gets harder to treat each employee as an individual because you tend to substitute other priorities for it. And because it becomes more time-consuming, you have to give it more thought and you have to think of more ingenious ways of how to do it."

One of those ways, Kelleher says, has been to increase written communication from the line to the corporate office; he himself serves as an ombudsman, fielding employee concerns and complaints and making sure they are acted upon. In addition, he sends out a weekly update, a monthly newsletter, and a monthly video, all addressing Southwest's values, traditions, and future. He is traveling more, visiting employees in new and old locations. "We also have gigantic parties," Kelleher adds, "where we bring in everybody from across the system. You have to have things like that."

But he says his most effective tool in maintaining his management approach at Southwest has been the creation of a Culture Committee, a group of seventy people drawn from all areas of the company, from pilots to clerical workers.

"We got them all together and we said, 'Now look, it's very important that this be continued, and we selected you because of your personality, your dedication, and so on. And we want you to be a missionary and an ambassador. We want you to carry the spiritual message of Southwest Airlines.' " (Apparently, the committee's members have taken Kelleher's mandate to heart. One of them, a customer service agent from St. Louis, recently canceled a two-week vacation to smooth tensions among employees in Detroit.)

But delegating the work of shepherding Southwest's people culture has hardly freed Kelleher's time for other tasks, and one senses he wouldn't want that, anyway. He says 70 percent of his time is spent handling the day-to-day crises of running a carrier—"another airline's pricing, another airline's scheduling, a political problem in Washington, whatever"—but the other 30 percent is spent on what he enjoys most, his employees. "They're fabulous, fabulous people," he says, looking around the Southwest lobby, its walls covered with photographs of everyone who works for the company. (The lobby is also decorated with a motorcycle displayed on a raised platform, a gift to Kelleher from a group of employees, its motorcycle enthusiasts.)

"Amazing things happen when you make people feel they are valued as individuals, when you dignify their suggestions and their ideas," he says, "when you show your respect for them by allowing them to exercise their own wisdom and judgment and discretion."

The success of Southwest, Kelleher says, isn't his. It belongs to his employees. With all due respect, his employees might just say he has it backwards.

THE HUMAN ASSETS APPROACH:
MORE THAN BEING A "PEOPLE PERSON"

Just as most business leaders describe themselves as strategists or visionaries, so do they often use the term "people person." Most CEOs and presidents are extroverted, they enjoy socializing, they like conversation, they possess a certain personal interest that draws others to them. But while human assets management might benefit from a CEO with these characteristics, as an *approach* it supersedes personality. Instead, organizations where people management is the main vehicle for adding extraordinary value are built around a complex system of managing them. This system is comprehensive and permeates every facet of the company's drive for strategy and results. It begins with hiring and continues with training, development, and promotion policies, and, if need be, into firing. At its essence, it is a system built around values—corporate values—explicitly communicated, with the intention of every employee's incorporating them into action and deed.

The first example of a human assets company in this book is the international food and drink purveyor Grand Metropolitan, where Allen Sheppard lays out the company's shared values in his version of the Ten Commandments. GrandMet employees are encouraged to embrace change, to set impossible goals and meet them, to accept accountability. The company's policies and culture then reinforce these corporate imperatives. Employees, such as the twenty-six-year-old brand manager who invented the cinnamon schnapps drink Goldschlager, are empowered to take risks, rewarded when they pay off, and not punished when they fail. At PepsiCo and Gillette, human assets management is also a function of shared values reinforced by management policies and procedures. At Pepsi, Wayne Calloway believes that personal integrity ultimately drives financial success; at Gillette, Al Zeien wants employees to value global cooperation and expertise sharing, and to put the corporation's interests before those of any single business unit. Both men are deeply involved in hiring and firing decisions, in performance reviews, in career planning. Like Helmut Maucher of Nestlé, they travel continuously, meeting hundreds of employees a year, spreading the word on the way to think and act, demonstrating how they make decisions themselves. At Southwest Airlines, the values of humor, commitment, and humility are reinforced by routinely scheduled meetings between senior management and new hires, by the airline's system of goodwill "ambassadors," and by Herb Kelleher's monthly video and newsletter. While these kinds of management tools are used at other companies, at the human assets organization they are the priority, the defining medium for value addition. For example, in terms of career planning, human assets CEOs such as Eric Nicoli of United Biscuits often map an individual manager's career forward through two or three jobs. In companies managed by other approaches, this task is left to the employee's manager, to the human resource department, or sometimes to no one at all.

The companies in this chapter tell us something else about human assets organizations: managing people is not just about managing individuals but about the relationships between them. Jan Timmer of Philips Electronics credits management's involvement in and renewal of this delicate process for the company's turnaround. Eric Nicoli talks about people in his company liking one another as a prerequisite for success; happy employees are committed and motivated, he says, and a major part of his job is creating an environment where friendships flourish. Some human assets managers, such as Paul Fentener van Vlissingen of SHV Holdings, pick this approach not for business reasons but for philosophical ones. Implemented thoroughly and consistently, however, the results are the same: employees who know what is expected of them and are committed to that end.

The human assets management approach comes down to trust, development, and empowerment. It is a system that disseminates certain explicit values and then rewards those who embrace them, building an organization in which everyone demonstrates predictable, acceptable behaviors. With trust in place, senior management can empower employees to take action, sometimes along lines in keeping with company tradition, and sometimes quite new in direction.

This is the case at **Rexam** (formerly known as Bowater), the international packaging and coated-products company based in London. Chairman Mike Woodhouse notes that for the past seven years, Rexam was successfully managed through an "ROS culture"—

managers were challenged to produce steadily increasing return-on-sales figures. But a new corporate focus on organic growth rather than on acquisitions means the company must refocus its culture, too. "We want managers to build this company for the future, to think about long-term issues and long-term strengths," he says. His goal is to inculcate the values of "integrity, openness, and honesty" that he believes lead to a "build culture" through the characteristic human assets techniques of "talk, chat, persuasion, and reward." He visits Rexam factories regularly, has developed new incentive programs for managers, and spends a good portion of his time "taking my perspectives out there, and lending them to people."

When does a CEO choose the human assets approach? Again, industry type doesn't seem to force the issue. Instead, this approach is most frequently used in situations in which, because of local market knowledge, the business units are *better positioned* than the center to make strategy. Or when the key elements of long-term strategy are particularly self-evident, as Pepsi's Calloway asserts, or cannot be formulated with any intelligent certitude, as Eric Nicoli suggests. The human assets approach is, as Herb Kelleher notes, also powerful in businesses where superlative *execution* is the key to competitive advantage. Thus, the approach is employed at diversified global conglomerates like Nestlé, Sara Lee, and Gillette. These companies leave strategy to the business units, but control its fundamental direction and its implementation with the human assets approach—with the powerful tools of trust, development, and empowerment.

When *shouldn't* a CEO use the human assets approach? One critical answer: When there aren't enough challenges to fulfill the kind of empowered employees this management style creates. There is no point charging up the workforce, encouraging entrepreneurship and promoting independent decision making, when the business situation neither calls for nor rewards such behaviors. One CEO who faced this situation—and overcame it—is Amos Hostetter, founder of **Continental Cablevision,** the third-largest cable operator in the United States and the country's most global, with major operations in Australia, Argentina, and Singapore. Hostetter describes his version of the human assets approach as "finding the best people possible, even if they are potentially better than I am. I don't care, I want to find them, identify them, put them in place, give them the authority to make important decisions that really impact the value of this company, manage their careers so they experience every part of what we do, and make their compensation so attractive that they would never consider going elsewhere."

But what Hostetter has discovered is that keeping empowered people continually motivated can be daunting. "It can be hard to keep these people challenged," he says. He has responded with a compensation package for top-level executives that hands out ownership, making some of his most valued employees millionaires many times over. "But sometimes that also gives them the independence to leave and go sail a boat around the world," Hostetter remarks. "The compensation has to be psychic, too, and that's where really interesting business challenges come in. They mean a lot." Fortunately for Continental Cablevision, the company's recent international growth has been explosive, and it has provided the kind of new opportunities that support the human assets approach.

Finally, it should be noted that while many human assets CEOs remark that their management approach is, in a word, fun, of all the approaches in this book it is perhaps the hardest to implement in terms of time and energy. Human assets management can take up to a decade to inculcate, because it involves creating trust, values, and consistency and is based on personal knowledge and experience. But once it is in place, human assets management goes far beyond a CEO who happens to be a "people person" to create an organization consisting of focused employees, each one a "company person."

4

WHEN KNOWLEDGE IS POWER:
THE EXPERTISE APPROACH

Some liken the modern diversified conglomerate to a farm silo—in particular, a very large silo where three or four tunnels run down from the top, parallel to one another but never intersecting, so that grain from one never gets mixed with grain from another. In some conglomerates, the companies are run parallel to one another, entirely separate. Even if there were some benefit to mixing the grain, as it were, it couldn't be done. The tunnel walls are too thick.

It's a disconcerting metaphor, but certainly many people in business have seen it in action. (In fact, many of the CEOs in this book talk about inheriting "silo companies." Dana Mead, the CEO of Tenneco who talks about change in chapter 6, is one. Linn Macdonald, the man who turned around Noranda Forest Inc., discussed in chapter 8, is another.) Silo management tends to sprout up at conglomerates with several companies (or sometimes dozens) in their portfolios, companies making and selling unrelated products or services. For all the talk in business literature about the benefits of synergies between operating units, it sometimes seems that few organizations manage to realize them.

This chapter is about organizations where senior management adds extraordinary value by breaking down the walls of the silo's tunnels. They do it by designing and implementing programs that explicitly spread a specific *expertise* between business units, be it in marketing, manufacturing, technology, or distribution. They see the corporate office, headed by a committed CEO, as the only place in a conglomerate to champion and execute this critical job—after all, no one would expect a marketing professional from a division that makes air conditioners to *volunteer* his knowledge about, say, co-operative advertising to an executive in a conglomerate's cellular telephone division. The day is busy enough already, and how would you even do such a thing? Often the systems just don't exist.

Which is why these "expertise" organizations have invented or adopted systems, and why senior management devotes the balance of its time to monitoring and fine-tuning them. But this does not mean the companies featured in this chapter have large headquarters staffs. In fact, most of them have come up with original ways to spread expertise without enlarging the corporate office. "But it's a constant battle, to be honest," admits Robert Cizik of **Cooper Industries,** one of the CEOs we meet in this chapter, "because your headquarters people are constantly trying to build and take over, and the divisions are constantly pushing away." In other words, it probably would be easier to keep the silo tunnels separate, just as they are on the farm.

We will begin by taking a look at Cooper Industries, the Houston-based conglomerate comprising fifty-four business units, at last count. (The company buys and sells several companies a year.) Other CEOs who use this approach are James Ross, of the United Kingdom's telecommunications giant **Cable & Wireless,** and Haruo Naito, president of **Eisai,** a Japanese pharmaceutical company. A few years ago, Naito decided his company should adopt knowledge of the customer as its critical expertise, and to that end he sent 100 middle managers to work in hospitals and nursing homes for a year—performing, not just observing, tasks such as changing bandages and bedpans. This chapter will also take a look at **Motorola,** where the CEO adopted "zero defects" as his rallying cry and organized the corporation around it; **Saint-Gobain,** the French glass maker; **Pharmacia** of Sweden; the advertising agency **Ogilvy & Mather;** and **Anglo American Corporation,** the world's largest gold and diamond mining concern.

AT COOPER INDUSTRIES: "I'M NOT A
MANUFACTURING GUY, BUT. . ."

Several years ago, Bob Cizik and his wife, Jane, endowed a professorship at Harvard Business School specifically for the teaching of manufacturing excellence, though Cizik doesn't attribute his reputation as the dean of American industrial manufacturing to his years at the school. Quite the opposite; when Cizik graduated in 1958, HBS offered just one manufacturing class. "No one talked about manufacturing then; nobody talked about the guy who's down on the factory floor making things day in and day out," Cizik recalls. "People designed products, some other people sold them, the financial people kept track, planners planned—and the guy on the factory floor was just *expected* to turn out an automobile or something. No one seemed to realize that what he was doing was really important."

Cizik obviously disagreed. After graduating, he joined **Cooper Industries,** then a manufacturer of compressors for the oil and gas industry with annual sales approaching $60 million. Seventeen years later, he was named CEO, and today that same company sells more than $4.5 billion in products that span dozens of technologies and industries, from drapery hardware to voltage regulators. With 40,800 employees throughout the United States, Cooper also produces plugs and receptacles, as well as servicing the petroleum industry with engines and drilling equipment. The company grew through acquisitions that had a very clear focus. It was manufacturing expertise, carefully cultivated and aggressively disseminated between units through systems designed by Cizik and his senior executives.

"When I joined Cooper, I asked myself, 'Where is this company going?'" Cizik recalls. "There was an organization in place, of course. It had a lot of strengths and it had a lot of weaknesses, and I felt it was important for us to try and define and understand what they were, then mitigate the weaknesses and build on the strengths, and to take this company somewhere."

At the time, Cizik was officially the new man in the finance department, but he soon developed a close relationship with the CEO, who came to lean on him for ideas and eventually for the strategy that would create the Cooper of the next thirty years.

"I wanted to *build* something," Cizik says of the time. "I didn't think in those days in terms of 'creating value,' but that's what I was after."

Cizik's first initiative was to launch a campaign of diversification. With a narrow product line, all serving the oil and gas industry, the company was extremely vulnerable to economic cycles. "We had risk upon risk," Cizik says, and sales and profits fluctuated accordingly. Worse than that, he adds, "When we were at our low ebb, people could certainly come in and play financial games with us, which isn't a very pleasant place to be from a management point of view."

But the question was: Where to diversify? And why?

"We knew there had to be some thread or theme to control our diversification, otherwise we would just become a big, wild conglomerate," Cizik says. "And let me tell you, a lot of opportunities came our way. We were in the oil business, from the standpoint of being a supplier to it, and someone would say, 'Don't you want to get involved with this wonderful offshore lease?' And it took a lot of courage to keep saying no. Offers and suggestions came from every direction. And we would say, 'No, we don't know anything about operating that kind of business, thank you.' The feeling was, we had to stick with what we knew best.

"So we analyzed those talents, and what we realized was we had good engineers. We had good manufacturing. What we did well was we engineered and manufactured very, very fine expensive equipment. But a manufacturing *focus*? Around this time, manufacturing was really being frowned upon in the United States. We were the Rust Bowl. The Japanese were beating us, and so were the Italians and the Germans. These were bleak days for U.S. manufacturing companies.

"But we looked at ourselves, and we asked, 'Why?' There's no reason for it. We make the best damn compressors in the world. They're like Swiss watches, they're good, and we've got a good workforce. On the other hand, we realized that manufacturing in America had been ignored for a long time. Factories were being run by high school dropouts, even ours. We were good at manufacturing, but we could be a lot better. We could—if we made a really big deal out of making this a manufacturing company."

Cizik was the champion of that approach.

"I said, we're going to be a manufacturing company, one of the best damn manufacturing companies in the world. We're going to get on the pulpit and say manufacturing is not dead in the United States, and we're going to beat the Japanese at this, and the Germans and anyone else. After all, we were operating in the largest market in the world—the United States.

"I'm not a manufacturing guy," Cizik adds with a smile. He was an accountant with Price Waterhouse before business school, in fact. "But I knew it had to be done. We had to find a central theme to our diversification program, and I knew manufacturing was it." How did he know? Cizik pauses for a moment, then smiles again. "I guess being something of a contrarian has a lot to do with it," he says.

With this theme in place, Cooper then moved aggressively to buy companies that had strong manufacturing potential or capabilities—strong but decidedly straightforward capabilities. In other words, Cooper would not consider companies that made products involving high-technology electronics. Instead, the company began by buying a firm that made compressors, just smaller than the ones it already sold. Next, it moved into hand tools. Over the years, it has expanded into companies with more complex technologies, but never veering far from, as Cizik says, "milling and drilling, grinding and boring."

At the beginning of Cooper's shopping spree, Cizik spent much of his time reviewing potential acquisitions to make sure they stayed within the company's focus. He still does; he estimates that 20 percent of his schedule is devoted to this task. But his job also involves, in large part, the integration of these new firms, making sure they are part of the system that spreads Cooper's manufacturing knowledge. (Inside the company, this process is called "Cooperization.") Early on, Cizik decided not to fiddle with the marketing divisions of the company's new acquisitions. "No point centralizing marketing," he explains. "The more decentralized that function is, the closer the company can be to its customers." Other functions, such as legal, tax, and accounting, were absorbed by headquarters.

Which left manufacturing.

"How do you integrate manufacturing of all these new companies to really add value?" Cizik asks. "That was what we said we were going to do, so we had to come up with programs and systems to do it."

They did. The first, and perhaps most powerful, of these is the Professional Manufacturing Group, a SWAT team of experts drawn from various operations around Cooper, sent into existing businesses and new acquisitions to review (and often overhaul) manufacturing operations. The team works well, Cizik says, because "they are not a bunch of outside consultants running around." Instead, they are Cooper insiders, "with grease under their fingernails."

"These are people we have pulled out of the shops, and we put them in the group for three or four years," he adds. Moreover, they are motivated to make the most of their term with the group because they are told—as is everyone at Cooper—that the job of spreading manufacturing know-how is good for your career. It is, in fact, a key step to increased responsibility in the company.

Another tool Cizik uses to spread expertise is hiring what he calls "the right minds"—recent college graduates with engineering degrees. They have good technical minds, he says, yet they are still pliable. The next critical imperative is training them correctly.

"We don't want to teach them how to make spark plugs," Cizik explains. "We want to build minds that understand the important manufacturing concepts—scheduling, supervision, all that. We move them around the plants a lot, expose them to a lot of people who are very experienced and bright, expose them to a lot of technologies." That way, Cizik says, when they become managers, they have been steeped in the nuts and bolts of excellence in manufacturing, as well as Cooper's commitment to spreading it up, down, and sideways.

To reinforce this process, Cizik says he also spends at least 20 percent of his time "mentoring" the people in the company's upper ranks, keeping them focused on Cooper's manufacturing theme. "My job is to imbue some sort of philosophy into people," Cizik says, "and then it's the people, really, who go and do it. Not me, *they* do it." In this way, Cizik resembles the strategists of chapter 2. He tries not to get too involved in the day-to-day management of business units, functions, or even of crisis situations. His role, he believes, is to stand outside the fray, making sure an ever-sharp focus on manufacturing somehow manages to define it all. Simply put, this is the role of an "expertise champion."

At sixty-three, Cizik has announced that he will retire soon. You might expect him to be looking for a successor to follow his manufacturing lead, but he's not. Instead, he hopes the next CEO of Cooper Industries will be a champion of another sort entirely. It is time, he says, for the company to focus on marketing with the same undivided attention it gave manufacturing.

"For years, all the pressures have been to ask, 'How can we produce this product at its lowest cost? How can we deliver it better? How can we keep our on-time performance?' This may have been too limiting," Cizik says. "I think what needs to be done more is thinking about the customer. What is he doing? What are his needs? How is he using our product? How can we build a partnership with him?

"I think," says Cizik, "if I had twenty more years, I would really focus on that."

AT EISAI: "ENCOUNTERING MORTALITY" TO GAIN EXPERTISE

In 1988, shortly after Haruo Naito became president and CEO of the pharmaceutical company his grandfather founded, Naito gathered three of his most trusted advisers and asked for a prognosis of the business he now headed. The answer was not encouraging. **Eisai Company,** they said, was destined to fail if it kept going in the same direction. Sales and profits were fine, but the company's philosophy and strategy were not being imparted to the employees. They worked terribly hard, but didn't understand why. Products were produced, but none were best-sellers. The company was growing, but almost despite itself.

Naito took this report to heart, for in fact he had lived Eisai's problems as an employee himself shortly after joining the company in 1975, when sales were $178 million and profits registered $4.6 million. At the time, Naito had recently returned to Japan from the United States, where he had received his M.B.A. from Northwestern University in Chicago and worked briefly for another company. If he was looking forward to a positive experience with his family's enterprise, those hopes were quickly dashed. He describes his first assignment at Eisai's R&D division as "total chaos."

"We worked twenty-four hours a day. We never left the facility. I lived there, too," he recalls. "People were lined up at three A.M. to use the copy machine. But I was committed to it, and I wasn't going to run away."

His father retired in 1988 and Naito was selected to succeed him. He was forty years old, remarkably young to run a Japanese corporation, especially the sixth-largest drug maker in the country's burgeoning pharmaceutical industry. Competitors and allies alike were watching him, and Naito knew it. In fact, that was one of the reasons he asked for a prognosis of the business from his three advisers, who had been his friends for more than a decade.

"They had no advice," he recalls. "They just said Eisai was going to fail."

In response, Naito says he decided two things: he would not surrender to their prediction, and Eisai would change from a company driven by its existing customers—doctors and pharmacists—to a company driven by all its customers, which included patients and their families. Managers, he decided, had to become experts in customer desires, anxieties, and behaviors, then force that expertise through the organization. The result would be drugs that met an existing market need, instead of drugs born in a laboratory far from the actual users of the product. It was a radical concept for Eisai, which was known in Japan for its well-funded R&D division, and unusual for the pharmaceutical industry in general. But Naito decided the focus would give his company a competitive advantage, and at the same time give its 4,500 employees a reason to love their work and thrive at it.

"It's not enough to tell employees that if they do something the company will grow this much or their salary will increase this much. That's just not enough incentive," Naito says, perhaps thinking of his own experiences within Eisai's R&D division. "You have to show them how what they are doing is connected to society, or exactly how it will help a patient. If your organization isn't set up to convince them of those things, then I think you will never be able to motivate them sufficiently."

With a new patient-focused organization as his starting point, Naito spent several weeks trying to figure out how to make his managers "experts on the customer." He immediately dismissed the idea of a top-down directive, which, he says, always loses something in the translation.

"In a company like ours, even if the CEO declares that we will become this kind of a new company, it is understandably difficult for every last worker to consciously adjust their daily activities to carry it out," he notes. "That is why we needed the overwhelming support of the middle managers."

Naito says he decided to nurture about 100 managers—selected from 1,200—who thoroughly understood his message and concept.

"From the standpoint of making drugs, we certainly knew a lot about diseases and how they developed and spread, but we didn't know anything about the patient as an *individual*, with a personality and a history," Naito says. "We didn't know about their relations with their family or whether they were in need of specialized care in addition to customary pharmaceutical therapy. My question was, how can we really be producing life-saving drugs if we didn't ever encounter death outside our own families?"

His answer: let the managers do just that. Naito formulated a program that included a seven-day seminar, three days of nursing-home training, and three days of medical-care observation in urban hospitals, in distant mountain villages, and on remote islands.

"These managers experienced the difficulties involved in daily care of the elderly, such as diaper changing, and they had to see people who died during their care," Naito says. "They also cared for people who were in very severe and critical condition, both emotionally and physically."

After Naito implemented the nurturing program, field programs were established in almost every division. These programs involved more than 1,000 employees, each with the same goal of communicating the company's vision of its new, expanded customer focus.

At the same time, many of Eisai's staff members—in particular, its secretaries and laboratory support personnel—were also pushed out from behind their desks. Naito arranged for them to meet regularly with pharmacists, both in drugstores and at hospitals.

"Usually, these employees just answer phones or shuffle numbers," Naito says, "so they had no idea what their co-workers in sales were doing or what patients cared about when they bought their medications. Getting them out of the office was a way to activate human relationships and bring them a step closer to the customer."

Several other systems were also implemented by Naito to make Eisai an expert on its customers. The first was a seven-days-a-week customer hot line. "A lot of ideas have come out of this so far," he says. Another is the EI-Net, which company sales representatives use to exchange information they have gathered in the field about patient needs and concerns.

Eisai is now in the sixth year of Naito's plan to become the industry's end-customer expert, and he himself raises the question of how well it is working.

"At first, it was quite a task," he reflects, "getting people to move, to see their jobs in a new light. But now, our thoughts and values have changed. Of course, many managers still do not understand. People still go on about how this is a new sales record. But it is certain our philosophical backbone has changed. It is much stronger."

A tangible result, Naito says, is the new drugs for the global market that will be coming from Eisai in the next few years. (It typically takes ten to fifteen years to develop and test a prescription medication before it reaches the market.)

"In working in hospitals that deal with the elderly we have come to see their viewpoints on medication, and we have become familiar with the conditions in which they live and we can see now there are problems with the way the system operates."

Eisai, today a company with upwards of $2.7 billion in revenues and $190 million in earnings, is currently developing a drug to treat Alzheimer's disease, and is also working on medications for other afflictions of the elderly, taking into account cost as well as quality.

Financially, Eisai will not see the impact of its reinvention as a customer-driven enterprise for several years. But Naito says he believes "if we stick with this pattern, everything should go well for us."

He speaks about the next two years of continuing to put expert systems in place as his biggest challenge, as a person and as a businessman. Such a change, he says, is something only a CEO could implement, not by his words but by forcing middle managers to change their area and scope of knowledge, and then spread that knowledge throughout the organization. His challenge in the more distant future will be to find a new area of knowledge for his managers to acquire, an area to add to their expertise about customers. "Otherwise," he says, "the work gets old and loses its meaning. You must never stop creating knowledge."

AT CABLE & WIRELESS:
CHANGING THE EQUATION WITH EXPERTISE

When James Ross was named CEO of **Cable & Wireless** in 1991, he analyzed what he calls his "inheritance," and concluded it was not something on which to bank the future.

That legacy—what we have called the "situation" in preceding pages—was a 120-year-old telecommunications company with 65,000 employees and operations in more than fifty countries. It was also a company without a clear strategic focus, without synergy across units, and without market approval. Cable & Wireless brought in revenues of $1.5 billion in 1994 with its phone, facsimile, and telex services, but without any distinct technological edge in a technology-driven business, it faced what Ross calls "profitless growth."

"The whole was substantially less than the sum of the parts," Ross says of Cable & Wireless, noting that the company's stock was at one point trading on the London exchange at nearly 40 percent below the value of its units combined. "The markets were saying the center was subtracting value, clearly."

In response to that message, Ross began seeking a new approach for the company that would change the equation and make its whole far greater than the sum of its parts. The one he selected was the management of expertise across business units, with a set of programs called the Federation. It is a term that Bob Cizik at Cooper Industries might also have used—it describes the concept of many divisions being united by a competitive advantage through a process designed and managed by the corporate office. There are two differences, however. First, Cable & Wireless has selected three areas of expertise on which to focus. And second, Cable & Wireless is still a work in progress. Ross has the philosophy and the systems in place; the approach's success now lies with the far-flung organization's acceptance and implementation of both. The company's future, Ross suggests, depends on it.

"Particularly for a company our size, if we remain fragmented—although the market might prefer that in the short term—it is going to be very difficult to survive," he says. "Unless we pool our resources, pool our ideas, and transfer experience, we are going to get swamped. Isn't that a pretty self-evident thesis? After all, we are up against formidable competitors."

Those competitors are one part of the Cable & Wireless inheritance, and they are formidable because so many of them have made technology their strength, and the foundation for their growth. Cable & Wireless, by contrast, grew over the years through acquisitions, buying operations in the Caribbean, Hong Kong, Australia, and South America. Many of these divisions were nationalized from the 1940s through the 1970s, Ross says, further discouraging innovation or any kind of information-sharing across borders. When the company was privatized in the 1980s, Cable & Wireless's then chairman had to "throw the company into the late twentieth century by the scruff of the neck."

His efforts, which included forcing P&L responsibility into the business units, changed Cable & Wireless's performance, but when Ross took over, the company was still considered one of the most low-tech in the telecommunications industry. Its key competitive advantage seemed to be the geographical spread of its operations, but that factor remained unexploited.

"We had a spread of assets and activities around the world, with very little logic lying behind how they had been built up and no rhyme nor reason to how they were being managed as a portfolio," Ross comments. "Our operating companies did not talk to each other. One person said to me, 'You mean I can talk direct from Hong Kong to Mercury [in England] without coming through the middle?' It was that culture completely."

Faced with this situation, Ross considered adopting the strategic approach, as described in chapter 2. Its appeal was simple: Cable & Wireless had no well-defined vision and needed one quickly. But ultimately, Ross decided against this top-down tactic because he believed it didn't make sense given the numerous and disparate national cultures within the organization. Moreover, Cable & Wireless holds a minority position in 80 percent of its divisions, and Ross notes, "You cannot manage that kind of portfolio by saying, 'This is how we are going to do it.' You can't dictate."

With the strategic approach eliminated, Ross says he confronted this question: Is Cable & Wireless bound to be a classic holding company, where the center adds no value except to decide what to buy and sell?

The answer was emphatically no.

"We want to be more than just a conglomerate," he says. "I mean, all our operations are in the same business. We have resisted over the years as a company, I think, very well all the temptations to diversify. And this is why we began inventing, or adapting for ourselves, the concept of the Federation.

"We think it will allow us to do something more than just manage, on behalf of the shareholder, a collection of investments," he says. "In order to do what? To add value to it. How do you add value? Do you add value by saying, 'I am going to have all my functional expertise and all my powerful individuals in the center, dictating or persuading people around the world what to do?' Or do you try and say, 'Let's leverage the strengths that we have in those independent business units and induce them, somehow, to transfer that knowledge and expertise around the Federation, so that eventually comes through the bottom line'?"

Ross chose the second option, which means he is in charge of "inducing" expertise-sharing. But first, he and his top staff had to decide which expertise should be shared. They selected three areas.

First was the servicing of multinational customers, in which Cable & Wireless has nearly 100 years of experience, though little of it communicated between business units. "This was an obvious expertise to choose, really," Ross says, "because by definition it is very difficult for an individual business unit to do on its own, other than by joining some other club of telecommunication companies."

Second was mobile phone technology, in which "we have an extraordinary collection of franchises around the world, some twenty-four," Ross notes.

And third was what Ross calls "capabilities"—the high-technology competencies that competitors own and that Cable & Wireless must acquire. By definition, capabilities are not one of the company's core areas of expertise, but Ross says they must be, and sharing information via the Federation is the only way to make it happen.

"We have an enormous learning curve to climb, and we had better learn our way up that curve," Ross says. "And the way to do that is not by fragmenting everything and getting each business unit to do everything totally in isolation but by finding some way across the Federation in which we can focus on a limited number of initiatives to develop."

So far, Ross has initiated five systems to jump-start the spread of expertise throughout Cable & Wireless. One is the transfer of personnel between business units, "and not just the people they want to get rid of." Another is the sponsorship of forums on a specific technical topic, attended by managers from many countries. Third, he has begun drawing to the corporation managers who are not British, in hopes that their country-specific expertise will now flow out to many other countries.

In addition to these steps, Ross says he himself has made the Federation's *continual reinforcement* one of his top priorities, constantly talking it up to employees around the world, in particular to business unit and functional directors. And finally, Ross has put muscle behind his call for expertise-sharing by changing the company's incentive system at its highest levels. For the first time, in 1995, the bonus of the top 100 managers worldwide was linked to achievement of the Federation's goals. "It's based on the American philosophy, 'If you pay for it, you get it,'" Ross explains.

He adds that he is eager to see how the organization responds to the new systems installed to promote the Federation; at the same time he is frustrated by how slowly the process is moving forward. The organization understands the principles behind the approach, he says, and many support it, but it takes a long time to shed an inheritance, especially one built over a century.

"Our inheritance is that this is a company that was started in the mid–nineteenth century by an entrepreneur who bet his personal wealth, his house, everything, on an unproven technology and won," Ross says. Now, the organization must make another bet: that sharing twenty-first-century expertise across fifty borders will leave a new legacy for the next generation at Cable & Wireless.

AT ANGLO AMERICAN: MANAGING SCARCE EXPERTISE WITH THE EXPERTISE APPROACH

To get a sense of the scope of operations at **Anglo American Corporation,** one need only look through its annual report—nearly every photograph is aerial. Such a perspective is the only way to capture the company's operations in action, from the massive vessel that recovers diamonds from the sea floor off Namibia, to the thirty-story nickel mine and smelter refinery in Zimbabwe, to the explosives plant so sprawling one frame cannot contain it all. Those pictures not taken from the sky tell a similar story about the kind of work being done: a huge open-arc furnace spraying sparks ceiling-high, a diamond drill rig that dwarfs the men running it, a zinc pressure leach treatment machine so large its controls and a half-dozen of its valves take up a room the size of an airplane hangar. By the time you read the text, it is no surprise to learn that Anglo American, with headquarters in Johannesburg, South Africa, is part of the largest mining group in the world. It comprises not only the company that bears its name, which mines gold, uranium, coal, base metals, and platinum in twelve countries, but also De Beers, the world's leading diamond producer, and Minorco, an international resources company. Anglo American also has significant industrial, financial, and agricultural interests. All told, the investment of the corporation itself—that is, not including De Beers and Minorco—was valued at $13.2 billion in 1994, and its total net earnings were $865 million.

The center's approach is expertise, but the situation giving rise to its choice is unique. Cooper Industries selected expertise as its focus because it already excelled in low-tech manufacturing. Eisai picked customer knowledge as its focus because none of its competitors had. Cable & Wireless chose three areas of expertise in order to keep up with its competitors. But at Anglo American, the center cultivates and aggressively spreads expertise in cutting-edge process technology because it must. The system of apartheid, although recently overturned, for decades kept the majority of the country's population uneducated and discouraged foreigners from filling the massive gap. In coming years, the pool of trained workers may expand, but since its inception in 1917, Anglo American has had to deal with a situation in which, simply, there were not enough technically trained men and women to staff all its operations simultaneously.

"Basically, in South Africa there is a shortage of people with skills and qualifications," says Chairman Julian Ogilvie Thompson. (He notes that there has been a shortage of finance as well.) In response to this dearth of qualified personnel, Anglo American developed a system that requires its core of technical experts to be always on the move, obtaining new technology skills, especially in mining, working within several different divisions, and sharing knowledge. "It's a pollination of ideas," Ogilvie Thompson says, "just like a bee moving around."

This pollination is achieved in several ways, first and foremost through a group of men and women called "consulting engineers." This group of highly skilled employees travels between Anglo American operations around the world, acting not as outsiders but more as line management wherever they go. The consulting engineers, for example, "pick up an idea from the chaps at Premier diamond mine, who are running the operations with skill," Ogilvie Thompson says, and "are able to transfer this idea to De Beers's group mines in Namibia or Botswana, really for free, adding value to the others."

The reason Anglo American benefits so much from this process, Ogilvie Thompson notes, is because from the start the corporation has invested so much of its finances in developing the most innovative process technologies. He mentions as an example a joint, twenty-year Anglo American and De Beers investment in deep-sea diamond mining. "We are doing this at depths of 120 meters plus, in very cold waters off Namibia—I mean, real Jules Verne stuff, tractors crawling on the sea floor, drill heads of seven meters in diameter.

"The problem is to develop a ship so that we have the shaft coming up into the ship in swells. You've got to have a mechanism that enables this shaft to stay rigid, drilling on the bottom while the ship rolls around in the swell. It is fascinating reading the reports of how they have improved the technology on a regular basis and now they can work three- or four-meter swells, and next year six-meter, and I think it will be nine-meter swells soon. This has the effect of increasing the amount of time you can work, which reduces the cutoff grade, which increases the reserves and extends the life, and makes the whole thing more viable.

"I mean, this is very exciting stuff, and we are streets ahead of everyone else, really."

The idea, then, is for this head start to be spread to other, related processes throughout the corporation. Consulting engineers serve that role, but the center reinforces it by purposefully moving corporate staff between operating companies. "Sometimes you might wonder if it is nice to be told that you are working with copper right now, and next week you'll be in South America, and next year you will be in Welkom," Ogilvie Thompson says, "but in a way it is a tremendous challenge." The result is that "you start seeing in the center, as the number two or three metallurgist, a man you and your wife had dinner with ten years ago when he was fixing up a new recovery plant in Nova Lima, south of Belo Horizonte in Brazil. You felt at the time this man was good, and now he's been other places, too."

To reinforce this point, Ogilvie Thompson notes the example of Graham Boustred, who is now a deputy chairman of the Anglo American Group. Boustred started in the company's heavy engineering business, moved on to coal, then into the industrial division, which includes iron and paper operations, as well as some agriculture, electronics, and construction concerns and a new mineral sands operation. In the case of the coal and industrial divisions, Boustred took relatively modest interests and developed them into major operations.

"When people say, 'Why don't you unbundle the whole thing?' "—meaning the Anglo American Group—"I say to them, 'What do you want? Do you want Graham Boustred to stay with Scaw Metals, or with steel, or with coal? Which do you want?' Because I am telling you, each one of those companies is to this day getting the benefit of this man's experience where he's moved around. When people move from one business to another, they take ideas with them."

In addition, Ogilvie Thompson says, the systematic movement of engineers and staff creates an internal culture, where information about process technology flows freely between divisions. Anglo American employees around the world pick up the telephone "and talk to each other immediately," he says. "There is a general feeling of being in one family—in the broader sense of the word—bound together by a general purpose: to make money and do things in a constructive way."

There is a means by which Anglo American implements the expertise approach, and it, too, arises from the corporation's unique situation. In addition to cultivating cutting-edge expertise within its own R&D laboratories and "forcing" its spread into and around far-flung operations, the center at Anglo American also works to create expertise by financing education and small business initiatives. It is, Ogilvie Thompson says, the work the South African government should have undertaken in the past, but did not. In total, Anglo American spent almost $100 million in 1994 on education and training, focusing in particular on funding scholarships for black students at science and technical colleges and supporting literacy programs. It also donated millions of dollars to build up the science and engineering faculties at several universities attended by the nation's black population. At the same time, the corporation's Small Business Initiative provided $27 million of support in the form of minority investment and contracts to 126 small and medium-size enterprises, operated largely by black businessmen and -women. These activities to create expertise and simultaneously promote a different, more equitable kind of society, Ogilvie Thompson says, "can only be done from the center."

With the installation of a new democratic government in South Africa, the particular situation that gave rise to Anglo American's expertise approach is now changing. (In fact, Ogilvie Thompson says that the new government, headed by Nelson Mandela, is strongly committed to taking up the kind of education and training programs the company itself has funded in the past.) But it will be many years before Anglo American sees the effects of this change with an influx of qualified personnel, ready and able to run mining operations from gold to copper, from Botswana to Chile. Only then will Anglo American know if it is best to focus the corporate center on another way of doing business or to stick with a system that charted it through a unique and difficult past.

AT MOTOROLA: "PERFECTION IN EVERYTHING YOU DO"

Anyone who watches the telecommunications equipment industry—in fact, most people who watch industry, period—have heard the mantras behind **Motorola**'s phenomenal success:

Six Sigma—The corporate quality program with the goal of only 3.4 defects per million parts produced. In other words, products as close to flawless as humanly possible.

10X—The corporate initiative with the goal of improving every process, in terms of cost and quality, by a factor of ten.

Minority Report—The corporate epistle that allows employees to speak out about the way things are done, challenging management not to miss any opportunity to achieve "zero defects."

Each of these mantras comes down to the clearly defined, relentlessly communicated expertise approach that for a decade has defined and driven Motorola, one of the world's leading makers of cellular phones, modems, semiconductors, integrated circuits, and a wide variety of other complex electronic devices and wireless communication systems. "Basically, it's all about perfection in every single thing you do," says Morton Topfer, who spent twenty-three years with the firm, including the last three as executive vice president.

"From manufacturing all the way through to the letters written by secretaries, *perfection.*"

To that end, Motorola's corporate center is completely focused on creating the knowledge that leads to superlative quality and systematically spreading it throughout the organization. It accomplishes these objectives through product, process, compensation, and hiring policies, as well as required annual training programs for every one of the company's 133,000 employees at the worldwide campuses of Motorola University. In addition, every division is routinely graded by a cross-functional quality SWAT team that awards a numerical score to be publicly compared to those of other divisions. New products that don't measure up to quality standards are flatly canceled. There is even an international competition for employees to design the highest-quality product solutions for customers. Winners receive gold, silver, and bronze medals in a companywide ceremony.

"Motorola is a company of believers," says Topfer, now vice chairman of Dell Computer. "Whether or not you focus on zero defects is not negotiable. Everyone does because it works." Motorola's revenues have grown at a compounded annual rate of 18 percent over the past five years, from $9 billion to $22.2 billion in 1994. In the same period, its net income has grown 24 percent a year, increasing from $498 million in 1989 to $1.5 billion in 1994. It is the market leader in the growing wireless communication equipment market, and holds dominant positions in the other markets it serves. In virtually every case, its competitive advantage is the cutting-edge design and construction that creates products that work better and longer than anyone else's.

If Motorola is a company obsessed with quality as its defining expertise, Topfer says it can be traced to a one-word business situation: Japan. Fifteen years ago, the company discovered that the pagers it sold in Japan fell far short of Japanese quality requirements. "In order to become a supplier to NTT, we had to make a tenfold improvement in quality," recalls Topfer, who was running the paging business for Motorola during this period. "And in fact, a lot of people in engineering told us it couldn't be done. But there was no alternative. If we were going to be a supplier to NTT, we had to make crystals and pagers that never broke, which was unheard of in those days. We told them no was not the answer. No was unacceptable. They had to go figure out how to do it."

They did, redesigning the crystals to overcome the technical problems that created their flaws in the first place. "The engineers figured out a new mounting mechanism that allowed us to drop crystals from five feet and didn't break," Topfer says. "The situation forced them, and us, to a creativity we should have had before."

This single experience, of course, didn't transform Motorola in its entirety, Topfer says, but it did start the momentum that came to a head several years later at a senior management retreat in Tucson, Arizona. The meeting was supposed to be a "love-in," says Topfer, and it was, because the company was doing well financially. But on the last day, at a session led by then-CEO Robert Galvin, one senior manager stood up and told the group, "Motorola quality stinks. It doesn't hold up to Japanese quality, and everyone in this room knows it. If we don't do something about it, we're headed for trouble."

In the silence that followed, "Galvin didn't say a thing," Topfer recalls. "But he went back and thought about it. He was a visionary. He saw that this guy was right. We had seen proof of it." Soon afterward, Galvin and his corporate team designed and launched the quality programs that would come to transform every aspect of the corporation. They created Motorola University, for instance, and made forty hours of technical training there each year a requirement for every employee, with classes focused on the achievement of zero defects through research, design, and production processes. As a result, Topfer says, "people on the production line in Malaysia are knowledgeable about Ishekawa diagrams and all the other quality techniques, and I mean that a twenty-year-old who works in a factory can talk to you as if she's graduated from a university with a business degree." Other programs to spread expertise and communicate its importance as a defining principle of the company include the SWAT team mentioned above. Every two years, its members move into a division for a week, evaluating products and processes. "Every division's grade is known, and you don't want to be on the bottom of the list," says Topfer. "It's a powerful motivator and a powerful way to tell everybody, 'Hey, this is what's important here.'"

Galvin made the same statement in another effective way, Topfer recalls. During performance reviews with senior executives, "he would walk out of the room after the section on quality. That was all that mattered." The same message came across in compensation reviews and hiring, promotion, and firing policies. For all intents and purposes, "how much you paid attention to quality, how much you talked about it, achieved it, shared it with others, was what Corporate cared about," Topfer says. "It drove the company."

Not surprisingly, the success of this strategy was not lost on Motorola's competitors, and many moved to imitate programs like Six Sigma. (Companies in other industries have as well.) No company has surpassed Motorola at its own game, but attempts to do so raise the fundamental challenge of the expertise approach. It adds extraordinary value only as long as the expertise at its core is proprietary. Can this be done in this age of widely accessible information, disseminated by a mobile workforce and international communication tools such as the Worldwide Web? Every company choosing the expertise approach must address this question.

It appears that Motorola has. While maintaining its commitment to Six Sigma Quality, the company recently announced it will now focus on new concepts, collectively called Renewal. It will not, however, widely share what this means or how to achieve it. In fact, in his letter explaining why he would not participate in this book project, President and COO Christopher Galvin wrote, "Strategically, Motorola has become such an often benchmarked institution that we will choose to be less open on discussion of our new concepts . . . than we were with Six Sigma Quality." The reason, Galvin notes, is that the company intends for Renewal to be the source "of some significant future competitive advantage." The company does not intend to give that away—and in that, it shares a critical lesson for all expertise organizations.

Expertise, as a source of success, must be protected. And when that can no longer happen, management must assess the new situation and swiftly change either its expertise or its entire approach.

AT OGILVY & MATHER: EXPERTS IN
MAKING BRANDS MATTER, ITS OWN INCLUDED

Ten years ago, when a weakened economy, the growing popularity of generic products, and marketing devices such as cash-back promotions and store coupons combined to hand the advertising business what Charlotte Beers calls "its first comeuppance," some industry observers suggested that ad agencies had begun their demise into irrelevance. Consumers, they said, were no longer loyal to brands; ad agencies had nothing left to sell.

"The feeling back then was that we weren't so valuable anymore, that we had been reduced to discount suppliers," says Beers, who at the time was chairwoman of the American Association of Advertising Agencies and the CEO of the Chicago agency Tatham-Laird & Kudner. "But I personally thought we continued to be an invaluable resource, an indispensable partner. Ever since that time, I've been focused on the unique quality that an advertising agency offers, and that fuels what we're doing today at **Ogilvy & Mather.**"

What they're doing at the world's sixth-largest ad agency—one with upwards of $6 billion in annual billings—is an example of the expertise approach at its essence. Beers, the company's CEO since 1992, serves as a relentless, impassioned champion of the value of brands.

"I believe in this more than anything I've ever done," says Beers of O&M's focus on becoming, in the words of the company's vision statement, "the agency most valued by those who most value brands." Her focus on brand expertise has guided Ogilvy out of a difficult period of declining billings and reputation into one of a revitalized identity and major new worldwide account gains, including Kodak Digital and Applied Imaging, Wilson Sporting Goods, and KFC International.

The largest of these new clients came aboard in 1994, when Ogilvy & Mather won IBM's worldwide advertising business, worth an estimated $500 million. The computer giant dropped more than forty other agencies to consolidate its global advertising with O&M in the largest switch in advertising history, and a clear signal that Beers's and her agency's commitment to brand expertise not only had wide appeal but could be delivered by the organization.

"IBM needed a partner who could help them unify and leverage the IBM brand worldwide," Beers says, "and our particular expertise is that we have the resources and the 'weapons,' if you will, to understand and enhance that relationship between the user and the product, to place it meaningfully and respectfully in people's lives. That, after all, is how a product earns the right to become a brand."

By "resources," Beers is referring to the "mavericks, dreamers, poets, writers, frustrated filmmakers—people who love ideas and are mostly fascinated with human behavior," who work in the company's 272 offices worldwide. (O&M has about 10,000 employees in total.)

And by "weapons," she specifically means the tools O&M uses to create its expertise, among them the Brand Audit, the Brand Probe, and the BrandPrint. Together, these and other tools put into practice the overarching philosophy of Brand Stewardship that guides O&M. It is a process that assigns advertising the role of uncovering and enhancing the critical, but sometimes ephemeral, relationship between a branded product and its user. As with other clients, when O&M pitched itself to IBM, Beers says, it wasn't pitching a particular advertising campaign. Instead, "We were offering unique expertise in understanding that relationship and turning it into advertising on a worldwide canvas."

The most visible result for IBM to date is the Solutions for a Small Planet international brand campaign—a series of quirky, amusing, subtitled vignettes of unlikely individuals discussing their excitement over IBM products. One television spot features two Czech nuns sharing their desire to "surf the 'Net," referring to the Internet; another depicts two middle-aged, arty-looking Frenchmen walking along the Seine, musing over computer memory capacity. It ends with one man exclaiming, *"Incroyable,"* with the subtitle below it reading, "Cool."

"The goal of the Small Planet campaign is to help IBM be perceived as a friendly resource for all kinds of people all over the world, not a big business institution," Beers explains. "Research tells us this campaign is doing that remarkably well, and the Brand Stewardship process helped get us there. Our team and IBM's team were so closely agreed on the intangible as well as tangible aspects of the brand-user relationship that there was a very clear understanding of what the advertising had to do."

One of the ways O&M reaches that kind of understanding with its clients is by working with them to create a BrandPrint, a distillation of the brand in words and sometimes images—"down to its rock-bottom truth," as Beers describes it. A BrandPrint can be as short as one paragraph, but it conveys "the full significance of the product in the user's life, and is so exact as to be like a fingerprint." (For competitive reasons, O&M does not reveal the BrandPrints of any clients. As is the case with the other companies in this chapter, Beers notes that expertise is only powerful if it is proprietary and in daily practice throughout the company.) "It's hard to write one of these, very hard," Beers says of a BrandPrint, "or picture it. It forces you to make inferences and hypotheses. It causes you to speak to the emotional underpinnings of the facts."

As an example, she points to O&M's recent campaign for Jaguar. As the legendary blues singer Etta James croons "At Last" in the background, the words go "At last my love has come along" and viewers are enticed with sumptuous footage of the luxury car in motion. With a nod toward the car's former quality problems but reinforcing its long-standing reputation for unique design, the tag line of the commercial is: "We've kept what you love. The rest is history."

"The heart of the BrandPrint we discovered for Jaguar is an appreciation of originality, both in the users and in the essence of the car itself," Beers says. "This led to advertising quite unlike anything else in the car category, but perfectly suited to Jaguar."

Another example of a BrandPrint at work is O&M's campaign for Dove soap, which its maker, Unilever, has used to expand sales of the product globally. The commercials feature testimonials from real women—residents of the country where the advertising is being shown—talking informally about their lives and their affection for Dove.

"This is a successful campaign because it speaks to the integrity of the relationship between the user and the product," Beers says. "Of course, women want to look their best, but in these ads, Dove doesn't overpromise. The product is about attainable miracles. The Brand Stewardship process allowed us to maintain the honesty of that relationship, and that power resulted in stunning sales share as we rolled out into sixty-four countries in two years."

Along with the BrandPrint, Brand Stewardship includes the two tools mentioned above, the Brand Audit and the Brand Probe. The first of these is O&M's method of analyzing and defining what it calls "the genetic code" of a brand—that is, the cluster of feelings, impressions, connections, and opinions that blend together to form the consumer's perception of the brand. It involves copious amounts of market research, some of it standard for the industry, such as identifying the target audience, competitor analysis, and usage patterns. But much of it is less so, such as consumer research techniques that get to the answers of such subtle questions as, How does this brand make you feel about yourself? How do you feel when others see you use this brand? What memories or associations does this brand bring to mind?

A Brand Probe goes one step further than the Brand Audit, involving market research techniques that again are proprietary, but Beers allows that they involve "dynamic scenarios, and sometimes very indirect and subtle dialogue to get at how consumers truly feel about a brand."

The Brand Probe is often used for brands in transition, or as in the case of IBM and American Express, to cut through vast quantities of complex and sometimes contradictory market research.

"Most clients have more data than anyone can ever use about their brands. The complexity can be enormous," Beers explains. "So the trick is to find the one or two things that make the brand relationship significant in the huge array of data. Brand Stewardship is the focusing element. It is the discipline that allows us to bring out the relationship between the product and the user that is constant as opposed to variable." The result? Advertising that shows the consumer "in a thousand nuances, tone, music, and conditions, the nature of the relationship" the client wants to promise, says Beers.

"There could have been a million executions for IBM or Jaguar or Dove," she adds, "but Brand Stewardship won't allow that. This process helps us and our clients develop a common language and a common vision, allowing us to go forward and develop advertising that captures the value of the brand."

Few in the industry could have predicted that Beers would be able to make such a statement when she took over O&M three years ago.

"Nobody hires an outside CEO if things are going well," she remarks in an accent that evokes her upbringing in Texas, the daughter of a cowboy. "I felt one of my first goals was to remove the word *beleaguered* from in front of Ogilvy & Mather's name in every press report."

The term stemmed from troubles that first emerged at O&M after the stock market crash of 1987, when many large companies began to trim their advertising expenditures. It was also in this period that the consumer's apparent acceptance of unadvertised store-brand products and the success of promotional marketing threw the entire industry into chaos.

Though hard hit, O&M still had many assets, chief among them its enormously successful history as a source of bold and innovative ideas that don't just entertain, but sell as well. Under the leadership of its legendary founder, David Ogilvy, the agency created such well-known campaigns as American Express's "Don't Leave Home Without It" and Maxwell House's "Good to the Last Drop," and developed the images that sold Barbie dolls, Shell gasoline, and Hathaway shirts, with the man in the black eye patch. Even after Ogilvy's retirement, the company continued to prosper, expanding globally and into new ventures, most notably direct marketing.

But by the early 1990s, O&M seemed to have relinquished its verve and its direction. In 1989, the company had been acquired—through a hostile takeover—by WPP Group, a British marketing services company, which already owned the J. Walter Thompson agency. Some of O&M's most senior managers and top creative and account executives resigned after WPP took over, and an era of conflict, political infighting, and distrust ensued. Major accounts, such as Unilever and Shell, withdrew some assignments from Ogilvy, as did Campbell Soup and American Express.

By the time Beers arrived, O&M had lost some of its own confidence, and the industry's as well. The agency was perceived by some as indifferent and disconnected from consumers, perhaps the two harshest criticisms for a company in the business of getting buyers excited about a product. Ogilvy & Mather was buttressed, however, by the perception that it had the best network in the world for international communications, which ironically wasn't its greatest strength at the time. "In fact," Beers notes, "we had a fragmented group of offices that had lost their sense of being a network."

Beers sized up the situation swiftly, and not unlike the turnaround CEOs profiled in chapter 8, she moved for change at the same pace. First, she listened to client complaints about what O&M had done wrong. "It was an impressive list," she notes wryly. "But I said, 'We're not going to do that anymore. Now, let's decide together what we need to get done.'"

At the same time, Beers began to crystallize the concept of Brand Stewardship through conversations and meetings with key O&M managers around the world. This group, who shared her excitement, was vital in helping to develop the concept, but Beers recalls that she encountered "great indifference or complete befuddlement" when they first introduced the concept to a wider circle within the organization.

"There were many things about this company that were working rather well, so how do you introduce a new order?" she notes. "While there's always a group of people who are aware, insightful, discerning, and thirsty for change, there are not many." In the following months, Beers asked those managers who zealously championed Brand Stewardship along with her to be her "counselors and closest agents," and urged them to sell the brand-expertise approach internally. Meanwhile, Beers herself was selling the concept to clients and getting a response markedly more enthusiastic than from within.

She remembers, for instance, describing the idea of Brand Stewardship in a speech to 300 top managers at Philip Morris, only to be greeted with applause so thunderous that "I actually turned around to see if someone had joined us up on stage, because we were not accustomed to success at that stage.

"We had agreed that day that the brands at Philip Morris Companies had untapped, unlimited potential; that their brands had life beyond literal, linear, factual data. They understood, and that was very exciting for me, for all of us."

The same kind of excitement is now building momentum among O&M's own staff, Beers says, as more and more people understand the concept of Brand Stewardship and its power to create better advertising. Part of that comes from seeing the concept in action, but it also comes through the company's "missionaries" continuing to spread the gospel of brands through videotaped speeches, brochures, training sessions, open-discussion forums, case histories about successful Brand Stewardship campaigns, and a handbook translated into ten languages including Korean and Portuguese. When we spoke with Beers, she was about to leave for London to participate in a master class on the topic with twenty-five Ogilvy executives from around the world.

Still, sounding a common theme with other expertise-approach CEOs, Beers notes that being the organization's primary champion of a cause inherently requires her full attention, and shows no signs of letting up.

"I had thought that I could start this, get it going, and then move on to other things, because I would have preferred to move on to some other issues in the company," she remarks. "But I've never been able to let it go."

David Ogilvy himself has sent her notes, she says, asking, "Are you going to do something beside the brand thing?" And she has had to reply, "Not till it's done." Indeed, a senior management task force is now designing a "second wave" in Brand Stewardship in order to keep the expertise fresh and relevant, just as some other companies in this chapter—in particular, Motorola—have had to go through a similar renewal process. As we've noted, such is one of the recurrent challenges of the expertise approach.

But while Beers acknowledges this, she is hardly daunted. Successfully enhancing the emotional relationship between a product and its user—the art of selling the value of a brand—is the "guiding interest" of her career, she says. "It's not just that it's marketing. It's that marketing is one of the most interesting aspects of how people behave with one another, and I find that fascinating. You can get me in a briefing on some obscure product that I will never use, and I'll still be fascinated by how people respond to it."

At Ogilvy & Mather, Beers has sparked that same fascination in her employees and her clients, rebuilding—and revitalizing—an organization with the expertise approach.

TWO NEW SITUATIONS, TWO COMPANIES TURNING TO EXPERTISE

For more than a decade, the industrial group **Saint-Gobain** has received accolades for its sophisticated, fast, and accurate financial control systems, considered by some to surpass those at any other French business organization. And while president Jean-Louis Beffa himself lauds the company's reporting system for the critical information it provides to his office, he also says he believes that controls shouldn't be the primary way the center adds value. Instead, he says he is turning his organization into one where the center devotes its energies and resources to increasing knowledge about cutting-edge process technologies and implementing programs to circulate that knowledge across divisions. In other words, Saint-Gobain is the story of a company moving from the box approach to the box approach *plus* expertise, in particular expertise about glass-making processes.

Saint-Gobain was founded in 1665 and first gained fame as the company that made the mirrors for the spectacular Galerie des

Glaces at the Palace of Versailles, home of Louis XIV. Today, it operates seven main businesses, including flat glass, building materials, industrial ceramics, and abrasives. It is among France's largest companies, with sales in 1994 of $15 billion and net income of $940 million, and is known throughout Europe for its modern control system, which serves as the model for many other major organizations.

"The reporting system is very good for some things; it gives you a very good sense of the world economy and helps you analyze the economic situation for each business, for example. Also, it is very helpful in the decision-making process, and it gives us a common language across countries for every business," Beffa says. But, he adds, the data provided by the system "are a thermometer, not a goal." Corporate needs accurate financial information about business unit performance, but having it can't be the raison d'être of senior management.

"What is the point of Corporate?" he asks. "The point is to keep the businesses from becoming commonplace. The point is to keep the businesses not just growing but with as wide a distance as possible in front of the competition. These ideas are not new; almost any CEO will tell you them.

"So what is special about how Saint-Gobain does it? It's this movement for acquiring knowledge and experience from the divisions in order to take advantage of it and to communicate with the divisions the experience of others."

The "movement" Beffa refers to resembles the programs at many of the other expertise companies in this chapter, such as frequent cross-divisional meetings and an R&D office supervised by Corporate so that synergistic processes are developed and information about them disseminated. More specifically, the corporate office at Saint-Gobain allocates funds to the R&D sections of each division, regardless of its financial capabilities. In this way, the center drives the expertise approach through the organization by making sure rich divisions subsidize less lucrative ones when their research is deemed strategically important to the entire group. This said, Beffa notes that his corporate office, like that at Cable & Wireless, is just beginning to focus on the expertise approach, but it intends to increase its prominence.

This does not mean that Beffa intends to decrease the prominence of Saint-Gobain's "box." The two approaches, he says, work well in tandem. "It's funny, because we started a fashion," he notes of the company's control systems. "People think a firm that can announce its results at the end of January must be a well-kept firm in which there are no surprises."

But in a truly well-kept firm, Beffa says, the center must know what's going on behind the figures, and beyond that, it must be involved in making the figures as good as they can be. At Saint-Gobain, the expertise approach is the means to that end.

Another company that is in transition to the expertise approach is the Swedish pharmaceutical giant **Pharmacia,** which has outgrown the strategic approach that guided it for the last decade. With new business challenges, its CEO Jan Ekberg has selected six intertwined areas of expertise to guide Pharmacia through the next decade, or until another change is required.

The Pharmacia story began in 1986, when Ekberg, then CEO of a relatively small, domestic drug company called Kabi Vitrum, determined that he had to vastly increase the size of his operation if it was to survive. Large companies, clearly, were coming to dominate the industry because only they had the money and scientists to develop new treatments, which could take upwards of ten years and millions of dollars, as well as the distribution systems to get them into international markets. Kabi Vitrum was a successful niche player, but "I sensed we were headed into, not out of, a tunnel," Ekberg recalls. "We were facing the classic dilemma of being stuck in the middle—subscale in a fast-growing industry where giant competitors could enter our core segments and simply invest us out of business."

Ekberg came back from a vacation, he remembers, convinced he needed to "grow Kabi Vitrum five to ten times in five years" through acquisitions. He met his goal, mainly through the implementation of the systematic strategic approach described in chapter 2. Ekberg himself dubbed the process Play Out–Play Back. "I outlined the strategic objectives for my management team. That was 'play out.' They were asked to come back—'play back'—with the options and possible actions. It took several iterations and it involved the whole of top management."

In 1990, Kabi Vitrum merged with the Pharmacia Group, with $2.5 billion in annual sales, and in 1993, the merged entity purchased Farmitalia, a large Italian pharmaceutical concern. The next two years were spent integrating the companies into one organization, with all the growing pains and cultural clashes that process entails. With the process complete in 1995, Ekberg decided it was time to focus the company on its second phase: competitive advantage through expertise.

He and his management team spent many hours discussing the changes affecting the pharmaceutical industry, "such as managed health care and deregulation, and others, which are changing the rules of the game in a fundamental way in our business," Ekberg says.

"We knew we could no longer focus on growth in the traditional sense. New challenges were facing us, not in terms of products but in terms of consumers. We realized we had to master what was happening to the user of our products, or else we would simply and slowly fade away from the marketplace."

Soon thereafter, Ekberg and ten of his top managers went on an off-site retreat with a long list of possible areas of expertise for Pharmacia. "We debated each one, redefined some, bundled others, dropped many," he says. "Many long evenings later, we finally arrived at six core areas of expertise." They are health economics, disease management, R&D, general management, project management, and marketing.

With the six areas determined, Ekberg designed and implemented a program to introduce the expertise concept to the organization. His experience as a strategic CEO was useful; he rolled out his new approach using Play Out–Play Back. Again, he says it worked; the company is committed to the change.

"In industries like ours, where you find a lot of turbulence," Ekberg explains of his transition to a new approach, "you must change rather than be changed."

THE EXPERTISE APPROACH:
POWERFUL WHILE IT LASTS

In this chapter we have met CEOs who define the center's role as identifying the expertise critical to competitive advantage in its industry, nurturing it, sometimes increasing it in scope, and actively disseminating it between business unit "silos," up and down the hierarchy, or among employees. (Some companies, such as Cable & Wireless and Pharmacia, identify more than one area of expertise, but these multiple choices are, in both cases, intertwined.) Expertise, these CEOs told us, comes in a variety of forms. At Cooper Industries and Saint-Gobain, for instance, it is leading-edge knowledge about manufacturing processes. At Eisai, President Haruo Naito made insight into the customer's "extraordinary experience" his company's special aptitude. Motorola is a company driven by an expertise that cuts across functions, products, and processes: quality.

Regardless of what expertise is at their core, though, the organizations in this chapter share common processes, spreading expertise through focused, rigorous programs and well-defined policies: Eisai's field training of middle managers in hospitals and nursing homes, for example; Cooper Industries' manufacturing SWAT team; Motorola's quality-linked compensation; and Anglo American's transfer of managers between countries and divisions. The relentless drive for shared knowledge in expertise organizations also becomes part and parcel of the corporate culture. In mature expertise organizations, managers communicate openly the technical, marketing, or other relevant skills, or even challenge management about how well the selected expertise is being achieved, as in the case of Motorola's Minority Report. In nascent expertise organizations, such as Cable & Wireless, Saint-Gobain, and Pharmacia, the chief executives assert that such a fluid, honest exchange of critical information is exactly what they were after in adopting this particular management tactic.

The expertise approach, however, is complicated. As the Motorola example suggests, expertise is a competitive advantage only as long as it is proprietary. (At Cooper, too, Bob Cizik hopes his successor will change the company's focus from stable manufacturing processes to marketing.) Certainly, some types of knowledge can be kept exclusive; it would take years of on-site experience as well as many millions of dollars in R&D to match what Anglo American knows about deep-sea mining processes. But we live in a society in which information moves swiftly and easily, over phone lines and computer networks, via employees switching companies and continents, or through reporters, Wall Street analysts, and academic researchers. Every company that selects the expertise approach must be aware of this challenge.

In addition, they must be aware that to adopt this approach is to commit to becoming world class in the targeted area of expertise. It is not enough to select a corporation's focal point. An effective expertise company must also design and implement original, creative, and meaningful programs to make this focal point a competitive advantage. They must, in other words, be the most expert in their area of expertise.

When does a CEO choose the expertise approach? The first answer is, when a certain expertise can be a source of significant competitive advantage—when it matters to the customer. The second answer is that the expertise approach is powerful only when it can be kept proprietary for a significant period of time; there is no point relentlessly developing knowledge that gives a company the edge only for a few months or a year. And third, the expertise approach is best applied in companies in which the divisions are in similar businesses. Anglo American may sell copper and diamonds, but its operations are largely concerned with mining. Motorola makes many different products, but wireless electronic technology links them. Eisai and Pharmacia sell medications across a number of continents, but its consumers are all exactly the same in what they want: good health.

Finally, this approach matches business situations in which the pace of change is manageable enough to accommodate the development of a critical expertise, a process that can take many years. This is not to say that expertise can't drive organizations in fast-changing industries, but if that is the case, management must stay far ahead of the wave or be prepared to change direction when it hits the shore.

5

"THE GREATEST FREEDOM"...

INSIDE FOUR WALLS:

THE BOX APPROACH

Not long ago, senior management at **HSBC Holdings** decided to compile a report card on themselves; they wanted to assess their own strengths and weaknesses, and determine what range existed in the types of people at the top level of the huge international commercial banking firm. As part of this effort, twenty-five senior managers took the well-known Myers Briggs psychometric test, which measures personality traits. The results came back a few days later, and Group Chief Executive John Bond remembers being startled, not by the range of personalities running HSBC but by the fact that all of the men analyzed were, in fact, extremely similar in terms of values, behaviors, and skills.

But did these results alarm Bond? Not at all. "It is," he reflects, "the best way you can run a company. I can sleep well at night knowing that the guys lending money whilst I am asleep think the same way I do, and are the same type of person I am." That type of person is someone who lives by the same rules, policies, and beliefs as Bond does, and the type of organization he runs is what we have come to refer to as a "box." Though this name perhaps implies a negative value judgment, it shouldn't. As the examples in this chapter show, the box approach, correctly applied, appeals to many employees and suits their organizations to powerful ends.

Simply put, a box company exists when the "center"—usually the CEO and his top staff—institutes a set of corporate rules, procedures, structures, and/or values, and uses these as boundaries for the performance of all employees. As we said in the introduction, virtually every company has a box, for every company has procedural, financial, and cultural control systems. But the companies we focus on in this chapter are those in which top management has made the box the *focus* of their value addition. In other words, in these companies, creating and maintaining the most effective box defines the center's role; it is at the fore of top management's daily activities and long-term concerns.

We also noted in the introduction that boxes come in a variety of sizes, and can be hard, soft, or in between. In our interviews, for example, we encountered one company we called a "concrete" box, for the rigidity of its financial controls and the pink slips sent to the managers who didn't meet them. We also encountered a company with a staggering number of unwritten rules, all of them pertaining to cultural norms, such as how people talked to one another in crisis situations and how quickly one answered the telephone when a customer called. The underlying values at these companies differ, but both are boxes in that the center is the standard-bearer of explicit, self-reinforcing constraints that determine employee behavior.

It is, perhaps, easy to criticize box companies. Certainly, boxes that are too hard are unpleasant places to work, restraining human creativity and growth (and business growth, too). But there are strong arguments in support of this approach. First, it is a necessity in highly leveraged industries such as banking, where government examiners insist on strict controls to help them protect both the consumer and the company from insider theft, inappropriate risk taking, or illicit transfer of funds. Beyond this is something John Bond mentioned; the box is effective in managing global corporations where no "center" can be everywhere, meet everyone, see every operation, analyze every problem situation. For the same reason, the box approach can make sense in highly decentralized companies. Moreover, box companies satisfy the personal and professional needs of people who enjoy predictability and structure. And finally, one great advantage of box management is the remarkable clarity it can bring an organization by delineating boundaries of behavior and demarking an over-riding "governing objective," as it is put by Sir Brian Pitman, chief executive of the United Kingdom's Lloyd's Bank, with 60,000 employees and upwards of $160 billion in assets. The governing objective at Lloyd's, Pitman says, is maximizing one goal: total return to shareholders. This particular measure arose out of months of high-level debate about the bank's strategy, products, and values in sessions that Pitman describes as emotional and sometimes contentious. But he says the process has paid off in the focus and energy it has spawned. "What this brought about really was a definition of the boundaries of the business: what you were going to do and what you were not going to do. It was no good people coming up and saying, 'We ought to have a flag in Cambodia, there's a lot of business there.' Now people know the question should be, 'Can we be in Cambodia and enhance the total return to shareholders?' Now, if you go to our operations in New Zealand, they think exactly this way. And in Germany as well. We have the clarity of a single driving force. There is no confusion. People go off in different directions if you let them do it—it's human nature." The benefit of a centrally driven organization with distinct boundaries, goals, and values, he says, is that people instead end up working together, often to more effective results.

In this chapter we will examine box companies such as **HSBC; Hewlett-Packard,** the electronic components company which employs a soft box; **BankAmerica;** and the French insurance conglomerate **AXA,** where a vice president of culture oversees a box that includes a company language. We will also hear from two CEOs from **British Airways** and the United Kingdom's **NatWest Group** who talk about the ways they mitigate the negative side effects of a control-based organization. Finally, this chapter briefly profiles **Nintendo,** the Japanese video game maker, which uses the box in tandem with the human assets approach.

HSBC: MANAGEMENT BY EXCEPTION

HSBC (HongKong Shanghai Banking Co.) Holdings is, states John Bond, a "bank where bad news travels quickly to the top." It is a description he offers without apology—indeed, with pride.

"This is not a bank where we spend a lot of time patting each other on the back and delivering good news," says Bond as he explains the organization he runs, which brought in profits of $5.1 billion in 1994, with an asset base of $323 billion.

"If I get a long-distance phone call," he adds, "it isn't to say, 'Hey, I made plan.'"

Instead, HSBC has a box so strong, with such firm walls and sharp corners, that the CEO and his top staff need only be alerted when something goes wrong somewhere in the bank's 3,000 offices in sixty-eight countries. That doesn't happen very often.

"We are used to having people do what they are expected to do. The rule here is do what you say you are going to do," Bond continues, speaking in the company's London offices. The founding member of the HSBC Group, the HongKongBank, was established by Scots traders in 1865, and has its headquarters in Hong Kong. "Make any mistake once and you can argue the reasons why you took the decision. If you make the same mistake twice it can be damaging to your health."

The result, Bond says, is a company "managed by exception"—he and his top staff focus on the exceptions to the rules. And the rules at HSBC are clear, specifically outlining everything from financial goals for each division along four dimensions, to the type of personal computer on every desk, from Jakarta to Buffalo, New York, where HSBC owns the regional American bank chain Marine Midland.

Sound stifling? Bond disagrees, pointing out that the clarity and consistency of the bank's box is exactly the reason why many managers choose it for lifetime employment. "In fact, what we have is the kind of teamwork that people spend their careers looking for," he says. Bond himself has been with the company twenty-nine years, almost all of them in the bank's international operations, including a stint turning around financially ailing Marine Midland in 1991 and 1992. "Many of the people in our upper ranks are people," he remarks, "who have wanted to make their whole careers with HSBC."

Moreover, Bond points out, given the banking industry, and the global reach of HSBC, no other type of management approach could work so effectively.

"Our viewpoint is very simple: there are very few original strategies in banking. It is a business of execution," he says. "We believe ours is a business based on trust, and by definition, trust is only built up over time." In other words, HSBC's box leads to consistency in performance by tellers and credit officers—branch to branch, country to country, year to year—and consistency begets trust. "The customers love it," Bond says firmly.

He also says the company's management approach is a function of HSBC's geographical dispersion and the radically different customs and demands of its markets. "It is no good me sitting here in London second-guessing what we should be doing for our women clients in Saudi Arabia," he explains. "Here at headquarters we constantly remind ourselves that over 50 percent of the profits of this group are made while we are asleep, so you can't pretend the head office is all-seeing, all-knowing, and making everything happen."

As an example, he mentions Malaysia, a country where HSBC has been for more than a century and has thirty-five branches—"big business, with more than $400 million in capital."

"The manager of that territory sits in Kuala Lumpur and he is responsible for everything. The markets. The relationship with the central bank. Major clients. The staff. Local auditors. He is absolutely in charge of running his business locally.

"But Head Office comes into play forcefully on the risk front. We approve acquisitions and information technology, which is vital in this industry. We manage high-level appointments and remuneration policy," as well as budget and planning goals.

The center controls overall risk, Bond explains, because it is the only variable it can and should regulate. Well-managed risk means smooth day-to-day operations, the main concern of headquarters. Asked about strategy formulation, Bond quickly agrees it, too, should concern the center—of *other* companies.

"Blue-skying is not the way we spend our time in our organization," Bond elaborates. "This comes out of our history. Nobody could have 'blue skied' that we would lose thirty-two branches in China on October 1, 1949." He shakes his head, reflecting on how some of history's most momentous events have transformed his bank. "We have been asked to leave Indonesia, and asked to leave Burma as it was, and then let back in. That is why we don't believe it is a particularly productive use of our time doing a whole lot of 'what ifs.' We do spend a lot of time thinking about the future of various economies, but we don't spend a lot of time thinking about what the world will look like in 2050 and how commercial banking is going to fit in."

But Bond and his staff do spend a lot of time maintaining and improving HSBC's structure, rules, and other control systems.

Perhaps the controls are nowhere more strict than in the company's information technology system, which Bond describes as "absolutely vital to the company and the industry." HSBC operates two main computer systems, one for its large operations, the other for its smaller ones. Both are designed by a small staff of experts under the eye of headquarters. Local branches can adjust the system in minor ways, but "what you *cannot* do is tinker with the core accountancy system," Bond states. He is urbane and engaging in conversation, but one gets the sense he does not suffer fools gladly. "You cannot," he says, "tinker with the profit calculation and the mainstream elements of what makes a bank tick.

"Every unit writes a technology plan each year on what they plan to spend on development, what they plan to spend on operations, and what equipment they plan to buy," Bond continues. "That is reviewed down to the last PC here, and we will say, 'You don't need to buy a new PC in Malaysia; we can supply it from Indonesia, where we have a surplus because we are closing a branch there.' We control the movement of equipment around the world from London, and I can assure you it is a very detailed plan, but it isn't very popular.

"It is the way we run our business; we start from the position that a company can spend unlimited amounts on technology, and if you delegate the power to spend, it can be infinite. We control that expenditure, and we try to keep it at around 12 percent of total expense. We think that is the right level."

Bond and his staff also set financial goals and controls for the far-flung bank through what he calls "a disciplined planning process."

"Meeting your plan is very much a part of HSBC culture," he adds. "It is an unhealthy thing not to make plan."

Bond says HSBC offices in each country must live by four rules. First, they should not present a plan in which costs are rising faster than revenues. Second, no plan should have a cost-income ratio of more than 60 percent. Third, no plan is permitted to have net income rising slower than risk-rated assets. And finally, each plan must show that noninterest income is moving toward 50 percent of its total revenue.

How top managers meet these yardsticks is "entirely up to them," Bond says, echoing a common theme in box companies about the freedom afforded to managers within the framework set by head-quarters.

In addition to its numerical yardsticks, HSBC also requires its divisions to present strategic plans every three to five years, not of the blue-sky variety dismissed above but plans that demonstrate HSBC management in each country is thinking about where the economy is going, the resources it needs, the political environment, the money supply, and local competitors. Strategic plans and annual operating plans are compared by headquarters, Bond says, and if there are exceptions, then the managers need to explain them. But managers who misplan—or worse, who are making a loss—get the most attention. "We spend a lot of time looking at them," Bond says, and you get a sense looking is not all he and his top staff are doing.

Bond also examines every acquisition proposed by either HSBC's country managers around the world or intermediaries, which amounts to about three a week. Since he and his top staff are "dead opposed" to committees, this usually means that the group chairman and he or one or two other top executives scrutinize each proposal, deciding if it should be pursued or if it is something that "doesn't fly."

Finally, Bond says the center at HSBC manages the remuneration policies that cover its 100,000 employees, based on the Hay grading system. "In fact, getting the right management in the right places is probably the most crucial task we have," he says. To that end, he travels nearly one-third of the year, meeting managers and getting a feel for different operations, then trying to determine what would work best for HSBC.

Bond concludes by referring back to the personality test that showed he and his top executives were remarkably similar, and suggests that it might be, in fact, a welcome result of HSBC's consistency, predictability, and clear structure—its box.

"It's not because we are all yes-men, although that would be a cynical viewpoint. Nor are we control freaks, focused on rules for no reason except that they are rules. Rather, it is simply because we have worked together for so long we share the same value system, and we trust one another. We know that to run a successful banking group you must have that trust among the top management team, as well as control the expenses and have good asset quality. If you do those things right, you will succeed.

"We've debated whether this is a weakness—that there are no huge arguments about 'I want to go to port,' or 'I want to go to starboard.' And we decided that it is a strength, as long as we are aware that it could become a weakness," Bond says. "But we know we need new influences, people coming in from the outside. You need enough people to challenge the status quo," Bond says, "but not enough to create a revolution."

HEWLETT-PACKARD: THE H-P WAY . . . A CULTURAL BOX

At first, Lewis Platt of **Hewlett-Packard** doesn't sound that different from HSBC's John Bond. Their industries may be different—with $25 billion in sales in 1994, H-P is a dominant force in the computer business, producing and selling high-technology products from laser printers to fiber-optic transceivers—but the role of headquarters is about the same. For instance, Platt argues, as Bond does, that the "center" simply doesn't have the expertise to supervise all its far-flung divisions and markets, which in H-P's case span 110 countries. "The businesses themselves operate pretty independently," Platt says. "They decide what products to develop, they decide when to bring them to market. They decide their manufacturing strategies, they decide how they're going to market those products, which channels they're going to use. So the notion here is that businesses run their own businesses."

The reason, says Platt, is the very nature of the electronics industry, with its breakneck pace of innovation. "We're talking about products that are on the market for nine months and are gone," he says, "and then you replace them with something new. I think we've tried to build an organizational structure, a way of managing the company, that's consistent with the business we're in today. I mean, when we look at 1994, 75 percent of our revenue came from products we introduced that year or the one before it. It just calls for a very light-on-your-feet superstructure. So I can't imagine being smart enough to run all those businesses or attempt to make decisions for all those businesses that are better decisions than they are making today."

What does that leave for headquarters to do? This is where Platt begins to sound different from Bond, who saw the center's role as managing risk by implementing strict financial, planning, and IT controls to mainstream day-to-day operations from one continent to the next.

By contrast, Platt, a low-key fifty-three-year-old, shrugs lightly when asked what responsibilities fall to H-P's top staff. He rattles off a few: tax, legal, environmental issues, purchasing, the annual report, insurance. "Sometimes," he adds, "I sit working with my managers on key decisions that they're making, and I'll challenge them if I don't like it.

"What other value does Corporate add?" Platt asks, and it is soon clear the question is rhetorical. "Not a lot," he replies without apology. "We don't try to. I don't feel bad about that."

But over the course of the next few hours, it becomes clear from Platt's description of his day-to-day activities that in fact his role is significant, and it is the role of reinforcing and maintaining H-P's box, a box consisting of *cultural* controls based on values and behaviors. It is ultimately, he agrees, a box as firm and self-reinforcing as the financial controls at the core of other firms, such as HSBC Holdings.

In an important way, Platt himself is the embodiment of the H-P box—or the "H-P way," as he calls it—which features loyalty to H-P and an honest, subdued, respectful personality. He's quite old-fashioned compared to the better-popularized, brash, eccentric, and outspoken personalities known to work at other high-tech Silicon Valley firms. Platt joined H-P's medical products division in 1966, shortly after receiving his engineering degree from Cornell and M.B.A. from Wharton. He later moved on to the company's analytical instruments unit, and in 1984, he became involved in the computer business. He was appointed to the top job in 1992, having never worked anywhere besides Hewlett-Packard. He drives a Ford Taurus, lives in a modest ranch home not far from H-P's Palo Alto, California, headquarters, and likes to fish in his free time. He speaks thoughtfully, but with enormous pride in H-P, which has been called the "company that gave birth to the Silicon Valley." He does not mention the company's phenomenal financial success in recent years, with revenues shooting up at a compound annual growth rate of nearly 30 percent since 1989, or its favorable embrace by the markets. He'd rather talk about trust—that is, how much he trusts the people who work for him and how they are all steeped in the culture that makes

H-P work as well as the H-P 12C calculator, seemingly in every other businessperson's desk, briefcase, or shirt pocket.

"Culture is a very, very strong thing," Platt says. "Therefore, you need people who are steeped in and strongly believe in the culture, who can spout the core values of the company because that's the way we really manage. When we say we have trust in and respect for our people, we really do. A lot of companies that are decentralized do it with a whole lot of checking and examining and second-guessing. But with us, it's run with what I call 'cultural control,' where people know the right thing to do.

"And I trust that they know the right thing to do," Platt adds. "I don't sit around wondering if they know what kind of decision to make in a particular circumstance. I just trust that they do, because of our core values." He lists those values as trust and respect for individuals, achievement and contribution, teamwork, and integrity, as well as flexibility and innovation—and he says that they work as a box because management has been living, breathing, and talking explicitly about them for thirty years. "I can't imagine ever having to change those core values," he says. At the same time, top managers have been equally explicit about the interrelated company "objectives" of profit, customers, growth, and citizenship.

"I come to work every morning honestly believing that all the H-P people are going to come to work in the morning and do their damnedest for the company. And not all my counterparts [at other firms] feel that way," Platt says. "I've talked to a lot of them who are scared of their workforce, or believe their workforce is going to screw them if possible. I mean, it's an adversarial position. I just don't have that when I come to work." H-P, it should be noted, employs 96,000 worldwide.

But how, exactly, does Platt guarantee his cultural box doesn't collapse? What does he do?

The first answer is that Platt sets the example himself, by his manner and also by his actions. He spends 30 percent of his time talking with customers. He spends another 30 percent of his time visiting H-P offices from Seattle to the Soviet Union. During these visits, he holds informal "coffee talks," in which he answers questions from any employee who has them. He then meets with the managers and their staff to review plans, projections, and products. And afterward, he makes sure he takes at least an hour to walk around the facility, stopping at desks and machines to ask, "Hi, how are you? How long have you been with us? What are you working on? What would you like to see changed in the company?" He explains that these chats, although sometimes brief, reinforce that part of the culture that values honesty and hard work.

In addition, Platt spends "tens of hours" each week responding to voice mail and E-mail. "It kills me, by the way, to answer all of them," he admits. "But those things are very important" in terms of spreading values.

"Yesterday I had a woman from Australia drop by," he elaborates. "She joined us in January, a few months back, just out of graduate school. She had some ideas about women's issues at H-P.

"She left here, and I don't mean to make this sound like my ego is getting away with me, but I think she left here dumbfounded that she could get an appointment with me. She had a couple of very good thoughts. I spent twenty minutes with her. And to tell you the truth, I do quite a bit of that. She walked out of here feeling like she belonged to a very special company. H-P managers do that kind of thing a lot—much more, I think, than managers at other companies."

Platt also reinforces H-P's cultural box in two other ways. First, he continues to support the system that rewards employees who have devoted their careers to the company. In other words, loyalty rises to the top. "The team that reports to me today has got to have on average close to twenty-five years of H-P experience. And not all of these guys are guys who are ready to retire; the mean age is around fifty. They really serve as a cultural basis for the company. And I'm sure all of them have an outstanding offer or two to work someplace else for twice as much money as they make today. But they can't imagine themselves working in a different kind of environment than this. I really think people believe this is a different kind of place. Maybe it's not as different as we think it is, but the important thing is, we all think it's different. Special."

The second way Platt reinforces the H-P cultural box is with a step few other CEOs might endorse, let alone organize. Once a year, he allows the business unit managers to vote on which functions in the corporate office add value and which don't. It's his way of reminding the organization of how much humility and contribution matter, even at the very top.

"Basically, the business units have the ability to vote on the level of services they get from Corporate, and they can vote it out of existence or say it should be half its size," he explains. "It's kind of a major housekeeping. We get rid of all those corporate functions that are getting too involved in decisions and second-guessing." It also speaks to his trust of those who work around and beneath him.

"Trust," says Platt, "is a great thing because it allows us to keep the infrastructure small, and it allows me to manage what I call the white spaces—the things that fall between the organizations. That's what I end up spending a lot of my time doing. I come up with projects that cross organizational boundaries, the kinds of things the businesses don't think about because they are focused on the business. Also, future things, things that bring together two or three or four of the businesses on a project no one of those businesses has identified on its own. And some of those have been really interesting.

"So I guess"—Platt hesitates slightly, apparently uncomfortable with the audacity of what he is about to say—"there is some strategic value added by the center after all."

AT BANKAMERICA—THE ANTI-BOX CEO IN A BOX

Richard Rosenberg, CEO of **BankAmerica,** knows his company is a box—he refers to it as such without hesitation—but in the next breath he explains all the devices he uses to "push the walls out as far as they can go." He scribbles personal notes to employees who have done good work, reads dozens of branch newsletters even though the misspellings drive him a bit crazy, and rehearses managers scheduled to appear before the board of directors. He is, for all intents and purposes, a human assets CEO stuck in the office of a box executive.

"I'm not a box guy. It's not my style," says Rosenberg, who at sixty-four has run BankAmerica since 1990. He is silver-haired and speaks with a directness often punctuated with laughter. "But there's clearly a box at BankAmerica. I don't think we can kid ourselves that there is not."

Again, the box is the answer to a distinct situation. BankAmerica, with 96,000 employees in thirty-seven countries, is a vast and complicated organization. With $215 billion in assets, it is the second largest bank holding company in the United States, making innumerable loans to individuals, businesses, and government agencies. It processes 20 million checks a day, and on some days processes almost 10 percent of all checks written in this country. In an average month, the bank fields approximately 15 million customer account inquiries. It operates some 5,500 ATMs in eleven states, processing millions of transactions a day. (In California alone, the number is 30 million.) "We've got big capital markets, big trading operations, huge wholesale operations, huge investments out there," Rosenberg says. "When it comes to financial service organizations, I would have to say, along with Citibank, we are among the most complex."

But what's perhaps more relevant than BankAmerica's complexity is the environment in which it operates—a highly regulated one. It is, says Rosenberg, the government's examiners that force his company (and all banks) into the box.

"We try very hard to give people on the line, people in the branches, as much authority and responsibility as possible," he reflects, "but even though in our heart of hearts we may know they are doing the right thing, we can't tolerate people doing the right thing if we know it violates regulations, although some of [those regulations], unfortunately, are rather obsolete and archaic."

BankAmerica is fortunate, though. Because of its successful financial results—its net income has grown at a compounded annual rate of 18 percent since 1990 to reach $2.1 billion in 1994—the government has cut it some slack. "They know there is a safety net there of capital and earnings," Rosenberg explains. Still, the box remains entrenched, he says, and he's found that his main job as CEO is making sure people don't get too comfortable inside its walls.

"The problem with the box is that people end up liking it," he says, slightly exasperated. "The hard part is not getting them to adjust to its limitations but getting them to take risks. It's not like people are banging on the walls and we've got the box too tight. It's that people don't want to take as much risk as we're prepared to allow them."

As a result, Rosenberg says he devotes at least 40 percent of his time to picking, training, and motivating people to "go to the edge of the box."

"It would be 60 or 70 percent of my time if it weren't for my community responsibilities," he adds, mentioning his commitment to community activities and charities such as the United Way, which he estimates takes up another 40 percent of his schedule.

How exactly does Rosenberg focus on developing anti-box box people like himself?

"I call on customers with them, I discuss special projects with them, and I have them appear before the board," he explains. "And one of my biggest challenges is distinguishing between the person who is the great presenter and the great manager. Sometimes they are not one and the same. You have to be very careful."

On many occasions, Rosenberg actually rehearses board presentations with those "great" managers who aren't particularly comfortable or persuasive in front of a crowd.

"That way, when it comes time for a promotion, you don't get the board saying, 'Isn't that the person who came in four months ago and couldn't answer our questions and was totally off base?'" Rosenberg explains. His goal, he adds, "is to find the potential presidents, not just the good presenters."

Rosenberg also spends hours each week defying the typical box's top-down authority structure by listening closely to as many employees as he can, listening to them for new ideas percolating from the bottom up. It is a task he accomplishes by reading dozens of newsletters from around the world. "Everyone with a PC on his desk puts out a newsletter in this company," he sighs, but it's with delight not frustration. "You know, we're killing a few more trees, but these newsletters are filled with new approaches for how they get a customer. I mean, some of these newsletters are pretty amateurish, and every once in a while there are misspellings that just grate on my nerves, but I've got to tell you, I wouldn't turn them off for anything."

After reading the newsletters, Rosenberg goes one step further. He personally spreads their customer-catching tips around the company. "Asia wholesale does not send their newsletter to the Southern California person who runs the branches," he says, "so I pass it along. That's part of my job."

Another major part, Rosenberg says, is motivating and rewarding the box-stretching employees he has selected, trained, and listened to. "My job is to make those people feel good about what they are doing, because believe it or not, man does not live by bread alone, although there has got to be bread." He describes overseeing 107 different incentive plans, but hastens to add that his motivational techniques are usually on a more personal level. He hand-writes notes to employees at any level who have made a contribution to the organization; he calls BankAmerica's PR department and asks them to feature outstanding employees in the corporation's weekly newspaper; and, he says, he sets an example by working "very hard" himself.

"I think—well, I *know*—this is going to sound very presumptuous," he elaborates, a bit hesitantly, "but I do think that corporations do take on, to some extent, the personality of the CEO. And I like to think the fact that I work very hard means that the people who work for me work very hard. They know what time I come in, they know how many days I travel—which pretty much is constantly. It's not something I boast about. They know it. And then it all comes back to who you pick. They follow that lead.

"But you've got to make them feel good about that," Rosenberg adds. "You can't pay people enough to work as hard and as intelligently as our people do."

One final way in which Rosenberg challenges the standard box is by *not* conducting formal performance reviews, a staple of most box organizations. "At the end of the day," he explains, "I know who did the job and who didn't, without all the forms."

He shakes his head at the conundrum he's found himself in at the height of his career, running a box but constantly coaxing people to push its walls as far as they will go without crashing down.

"We can't succeed by simply living in a box. I mean, with our heavily regulated environment, we *have* to have one, fine. But we can't succeed with that kind of mentality. We always have to think, number one, about ways to expand the box, how to make it bigger.

"Otherwise," he warns, "it becomes a coffin."

AT AXA GROUP: THROUGH THE VALLEY OF DESPAIR, TO REACH A COMMON CULTURE

If all goes as planned, some day in the near future a manager of the international insurance giant **AXA Group** will be able to say, "I had to go through the valley of despair, but with some TNT action, I was able to catch the train of the north"—and AXA Group managers around the globe will understand exactly what he's talking about. And one of them might even respond, "Better that than the trap of immobility."

The valley of despair, TNT action, the train of the north, the trap of immobility—these phrases are part of a new language of management used by AXA's top management team as part of perhaps the most unique soft box we encountered in our research. Like Hewlett-Packard, AXA's box is cultural, based on values shared across literally dozens of divisions worldwide, including the Equitable insurance company in the United States, but only AXA's box includes an invented language, hand-drawn symbols, detailed behavioral guidelines, and a university at a converted French castle devoted to teaching these subjects to thousands of managers. Because of this system, the hope is that none of AXA's roughly 50,000 employees worldwide will need a translator to know that "the valley of despair" is the rough terrain you must cover before reaching a difficult management objective, or that TNT action means rapid implementation of decisions, or that the train of the north is the vehicle that carries employees toward common corporate goals and values. (The trap of immobility is where people find themselves if they are unwilling to change—that is, a place that is worse than where one started.) The hope is that AXA's employees, divided by their own national cultures, will be united by a new and distinct corporate culture that promotes the competitive advantage of cross-border communication and information sharing.

"We all have words in our families that make us wink. You don't have to make long speeches—one word is said and it reminds us of something, and the others on the sidelines, they don't get it, but between us, these words speak volumes," explains Claude Bébéar, AXA's president, who has been called a "revolutionary gentleman" in the French media for his innovative business practices over the past several decades.

"That is the idea behind our language and our shared culture," Bébéar adds. "You see, it's very much knowledge of one another. Then, after that, when the people know the values and they know each other well, they do not hesitate to help each other and exchange ideas. The role of the center is to nurture this objective."

He adds: "Without a common culture, we would be just like some sort of holding company."

Bébéar stresses that the center at AXA also has another critical role: maintaining the company's hard box, similar to others in this chapter, with audit committees, complex accounting systems, a sophisticated employee ranking and classification system, specific corporate-set financial targets, and a strict reporting plan. Group strategy is set by Bébéar and his strategic committee in Paris, and then "sold" top-down around the world. Headquarters also allocates all resources and oversees a uniform information-technology system. This hard box is necessary, Bébéar says, because with $250 billion in assets under management, AXA faces many of the same financial control issues as major international banks. The opportunities for data manipulation (or theft) are enormous. "You have to agree squarely on how the figures are calculated, and you must agree on all the definitions," he says. "What is a premium? What is an accident? What is a mathematical reserve? We all agree on these matters" because systems in place close them to interpretation.

But Bébéar says this hard-box approach is not enough to guarantee every employee's actions, or enough to respond to the competitive situation AXA confronts in today's marketplace. He describes AXA's situation as one of increasing competition and product innovation, one that demands the kind of creativity a multinational corps of managers, put together, can bring. Moreover, AXA must be as decentralized as possible, he says, because insurance laws and customs vary so much with each country. All of these factors call for highly motivated employees who eagerly share "intelligence" and technical advice, Bébéar says—employees who possess AXA's values of loyalty, team spirit, pride in work, ambition, imagination, realism, and exigency.

There is one other reason AXA employees must display these characteristics, according to Françoise Colloc'h, AXA's director of corporate culture and communications. It speaks to the customer's fundamental distaste for the whole business of buying insurance.

"When you get insured, you give me some money, and you find that very unpleasant," Colloc'h says, "and in exchange, you have a promise that when something happens to you, we will be there. And when you come looking for us again, something unpleasant has happened to you. So the whole client relationship is a painful one, in comparison to, say, when you buy a car. Then, when you spend your money, at least you have something nice in return.

"But in insurance, the relationship between the company and the customer is basically negative," Colloc'h adds, "so in fact, the role of the individual [employee] is probably a thousand times more important than it is elsewhere." In fact, she says, employees can offer customers little beside the values AXA endorses, but they go far toward ensuring the company's goals of continued growth and profitability.

Bébéar and Colloc'h agree that it was AXA's growth in the first place that made the creation of a common culture necessary. Since 1981, AXA has doubled in size (in terms of assets and income) every four years, so what began as a small French insurance firm is today a collection of twenty-eight companies in Germany, Holland, Belgium, Canada, Spain, France, England, and the United States. (There are AXA companies in Hong Kong, Singapore, and Malaysia as well, and the group recently acquired one of Australia's largest insurance companies, National Mutual Life Association.) AXA also includes fifteen asset management and financial service companies in the United States and France, including the well-known Wall Street firm of Donaldson, Lufkin & Jenrette, and Alliance Capital.

The acquisition campaign propelled AXA's net income to $457 million in 1994, but it also created a profound sense of "culture shock," according to Colloc'h.

"People were merged and moved; they changed products, company names, and computers, often very quickly during this period," Colloc'h says. "And during this revolution, management was the least of our concerns because we had technical challenges all the time. And it's true that when you do not have a very cohesive, well-established structure, instead of managing, you have to solve problems."

But in the long run, to succeed—even to survive—you must address "the guiding principles of human relations," Colloc'h notes, and when Bébéar realized this in the early 1990s he changed her role from office director to director of corporate culture and communications.

"We needed to federate everyone, to find pluses in being together and prepare for the challenge of the future," Colloc'h explains.

Step one of the process was for Bébéar to define the company's overarching *business* principles, and then communicate them to divisions around the world. The principles were to concentrate on the insurance business without diversification; to honor obligations to clients, stockholders, staff, and the community; to remain an independent entity—in other words, to avoid being bought or merged; and to be decentralized in order to adapt more easily to local market dynamics.

The second part, the "federation" process—the process of creating a soft box—was to develop a specific AXA culture, and "this preoccupied us 200 times more than all the other" issues of human resource management, Colloc'h recalls. It involved long meetings attended by AXA human resource managers in which common values were debated. "The Americans would raise the subjects of sexual harassment and racial equality, and the European countries would laugh and say, 'We don't have this problem,' " says Colloc'h. Such disagreement was not uncommon as AXA tried to form one culture from so many disparate ones.

But the resistance didn't surprise Bébéar. He recalls that when AXA purchased 49 percent of the Equitable in 1992, the American company "had a concept that was very clearly that there were two or three hundred people who count. Those people were treated extremely well, they were coddled, and so on, and the rest were outcasts.

"We would have nothing to do with that," he says. "We explained to them that in our company, if we have 7,000 or 8,000 employees, we try to motivate every last one of them, and that every last one has his part to play."

The Americans, Bébéar notes, initially rebuffed AXA's cultural sea change, but soon adapted. The company's British acquisitions put up much more of a fight. "If you are pushing a culture that is not totally British, it is very difficult," Bébéar comments.

Finally, after months of discussion with managers from acquisitions around the world, AXA's corporate office published several documents about the company's culture for employees, among them a set of guidelines for "management style." It is exhaustive in the ground it covers, from salary policies to correct attitudes.

"AXA managers are positive and adopt a realistic, forthright, and pro-active attitude toward their work at all times," one section of the guidelines reads. "They avoid openly criticizing company policy, decisions made at a higher level or those made by another company or unit in the group." (The guidelines go on to say that constructive criticism is welcomed, as are suggestions to increase efficiency.)

The guidelines also outline why communication between units is so important for AXA's success, and advise, "AXA managers promote opportunities for staff to express their views, criticism, and suggestions about their work. They answer all questions within a reasonable time. They encourage staff members to meet with other group employees from areas outside their own area of responsibility, and to create relationships outside the strict framework of the staff member's own line organization. Such contacts in no way represent an infringement on the manager's authority."

The document concludes with the assertion that "management principles must not be purely theoretical," and urges managers to put them into practice. The comment is not without bite. A management evaluation process, developed at the same time as the guidelines, links professional goals and behavior goals, and determines compensation.

Over the past year, Bébéar and Colloc'h have also devoted a great deal of time to finalize the AXA language of phrases that includes "valley of despair" and "train of the north." Using an American system of 151 symbols and phrases called Modelnetics as their launching pad, they have created twenty-one of their own to describe management situations and values specific to AXA, and *not* specific to any one national culture. For example, an AXA language phrase called *L'esprit d'équipe*—team spirit—is depicted by the symbol "1 + 1 = 3." A line drawing of a small house, inside another house, inside another house, is the symbol for the AXA phrase *Le businessmen concept*—the concept of business, which communicates the principle that every AXA business unit should be managed as if it is independent, but that its needs should never take priority over the needs of the corporate entity, the AXA Group. (Some of the AXA language symbols are intended to amuse; the "trap of immobility," for instance, is depicted by a stick figure with a ball and chain around his ankle.)

Once the AXA language of management was created, Bébéar and Colloc'h were determined that it become the lingua franca of its common culture. The company already had its own training program, where executives were taught technical skills and competitive strategies, but Bébéar decided it should be changed from insurance topics to a broader curriculum about values. The new AXA university, located in a fifty-room castle in France's Bordeaux region, opened last February. Managers, in groups of forty, attended throughout the year.

"We spend the first five days letting people discover AXA's management style through case studies and role playing, and we also have five days of seminars on all the AXA management styles," Colloc'h says. "Purely and simply, we study like crazy there."

On a typical day at AXA University, managers are divided into multinational teams and work closely with a trainer and an AXA director on such topics as priorities, control, delegation of authority, self-analysis, and giving criticism. The curriculum at the school is supported by training materials tailored for each country, which employees can refer to on an ongoing basis.

People leave the university with "a personal action plan," Colloc'h says. "That means that when they go back and they say, 'I have a problem because I don't know how to delegate or set priorities,' or something else, their managers can give them the appropriate cultural training module for their country." Six months later, Colloc'h and her staff look again to determine how the manager is measuring up.

"We want to see that the program is effective," Colloc'h explains. "We are not doing it just to please ourselves."

But even in saying this, Bébéar and Colloc'h emphasize that AXA does not want to make its employees uniform.

"France is different, Spain is different, Italy also has its specifics," Bébéar says. "You have to take all that into account, but at the same time hold very firmly to certain principles, certain values which are the elements of a culture."

What AXA intends, Colloc'h adds, is to make sure people from each of its various cultures understand each other, communicate with each other, and consider each other with "tenderness."

She tells a story about an international team of computer specialists who went together to the United States when AXA acquired the Equitable, in order to adapt its information systems to the rest of the organization. For three months, the team worked intensely, and when it was done, it returned to Paris for a presentation about its accomplishments.

"It was really a revolution, what they did," Colloc'h recalls, "they did so much." But at the end of the meeting, they told us, 'There is still one point on which we could not reach agreement,' and then put up two slides, one with a coffee mug and the other with an espresso cup.

"They said, 'Working together—okay, but drinking one another's coffee, that's very hard.'

"You see," Colloc'h says with a smile, "we can do fabulous things together, as long as we respect one another's culture."

OTHER BOXES, OTHER VOICES

Like Richard Rosenberg at BankAmerica, several other CEOs we spoke with described the unique ways they have devised to mitigate the sometimes negative side effects of managing through control systems, however soft. Rosenberg spoke of his efforts to disseminate new, grassroots marketing ideas throughout the organization by circulating employee newsletters among far-flung divisions. Other CEOs worry not so much about spreading expertise as they do about facilitating communication between levels, namely the line and the corporate office. Both Derek Wanless of **NatWest Group** and Sir Colin Marshall of **British Airways** note that box management often means that critical information gets filtered on the way up. Only very bad news is heard, while important suggestions, insights, and criticisms—"the moaning," as Marshall calls it—are silenced. Both executives have devised ways to break this pattern, for they believe those voices contain messages that even a box organization must acknowledge.

At NatWest, one of the United Kingdom's "Big Four" banks with total assets of $250 billion, Wanless gets close to those voices by devoting, by his estimation, 30 percent of his time to the human assets approach. At NatWest since 1970, Wanless says the change in his schedule is new, and comes in response to his sense that he was getting only "sanitized reports" from inside the organization, since control systems, by design, alert management only when someone steps outside the box's boundaries. Those reports "don't tell you much about what is *really* happening," Wanless says. "It is only by getting out and around that you can see and feel it. I have always done a bit of that, but the percentage of my time spent that way is up very sharply, and it might increase more."

To get out and around, Wanless says he has delegated the maintenance of NatWest's box to several of his senior staff members, while he himself has taken charge of running several employee teams. One of them consists of the group's top 100 managers, and its purpose is to examine the group's future strategy. The other teams, about ten in number, are composed of six to eight "young, lively" managers from all sectors of the group, and they address a variety of topics selected by Wanless. "We ask, 'Diversity—what does it mean for us?' And 'A learning organization—what does it mean for us?' " Wanless says. "Or we put together a team to examine global trade finance, which we have never actually addressed as a business." The teams investigate and debate these issues and then meet with Wanless, who continues the discussion with them. "The ideas that come bubbling out of these teams are light-years better than what we've had in the past," he says, "because we've broken out of the box."

Like Wanless, Sir Colin Marshall of British Airways also sees one of his roles as pushing out the walls of the box, but he notes that it is a task undertaken with extreme vigilance, since lives depend on his center's strict controls regulating safety. The carrier's corporate office maintains tight regulations over hundreds of routes crisscrossing the globe, the international transfer of millions of dollars each day, and the utilization of expensive assets—that is, hundreds of airplanes. None of these jobs can be pushed down the line or out into countries, Marshall says, making British Airways, with $9 billion in sales in 1994, "one of the largest single-center businesses in the world today."

"We have had a number of attempts to decentralize the business in the past," Marshall notes, "and almost every time we have done it, we have had to pull back and recognize that this is a very centralized organization." Yet at the same time, he adds, British Airways has successfully pushed accountability for advertising, pricing, and other non-safety-related operational and business matters into the field, significantly reducing the bureaucracy that can easily build up in a box organization.

Marshall also uses another technique to make sure British Airways' box doesn't get too small to be effective, both as an employer and as a competitor: he calls it "listening to the moaning."

"As I go around the world, I hear various of our managers saying, 'If only I could get another aircraft to fly on this day to this particular route,' et cetera," Marshall says. "For instance, I was in Japan last week, and our manager there badly wanted some extra services to Osaka. But you know, we have to weigh that against the cost of taking the aircraft off some other routes, or alternatively, of acquiring another aircraft. If we acquire another aircraft, you are talking about 100 million pounds (roughly $150 million) for a 747 these days, and you want to make damn sure that you are going to get a return for that extra investment."

But Marshall doesn't object to being asked to make hard trade-offs or major investments. These requests often contain the "new ideas and new proposals" the center needs to hear, so that the whole organization can keep its cutting edge.

"We don't believe that where we are today is where we should be or where we would expect to be tomorrow," he says. "It is a constant process of improvements and, as a result of that, we do get a lot of feedback coming from our managers, and I suppose that is why I constantly hear managers moaning about the degree of central control. We encourage them to do that, to moan. It gives us an opportunity to get into dialogue with them."

To hear this "moaning" on an ongoing basis, Marshall says he travels frequently, meeting one-on-one with managers and specifically requesting their criticisms. Moreover, over the past five years, the company has held 110 seminars, each with twenty-five managers, and at each one "I spent two to three hours just sitting there talking with them about various aspects of the business," Marshall says. More such seminars are planned, all focused on "people giving us their viewpoints."

Asked if this process will truly generate honest responses, Marshall says British Airways employees, some so accustomed to strict control management they were originally reluctant to speak out, now know "they aren't going to get slayed if they come up with a criticism." To prove this point to the organization, Marshall says he has fired senior managers who haven't listened openly to criticism, and has promoted iconoclasts who have challenged the system.

What he has created is a box with an unconventional system, a system that amplifies "moaning" within its walls.

"We have kept reassuring our people, kept on encouraging them that this is what we believe in," Marshall says. "This is what we want to have."

Finally, we come to **Nintendo,** the leading Japanese game maker, where two approaches that don't often go together are in play: the box and human assets management.

This combination is a response to an unusual, almost contradictory situation: success in the entertainment software industry requires enormous creativity from designers to guarantee interesting, original, and fun games; and it requires rigid quality standards to guarantee flawless computer code. In addition, the president of Nintendo, Hiroshi Yamauchi, forbids graphic violence to be shown in products marketed under the Nintendo name. (The company, with 1994 sales of $4.7 billion and net income of $510 million, sells more than 2,500 titles, but is perhaps best known for the extremely popular Famicon, Game Boy, and Super Famicon systems. Its Donkey Kong Country is the fastest-selling video game ever.)

The first of Nintendo's business exigencies—the need for creativity—might suggest a "people" company in which employees are given their freedom and empowered to make with it what they can. And in this way, Nintendo even supersedes some of the full-blown human assets companies described in chapter 3. Software designers are hired based not on their education, grades, or training but on what Yamauchi calls "their individual nature." Once employed by Nintendo, these designers are given free rein with their time. "We never put a time limit on the development of products," Yamauchi says. "The production of software is a delicate thing. If you rush it, the result won't be a show at all, but something worthless. So we always tell the developers to work on it until they feel it's finished."

In the meantime, Yamauchi says, it is best for management to keep out of the creative process. "We have kept quiet even when people go to see a movie or play during work," he notes. His reason: "There are only a handful of people in the entire world who can produce the software people want." They must be managed with great care, which at Nintendo means with great personal freedom.

Such freedom, however, does not extend to other aspects of the company, and this is where Nintendo's box can be seen as the vehicle for major value addition. Yamauchi has installed strict quality controls for all internally produced software, and even stricter ones for the software it licenses. All its software is evaluated and ranked on five quality dimensions by a select group of experienced video-game consumers. The company requires all licensees to work closely with Nintendo as a team, not as a mere supplier. Bad code or slipshod production, Yamauchi explains, can destroy an entertainment company as quickly as boring games. A winning enterprise can have neither.

Finally, Yamauchi's box extends to the content of Nintendo's product offerings, in the form of strict guidelines that forbid designers from depicting anything that is "against public order or morals," and that covers a lot of territory.

"We forbid anything that would be harmful to anybody," Yamauchi adds, noting that "decapitations and lots of blood" are common in many American games. "I will not have products that are violent, excessively stimulating, or too strong. This is established as the opinion of Nintendo's top management. You must demonstrate self-control."

While preventing unruly behavior, mainly on the part of adolescent boys, is not the goal of any other control system we have seen, Nintendo's ethical box is, in fact, quite similar to many others in this chapter. It is about corporate values, and the center making them explicit for the organization so as to control how people act and think. What is different about Nintendo is that its box works so well in tandem with the human assets approach. That's different, but not surprising, given management's clarity of purpose and consistency of application. Together, they make two approaches as powerful as one.

THE BOX APPROACH: CONTROLS, CHALLENGES, AND RESULTS

Our definition of the box organization frequently prompts a response something like this: "That's my company *exactly*. Hundreds of rules, and no one pays attention to you unless you break one."

Given the prevalence of box companies—fully a quarter of the companies in our interviews fell into this category—the person speaking may be right. But every company has a box; every company has controls, both hard and soft. The companies in this chapter, and all fully realized box organizations, are the ones in which the CEO and his or her staff make controls the defining medium of value addition. At HSBC Holdings, John Bond explains that customers put a premium on trust. Thus, his organization is relentlessly driven to deliver that, and it does so with strict controls that guarantee predictability, conservatism, and accountability. At AXA, President Claude Bébéar has identified shared expertise about insurance products as one of the company's key success factors. Yet the geographical diversity of his corporation stands in the way of fluid and frequent cross-border communication between managers. In response, AXA has built a box of common values, spread by a unique language and reinforced with extensive training programs. Hewlett-Packard has stood for quality and cutting-edge technology for decades. CEO Lewis Platt says credit is due to the "H-P way," long-standing cultural norms that overtly reward the kinds of business thinking and behaviors that result in superlative products. Indeed, every organization in this chapter is an example of the corporate center's designing and implementing specific guidelines as the means to extraordinary value.

These companies are also evidence that the box approach does allow freedom, albeit within walls. As Daniel Cardon de Lichtbuer, president and CEO of **Banque Brussels Lambert,** puts it: "We set guidelines, we draw lines, to provide a frame of reference, and we leave our employees pretty decentralized in the way they can act within those lines." Adds Lichtbuer, "Do they play with four defensemen or two, or with two offensemen or three? I would say that as long as the results are satisfactory to us, that is rather unimportant to headquarters. If results are good and obtained properly, we give our local directors the greatest freedom, but within a framework."

This chapter has also suggested that box management, despite the constricting implications of its name, is neither good nor bad by definition, and in fact, many people prefer working in this kind of environment for its security, in terms of the clarity of the expectations it sets and how it rewards employees. The box approach is perhaps better than any other at explicitly setting goals and performance standards.

When does a CEO choose the box approach? Clearly, boxes are employed in industries where risk management is a competitive advantage, such as banks and airlines. They can also work well when fast, honest, and continuous communication is a key success factor and cultural rules can make that happen, as is the case at Hewlett-Packard and AXA. The box approach appears to fit particularly well with situations where the customer demands unassailable consistency. And finally, boxes can add value when swift and radical improvement of standards or performance is needed. (This subject is examined in chapter 7, on companies in crisis.)

This said, it is important to note that the box approach carries with it a number of management challenges. These companies must work hard to keep creativity alive within their walls. In mature box companies, such as BankAmerica, British Airways, and NatWest, this is one of the center's most demanding and value-added roles. Some box companies can confuse performance goal and reward systems with personnel development, which involves training and career planning. They are not the same thing, and one without the other can undermine employee effectiveness. Finally, it is critical that the box CEO get the dimensions of his construct right. If the walls are too close together, an organization can be crushed by bureaucracy, regulations, and status quo behavior; too far apart, and the box loses its control and its fundamental efficacy.

But ultimately, even with its built-in challenges, the box approach serves a critical purpose for the shareholder because effective controls, in the form of accurate accounting and reporting systems, can free management to focus on important, overarching competitive matters, such as a company's strategy and future. One executive who speaks to this issue is Sir Alistair Grant, chairman of the **Argyll Group,** owner of Britain's Safeway and Presto supermarkets. "Now that the business is tightly run," he explains after describing Argyll's extensive financial control system, "we are looking more at big issues. We are thinking more long term, conceiving how we should grow, how much money we should put into refurbishing old stores, how we should move in terms of information technology, what new products we should look into, whether we should pursue new business initiatives, such as petrol or pharmacies."

Now that Argyll's control systems are fully and effectively functioning, "the days of red-starring everything that did not meet planning are past," says Grant. "And now we can get to the most important job of sitting on your own and thinking, with a blank piece of paper in front of you, conceiving a new way of looking at things." In the long term, it is this kind of thinking, Grant says, that separates a good company from a superlative one, in which return on shareholder investment surpasses the market average.

If the box approach can make this happen—and it often does—its difficulties are worth the challenge they pose.

6

UPENDING THE STATUS QUO, "TOUCHING THE SACRED": THE CHANGE-AGENT APPROACH

B ack in 1993, when J. P. Bolduc was named the first nonfamily member to run the international industrial conglomerate **W.R. Grace,** it didn't take him long to realize he had stepped into an organization that had been run with the box approach, but hardly as a means to creating extraordinary value. Instead, the company's rigid rules, processes, and culture were so constraining that anyone who spoke out to challenge them got his shirt, as Bolduc puts it, "splattered with blood."

Bolduc moved swiftly to make Grace into the antithesis of a hard box, using what we call the change-agent approach. In this approach, the center becomes the vehicle of the organization's radical and continuous transformation. Though many of the 161 executives we talked to in our research mentioned the importance of continuous improvement, the executives in this chapter stand apart because they identified the *complete overhaul of practically everything* in their companies as the most important role of the center—its medium for adding extraordinary value. These were not CEOs in turnaround situations—CEOs faced with bankruptcy, liquidation, or shareholder revolt. They were, instead, executives who, peering into the future three, five, or even ten years off, saw that they would be turnaround

CEOs if change, as a nonstop process and a culture, did not come to define their organizations. And yet to create that change, many of them adopted the urgency of so-called firefighting CEOs. For as a group, they were unanimous in saying that they have found it much easier to decide a company needs to change than to actually make that change happen.

They also agreed that changing a corporation is a messy process, replete with stops and starts, and can often require a protracted period of "flying blind," as Sir Iain Vallance, chairman of **British Telecommunications,** puts it. Vallance guided BT through a decade of complete overhaul, as it went from a state-owned monopoly to a publicly traded company facing a competitive marketplace. In the process, twelve layers of management were reduced to five, the workforce was cut from 240,000 to 140,000, reporting and monitoring systems were revamped, job responsibilities were redefined, and strategy was designed.

"Everyone thought that within a year or two it would come out all right because you got access to private capital, and you brought in a lot of management from the outside," Vallance recalls. Instead, BT struggled long and hard with a characteristic challenge of change organizations: striking the right balance between new ideas and control. An early corporate program encouraging the former—nicknamed Let a Thousand Flowers Bloom—resulted in "a load of weeds, frankly," Vallance says, "because we hadn't grasped the essential thing about a telecommunications network company, which is you have to be run as an integrated firm." The company swung to the other extreme, a rigid form of financial control, before landing at the place between the two that allowed BT to reinvent itself.

"There was a period early on where we were very much flying blind," Vallance comments, "because the change was so dramatic and it went right the way down through the organization to touch everybody. Fortunately, we didn't come to ground."

Like many others in this chapter, Vallance believes that the trauma of change demands a certain type of leader. "A very strong and central hand is required," he says. "Once the structure is in being, once you get the new systems and new processes chuntering on, then you can take a more backseat approach. But while the change itself is happening, you cannot."

And with that role can come controversy, or so some of the following stories seem to suggest. J. P. Bolduc of W.R. Grace is a case in point. After four successful but tremendously challenging years redirecting the company, he resigned abruptly over major differences in philosophy and style with the company's leadership. Change—swift, thorough, and radical—has a way of doing that.

Along with J. P. Bolduc's efforts at Grace, this chapter also examines the change-agent approach in practice at **Goldman, Sachs & Co.,** the venerable blue-chip Wall Street investment banking firm, long known for its conservative, gentlemanly approach to business. Stephen Friedman helped Goldman Sachs break that mold, becoming a place where the aggressive and the innovative are well rewarded. In addition, this chapter profiles the change-agent approach that revamped the way of doing business at the American gas and automotive parts giant **Tenneco,** and at two Japanese companies, **Mitsui,** the world's largest trading company, and **Canon,** maker of cameras, fax machines, and printers. We also take a brief look at **National Australia Bank,** where CEO Nobby Clark made his defining role moving the organization from a hard box to one defined by flexibility and creativity. The chapter concludes with some compelling insights on the nature of change by Ken Chenault, vice chairman of **American Express,** a company that has seen its share of dramatic change in the past several years.

AT W.R. GRACE: NO MORE BLOODY SHIRTS

We begin this chapter with a profile of J. P. Bolduc because of all the executives in our research, he embraced the change-agent approach with perhaps the most zeal, vowing to transform the 141-year-old company he inherited from a cramped and constraining box into an entirely new organization infused with new ideas and flexibility. When we spoke with him, he was on the way to achieving that goal, and although some inside **W.R. Grace** seemed uncomfortable with the pace of change, the markets certainly approved. Bolduc's initiatives were heralded by many Wall Street analysts, and shares of the company's stock rose from $17.50 to $45, or more than 150 percent, during his tenure.

But by early 1995, Bolduc's continuing differences with the company's leadership over his style and philosophy were reaching a head.

At the same time, according to newspaper reports, Bolduc was feuding with Chairman J. Peter Grace over whether the company should report to the SEC a number of costly perquisites enjoyed by Grace himself, as well as some transactions between the company and one of Grace's sons. Finally, in March, Bolduc handed in his resignation. Reaction from the company's major institutional shareholders was fast and angry, and in the months afterward they pushed through some major changes themselves: the company's board of directors was reduced from twenty-two to twelve members, J. Peter Grace was forced to resign as chairman of the board and as a director, and National Medical Care, Grace's largest subsidiary with annual revenues near $2 billion, was put up for sale. But even with these efforts, Bolduc's radical campaign for renewal of W.R. Grace as an organization was interrupted, perhaps forever.

Bolduc's relationship with Peter Grace was not always contentious. The two men met in 1983 when Bolduc was asked to run President Reagan's task force investigating waste and inefficiency in U.S. government operations. The group, comprising 160 top-ranking CEOs and 2,000 private-sector volunteers, was chaired by Peter Grace, then CEO of the company bearing his name. The two men did initially clash in opinion and style, but they soon came to like and respect one another—so much so that in 1983 Grace asked Bolduc to leave the consulting firm Booz, Allen & Hamilton for his company. By 1986, Bolduc had become vice chairman and CFO of W.R. Grace, and in 1990 he was named COO and president. When Peter Grace retired two years later, Bolduc, fifty-three years old, became the first CEO of the company not related to its founder.

When we spoke with Bolduc in late 1994, he referred to the Grace family and its legacy with reverence, pointing out that the company had paid dividends in 278 consecutive quarters. In its long history as an international conglomerate, he noted, W.R. Grace had moved in and out of hundreds of businesses, usually at a profit, from shrimp farming to restaurants, from textiles to airlines. Its earnings growth had been steady but slow, and at times unspectacular, but it had never posted a real loss. But Bolduc also stressed that he took the job of CEO deeply believing that W.R. Grace needed to change.

"The way the company was led and managed in the past was the right way to operate for the times in order to survive and succeed. I probably would have done it the exact same way," Bolduc said, "but we knew as soon as we began, that with the [Berlin] Wall coming down, communism moving out, and global competition setting in, what worked in the past was not going to work in the future."

When Bolduc looked into the future he saw a marketplace that might reward diversified companies, but only if they focused on certain core technologies and competencies. He saw a marketplace demanding that corporations manage across their divisions for synergies and shared experiences. He saw a marketplace where low-cost, high-quality producers were the only survivors, where companies that expanded into emerging markets such as Latin America and the Far East would excel—providing they did something about their costs. He saw a marketplace that called out for diversity and inclusion in corporate management across ethnic, gender, and racial lines.

"In the future—but really, even right now—shareholders have a different view, a different kind of interest," Bolduc explained. "If they can get 20 percent return in India, that's where they're going to invest, not in some American company that's getting 3 percent.

"And competition is changing, changing wildly. The walls of communism are largely down. That's terrific, but it means there are potentially forty new Japans out there. Competing in the global marketplace is going to be even tougher for Americans than before. Why? Well, our quality of life—our standard of living—is so high, people expect wages and benefits that are unheard of in the rest of the world. Even those on welfare in this great country are in the upper tenth percentile of the world's population in terms of standard of living. People in other countries work hard and long; they're hungry and they have 'fire in their belly,' and they're well-educated and in many cases multilingual. And they can produce a quality product for half of what it costs us. And that's not even mentioning the cost of employee benefits, environmental compliance, and litigation that American companies face each day. Do you think companies in the former Soviet bloc or China or India have to spend $50 to $100 million on environmental compliance or legal fees every year? Hell, they're only beginning to develop their environmental laws and their legal systems."

Given the new economic world order, Bolduc said he knew he had to create a new W.R. Grace, a company characterized by openness, creativity, flexibility, and boldness. Immediately he and his top team began to spread his message. Their days were filled with speeches and with meetings with employees and shareholders, analysts and managers, addressing the company's new strategy, structure, and systems. They even made several videos and public pronouncements declaring the company's new mission and values and had them sent to company divisions around the world.

The initial reaction, Bolduc recalled, was "a big yawn." Grace was a company so deeply entrenched in its tradition of bureaucracy, hierarchy, and "staying inside the sandbox" that most of its employees simply shrugged off "the New Grace" as new CEO saber-rattling. But that was not enough to stifle Bolduc and his new senior management team.

"Nobody believed what the hell we were trying to do," Bolduc said, "so it became clear we had to break through the sound barrier."

To do that, Bolduc and his team began to accelerate the sale of several noncore businesses in the Grace portfolio—businesses that Bolduc and his staff had determined didn't make strategic sense. Many of them, Bolduc says, were "sweetheart businesses that people liked." Some were very profitable. One of them, a Belgian mattress-ticking manufacturer, held the largest market share in the world, and posted a 22 percent return on capital. Bolduc sold it because it was in the textile business, and that wasn't where Grace was going in the future. (Instead, the company was going to focus on six core businesses, five of which fell into the category of specialty chemicals.) The sale of the mattress-ticking company, and others like it, put the company "into cultural shock," Bolduc recalled. "When we first announced we were going to do it, those inside and out said it would never happen or that I wouldn't survive."

Next, Bolduc and his team concentrated their time and energy on another project: integrating functions across divisions. Hundreds of transportation offices that arranged employee travel were collapsed into one unit. Horizontal communications between Grace's product lines and R&D groups were affected by changing where and how the company's scientists and engineers worked. Moreover, the old corporate structure that built walls between countries and products was replaced with a completely new matrix system that meant Grace would service each customer globally, with the same products and one "corporate face." The reorganization rearranged managers along global product lines and away from divisions, eliminating five levels of management in the process and putting a renewed focus on the customer. Its impact was felt in every corner of Grace worldwide.

With the divestment and restructuring plans in motion, what followed next was a year of concentrated global travel for Bolduc and the senior managers he called his "policy cabinet." First they met with hundreds of key managers, prodding them to develop their global product line for the year 2000, as well as a strategy that explained, in persuasive detail, why their business should remain part of Grace. Next, they focused on employees beneath the executive ranks.

"During the first two years of restructuring, I met with every single employee group I could get my hands on, spoke for twenty, thirty, forty minutes. After we'd given them the 'why' for change," Bolduc recalled, "I'd take my jacket off and say, 'All right, have at me. Let's talk about the company, its future, your job, your career, and your future. Let's talk about how you can make a difference, how you can make Grace a better place in which to work and live.' Some of the sessions would start at seven o'clock at night. We'd have dinner, and by eight o'clock, I'm on the podium. Nine o'clock I'm wrapped up, and then we'd go with questions and answers for however long it took—sometimes until one or two in the morning."

During those sessions, Bolduc and his team laid out where Grace was headed: it was going to become a company where employees participated in the change process and moved frequently between functions, product lines, and countries. It was going to be a company where people would be paid for performance, regardless of tenure. It was going to be a company where mavericks were promoted, where "thinking outside the box" was rewarded, where showing up simply wasn't good enough. It was going to be a company rededicated to customer service, a company intent on "drawing the market to it," instead of waiting for the market to come its way. All the old bets were off, Bolduc told the employees; the Grace culture would forever be changed.

"Employees were upset, employees were concerned," Bolduc remembered of those late-night sessions. "People would say, 'I don't want to change, I'm happy with what I'm doing. I don't understand what you're trying to do to the company or why. I have no interest in learning about other product lines or other parts of the company. I've been researching a project for seven years, and now I'm told we're not going to do that because it's not a core product, so where am I to go?' There were a lot of real people issues that had to be dealt with. A lot of concerns that if you've got a heart at all you had to listen because they were all hardworking, dedicated, competent, and capable people, who were now going to be directed in a whole new scheme—a new culture—and a whole new set of behaviors, values, and strategies."

Perhaps what upset employees most, Bolduc said, was the new incentive plan he put into place. In the past, Grace had a tradition of regular salary increases and predictable bonuses. No longer.

"We told people we wanted to differentiate between the performers and nonperformers. We wanted to reward and motivate the performers. We also wanted to be fair to the nonperformers by assuring that constructive feedback and adequate training opportunities were available. But in the final analysis, we wanted the nonperformers to understand the new value system. We wanted them to salivate to get what the performers were getting, and after all that, if they couldn't or wouldn't perform and accept the new culture, then they ought to leave, because this was not the culture they were going to be happy with."

As a result, some people who had been handed bonuses for twenty or thirty years received reduced bonuses or none at all. Some left the company, others were fired. Yet others who had earned a small token bonus in the past began receiving meaningful bonus checks—some even exceeding their annual salaries.

Bolduc and his team also spent time redesigning and implementing the way businesses asked Corporate for capital to invest. In the past, when units wanted to build a plant, for instance, they were required to prepare an exhaustive document of fifty pages or more detailing the reasons, financial implications, and payback schedule. The entire process, from identification of need to the shovel in the ground, sometimes took upwards of twelve months. In Bolduc's vision of a fast, flexible company, this process was a dinosaur, a dangerous one at that. He and his top team informed managers that all capital requests were not to exceed five pages, and guaranteed an answer in thirty days, and then he put in place the people and systems in the field and at corporate headquarters to make that happen.

This new procedure helped the company redirect more than 50 percent of its capital from nonstrategic to core businesses. This again, he recalls, was another "culture shock," and not one that particularly delighted those comfortable with Grace's old ways. To them, Bolduc's change was too rapid, he admits, and too thorough.

But even with this kind of resistance, Bolduc told us that three-plus years into the company's change program, more and more people were beginning to understand and strongly support its purpose. "We think they understand that Grace has to change now," he said, "they understand that if Grace doesn't change and fails, Grace is gone and so, too, are they. I need them to think about this company twenty-four hours a day."

The goal of the change-agent CEO, he said, was getting employees to see that "the only security blanket we have is to live outside the sandbox."

"It's exciting," he added, "but we're still not there. In fact, we have a long way to go. I guess that was the one thing I underestimated—how long it takes to change people's behavior, attitudes, and how to deal fairly and equitably with their fears. But we're trying. We'll keep on trying for however long it takes."

Ironically, when Bolduc resigned, W.R. Grace was experiencing its highest earnings in over a decade. Operating margins had increased nearly 100 percent since he took over, cash flow was out of the red, and costs were down by hundreds of millions of dollars. Yet the day before his last with the company, he wrote to us of Grace's needing the courage to push change even further in the organization, perhaps breaking up more of its businesses. The company, he said, must "inculcate a sustained passion for continuous improvement."

It is up to his successor to see if it does.

AT CANON: BACK TO THE SAMURAI

He is sixty-eight now and considered by many to be one of Japan's premier businessmen, but Ryuzaburo Kaku has no second thoughts about his early days at **Canon Inc.,** when he was a devoted troublemaker. Then, as an entry-level employee, he "picked out the flaws" of the company and contacted the corporate office with his opinions.

"This is something that does not necessarily make one look like a good employee," Kaku recalls ruefully. Almost invariably, his detailed proposals for change were ignored.

But one day after Kaku had been with the company ten years and was working in the planning department, an aide of the president paid him a visit. Months before, Kaku had informed headquarters that he believed the company would run out of money in a year. At the time, no one listened. They were listening now; the company was to be restructured per his advice. As a result, Kaku was not promoted—the Japanese system of seniority prevents such leaps—but his comments were given more than passing notice. Over the next thirty years, he rose to the position he aspired to, he admits, "from my first days at the company as a young man."

Today, Kaku is chairman of Canon, the $19-billion maker of cameras and office automation equipment sold around the world. With 68,000 employees, the company holds a leading market share in almost every industry in which it operates. Kaku served as the company's president from 1977 until 1989, and during this tenure he finally got his chance to change Canon—to transform it from a traditional, centralized Japanese conglomerate to one of the country's most decentralized and least hierarchical firms.

Like many of the chief executives in this chapter, Kaku changed the course of his company because of a future he feared, one in which Canon was "just another ordinary big company" with no particular competitive advantage in either marketing or manufacturing. The company was growing bigger each year, but its growth was taking it further away from its customers. Its factories were sprouting up everywhere, but so were squabbles between plant managers about what should be made where. At the time, Kaku believed that Canon's global reach would continue to expand rapidly, as would the breadth and depth of its product line, but the Canon of his predecessor, a highly centralized organization where all major decisions, and many minor ones, were made in the president's office, was not ready for such an environment.

"How can management handle [it] when the president makes all the decisions?" Kaku asks. "Only a third of his day might be allocated to the camera business, another third to calculating machines, and another to copiers. But that kind of situation results in overwork that becomes just too much to handle. And the people lower down in the organization, the people who have to wait for every single management decision before they get on with their work, just get bogged down in their projects. You can see them forming a line down the hallway. . . .

"They come in with their presentations," he explains. "A presentation takes thirty minutes. Then they exit, and the next group, which has been waiting, comes in for their thirty minutes. No matter what the objective is, this is the most inefficient way to manage a company."

Kaku pauses for a moment before continuing. He is soft-spoken and shows his age, but his quiet authority remains undiminished. "One person, the president, might know all the necessary details about one group, but he would have to be close to a genius for him then also to have detailed knowledge about everything made and sold." He shakes his head. "Once I realized that, I knew we had to decentralize."

For various reasons, several other CEOs in this book have come to a similar conclusion—Lewis Platt at Hewlett-Packard and Helmut Maucher at Nestlé are two—but no others have done what Kaku did next. Instead of looking at other companies for guidance on a new organizational structure, he looked to history for inspiration. The result? Kaku decided that the "new" Canon would best succeed if it was managed as Japan was "managed" during the Tokugawa era of samurai rule, the period from 1603 to 1867 during which wealthy Japanese noblemen divided the country into domains and ruled the nation as a collection of prosperous fiefdoms, sometimes warring, but often coexisting because of pacts with many mutual benefits. The country overall was ruled by a shogun whose palace was located in Edo. Studying the Tokugawa period, Kaku says, "made me think one could do it that way now, too, because of the beauty of that system, with centralized power and decentralized control."

Kaku relates details about this era with such ease it is obvious that his knowledge of it, and decision to emulate it, was no lark. "One example would be the Shimazu domain," he says, referring to an area in southern Japan, centered on the city of Kagoshima. "The Shimazu lords handled everything pertaining to Shimazu. They were responsible for collecting taxes and the way in which taxes were collected. They looked after local administration and how the system of central power was maintained. They looked after agriculture, manufacturing, and land issues.

"The central government in Edo handled issues pertaining to *all* the domains," Kaku says. "For instance, it made the rules concerning how often the lords of the domains could see their wives. All wives were kept in Edo and lived near the castle. The Shimazu domain rulers had to come from Kagoshima to Edo every other year to see their wives. Then after fulfilling their duties in Edo, they went back to the country."

Wives? Kept in Edo?

Kaku dismisses these specifics as not relevant to his decision; it was the efficient and empowering division of authority during the Tokugawa period that made him select it as a model for Canon. Specifically, this meant that important decisions about individual business units had to be made in the business units, including decisions about marketing, manufacturing, and product development. It meant nothing less than a total restructuring of Canon's way of doing business. "It seemed clear to me the marketing companies needed to be independent," Kaku explains. "There was to be a Canon marketing company for domestic sales in Japan, another in the United States for American sales, and in Europe, a Canon company in Amsterdam for European sales.

"But then the European entity was to be further split up, so there was to be an English company, and a French one, and a German one. And then this arrangement was to proceed through production and development." Finally, Kaku decided, the business units needed to design and implement systems to supply their own capital instead of receiving it from corporate headquarters. He was cutting the cord, in effect creating a center that managed its subsidiaries by "simply looking on."

At the same time, Kaku was turning his attention to fixing the factory-squabbling problem that had plagued the company since its growth spurt in the 1960s. When he took over as president, Canon products were being built in whatever plants had the capacity, leading to constant bickering between managers. "And the one with the loudest voice usually carried the day," Kaku recalls. As much as he despised the arguing, he abhorred even more the waste of human energy on internal matters. "That was energy that could have been used in furthering outside goals," he remarks. "I decided what products should be built in which plants, and then dedicated the plants in that fashion. After that, the managers were left to run the plants as they wished." To his mind, Kaku says, this is the strongest example of the Tokugawa era's centralized power–decentralized control at work.

What did all these changes mean for Kaku on a day-to-day basis? He estimates that the decentralization, which is still evolving, took up ten years of his presidency. He describes his days as a flurry of many activities, with the actual conceptualizing of plans heading the list. He talks about forming global and cross-functional committees to execute the change, educating members about what he envisioned, and then spending countless hours hearing their comments, explaining to them many times the whys and hows of the new Canon in logistical and philosophical terms. He says he also spent many hours each week with Canon's human resource managers designing training programs that would prepare workers of all levels for what the decentralization and new dedicated plant system would involve. Each day, he recalls, included small steps forward, measured in inches, not bounds. He tried not to look too far ahead; the change was too massive to accept that way. "I looked at the direction we were going in," he reflects, "and then tried to grasp what could be done each day, and week, and year as it came. And then I thought about how to do it, and which strategies would work."

By 1981, Kaku says, the first stage of Canon's change was in place, and he paused briefly in his efforts to design what he called the Second Premier Company Plan. Again, he was spurred by a future that required organizational change, a future marked by economic friction between the United States and Japan, as well as Japan's enormous balance of payment surplus. Both issues, he feared, were certain to affect the value of the yen, and Canon had to change in order to insulate itself from the fallout. That change involved radically lowering the company's expenses, as well as determining where it expanded operations, how it expanded, and which technologies it developed.

Kaku describes his schedule in this period as one filled with meetings with the small groups assigned to determine how to cut Canon's expenditures. Even though a decade has passed, he can still rattle off the committees' acronyms and which "wasteful practices" each one targeted. ("The CPS committee, for example, would take care of such issues as wasted planning effort and unneeded equipment and buildings," Kaku says, "nine items in all.") At the same time, he developed a system—a first at Canon—for suggestions about cost cutting that flowed from the bottom up. By any measure, his efforts were a success. In one year alone, Canon cut $401 million out of its expenses.

But even as he was looking inward, Kaku says he was spending much of his time looking outside Canon, too, at the behest of the Japanese government, which was seeking to lessen tensions with the United States and counteract the rising value of the yen. As a result, Kaku devoted several days each month to considering proposals about where to build Canon's plants overseas. Decisions were made to build in the United States, Malaysia, and Thailand, as well as mainland China. He recalls the complications of these deals, with their lawyers, government regulations, and publicity, and laments that all their objectives have still not been achieved. Tensions between Japan and the United States, he notes, are hardly resolved.

Along with meetings about cost cutting and global expansion, Kaku says he used his time as president to determine Canon's technology strategy. But this was an area where he met less with groups and spent more time thinking on his own. "The top-down approach was used for this," he says. The issues were fundamental: what should Canon make, how much should it spend on R&D, and which competitors should it take on around the world?

Still, Kaku insists his final decisions on these questions came after discussions and consultations with other executive directors. The board would meet every day at 8 A.M. "When we got together, we talked about achievements and how we could improve every aspect of the business," he recalls. "At these meetings I also outlined the problems facing Canon in the future and explained the plans for change." The directors would openly respond to Kaku's comments, he says, sometimes challenging him, but usually offering suggestions and insight.

"In the end," he says, "I realized how valuable these meetings had been. They precipitated everything that followed."

In 1989, Kaku handed the day-to-day operation of Canon over to Keizo Yamaji, who continued the trend toward decentralization. (Yamaji passed his job on to Hajime Mitarai in 1993.) In fact, some industry observers believe Canon is the Japanese company that allows its employees the most freedom and latitude.

Kaku considers this his legacy. Speaking of his decades at Canon, he returns to his early days, when he pointed out Canon's "flaws" to the head office. He says that spirit has never left him. "Even in the midst of our biggest changes I tried to think from the point of view of an ordinary employee who is thinking of what he or she would do as president." If Canon is lucky, there is an "ordinary" employee thinking that way right now, contacting the corporate office with suggestions that someone is finding the time to address.

AT TENNECO: CHANGE, FAST AND VIOLENT (AND SORT THE BODIES LATER)

When Dana Mead arrived at **Tenneco** in early 1992, he thought his main task was straightforward enough: the survival and reinvigoration of a basically strong company. Tenneco—at that time one of the world's 100 largest diversified industrial companies with $16.6 billion in assets—boasted five divisions that were considered world class in terms of market share. Its pipeline business transported 14 percent of the natural gas in the United States, while Newport News, its shipbuilding division, was the sole supplier of the nation's fleet of nuclear-powered aircraft carriers and also built nuclear-powered attack submarines. With Walker mufflers and Monroe shocks and struts, Tenneco's automotive division owned some of the best-respected brand names in the industry. Its chemicals and packaging divisions had combined operating incomes of $148 million from $3 billion in sales. Only Case, the farm and construction equipment business, had experienced sustained losses. All told, Mead thought he was joining an enterprise well along the right track.

"Talk about gross ignorance!" he says now with a hearty laugh. Mead is the classic Army man—Pattonesque even—with a bold and self-confident manner, a booming voice, piercing gaze, square shoulders, silver hair, and disarmingly frank sense of humor. A former West Point professor with a Ph.D. in politics and economics from MIT, Mead worked at International Paper Co. for fourteen years before joining Tenneco. He recalls his first weeks there with a look of bemused amazement crossing his face, remembering how he and Mike Walsh, also new to the job, took in the situation at corporate headquarters. "I'm telling you, if we had been investment bankers or consultants, either one, we would have been fired for not doing proper due diligence before taking over," he says, "because the situation was severe. Much more severe than we could have imagined."

Mead describes the Tenneco he inherited as a diversified industrial company with basically attractive businesses but no strategy formulation process; a highly politicized capital allocation system; little communication between divisions to exploit enormous purchasing economies in steel, paint, or other common raw materials; no process to assess the company's massive environmental risks in the pipeline and chemical businesses; and compensation programs that measured and rewarded meaningless goals. In the automotive and some other divisions, for example, managers' bonuses were based on return on net assets. "Hell, that's a high RONA business, anyway. I mean, the assets are small pipe benders, welders, and stuff," Mead explains, exasperated. "They can pick them up, throw them in a truck, and then drive to somewhere else, rent a shed, and go in there and stack them. So, hey, surprise, they always had huge bonuses, and there was no one up here saying, 'Wait a minute, that doesn't make sense.'

"You know, from what we found, you could have written a book about gaps between a holding company and operating divisions."

The battle plan: change.

"Quick and violent," Mead says. "We were just going to do it, and sort the bodies later." (By "we," Mead means he and Walsh, who was chairman and CEO at the beginning of this period. Mead took over as CEO in February 1994, when Walsh stepped down owing to the effects of his battle against brain cancer. He succumbed to the disease three months later, and Mead added the chairman's title, but Mead makes it clear that they were partners—that they acted as co-pilots—until then.)

Starting in 1992, Mead and Walsh overhauled Tenneco, introducing a series of new systems and reinventing its culture. It is a story that in some ways resembles the others we have seen in this chapter. Just as many managers at W.R. Grace and Canon initially rejected the call for change, and many had to leave, such was the case at Tenneco. Just as J. P. Bolduc and Allen Sheppard of GrandMet had to aggressively sell their visions internally, so too did Mead and Walsh.

But both Grace and Canon are examples of change in which the CEOs wanted to destroy a corporate box that no longer worked, and replace it with an organizational model that encouraged more freedom and creativity. At Tenneco, the change Walsh and Mead initiated meant introducing new controls and codified systems in the form of explicit rules, procedures, and policies that essentially required the organization to reduce costs and build quality into production. The next step was to communicate, educate, and build a sense of commitment. "Our real accomplishment," Mead says, "was to energize and direct to common purpose the talent we already had."

Mead gladly takes hours to describe all the devices, programs, systems, and values that he and Walsh installed as part of the campaign for change. And after all that time, he ends with an example that perhaps sums them all up. It has to do with Tenneco's pipeline business, which ships nearly 9 billion cubic feet of natural gas every day, the largest share of it from the Gulf of Mexico to the Northeast and Chicago, in almost 20,000 miles of pipe. It is the corporation's biggest division in terms of profits ($415 million in operating income in 1994) and has always been one of its most prestigious because of its profitability in the industry.

But it was, Mead says, a business operating within an industrywide system that simply didn't make sense.

"In the natural gas transmission business, suppliers used to put gas in our pipe, gas that we owned by virtue of contract, take or pay. Stuff went through our line and we sold it to the people on the other end, Boston Edison, or whomever," Mead says. "We never metered it at either end of the pipe, so at the end of the year, we always ended up somewhere between 15 and 30 percent short.

"So then, the next step, we would go back and we would negotiate with both sides. We would say to the suppliers, 'You didn't put in as much as you said you did,' and we would say to the buyers, 'You took out more than you said you did.' And this process would go on forever," Mead says, sounding, not surprisingly, a bit incredulous. "And usually over a period of years, we would get the discrepancy down to 5 or 7 percent. That's the way the pipeline industry operated. Unbelievable."

Today, no one is allowed to put gas in a Tenneco pipe unless there is a buyer at the other end with a set price and a set take-away volume. Although this sounds simple, it's actually quite complex because the quality of the gas needs to be factored into the deal, and gas quality is both subjective and unpredictable. Mead says the Tenneco

Gas people are a "resourceful and resilient lot," but the transition has been extremely difficult: designing new systems, taking the wrinkles out of them, and working with suppliers and customers to use new forms of data. It took until early 1995 for the new system to get up and running.

Along with the changes in the gas business, Mead and Walsh also launched several management innovations that cut across the company's divisions. Foremost among these was a new cost-of-quality program, prompted in part by the reaction the team received when it asked the presidents of the business units how much money manufacturing and service failures were costing each quarter.

"We got a lot of blank stares," Mead recalls. "Then we told them we were going to institute quality programs. They told us they already had them."

If they did, they weren't working. Walsh and Mead brought in a specialized consulting firm that found almost $3 billion—22 percent of revenues—in failure costs. With that figure in hand, Mead went back to the business units and "confronted reality," he says. And not just with this problem, but everything else he deemed at less than world-class standards.

"We had to create a sense of crisis," Mead says. "The earnings were off by 20 percent of the existing targets when we arrived. How can a company with dominant market positions not be growing both its top line and its margins?

"We said, 'Something is *wrong.*'"

That's when Mead and Walsh introduced the concept of "operating cost leadership," which translated into the imperative that Tenneco's businesses had to make the highest-quality, lowest-cost products. Managers stopped staring blankly and started nodding their heads, Mead recalls. "Operating cost leadership" really meant something when the targets were "burnt into the budget." For instance, if he and an operating division president determined a division could get $100 million out of cost-of-quality improvements, that number went straight into the plan as a target.

"I had to be forceful," Mead says. "I just told them how it had to be, with the numbers and all. There were some protests that it wouldn't be possible to get those numbers out. I said, 'Just do it. Go into a plant and start pushing at the bottom. We just can't study this thing to death. We need results.'"

Mead held the divisions to the rules of the new program. Every division was (and still is) required to report on the cost of quality every month. "And they can't get away with a gross number," Mead notes, "you've got to give me one through twenty, or whatever the number is, of the programs you are working on and explain how you're going to get the $100 million or $200 million you need." In addition, divisions are required to provide detailed timelines for improvements. The progress must be documented with a figure, not promises. The divisions that have problems meeting the targets or have special issues requiring close attention are required to report weekly to Mead's senior staff meeting every Monday morning until the problem is repaired or the goal is reached.

"We have an agenda, and we put them through their paces," Mead says. "We had Case on the agenda for several months. Then we had the shipyard for about a year to discuss the effort to win approval for the latest aircraft carrier. We've had several sessions with both the natural gas company and the automotive parts company. These are action meetings, not show-and-tell. We try to make decisions about making the changes that are necessary. There can be no excuses."

"No excuses"—it is a term Mead comes back to repeatedly when he talks about the other kind of change he and Walsh built into the new Tenneco, cultural change.

"You know, you hear a lot about culture, but we decided ours had to be started from scratch, and it had to be a culture where there was no substitute for victory. We started this mantra: Results, not best efforts. And in making it happen, at times we had to be brutal. We said, 'There can be no excuse for not hitting your numbers.' And we built that into the culture so that everyone ascribes to it now."

How, exactly, did they build it in?

For starters, they instituted a form of peer pressure. Every month for two years, divisional presidents made presentations before Mead and the top management team and reported their performance. "The pressure this builds is terrific, and it works," Mead says. "These guys are very capable, and like all of us, they have their pride. No one likes to explain a shortfall." Managers who once came in with "why nots" now come with plans to, for example, sell off a joint venture that never made money. They'd been holding on to it, Mead says, because it was business as usual. But a relentless focus on results, and censure for not meeting them, redefines that concept.

A second change in the culture came when division managers were empowered to act, to make decisions, to take risks—albeit with corporate supervision. "We told them, 'We want you to *not* sit there until every opportunity disappears,' which this company was famous for," he relates, "because this place was so political a debate could go on for years.

"We told these guys, 'Just do it; we'll sort the bodies out later.' It took about a year for them to believe us."

Today, Mead says, managers understand him so well he has had to rein them in with some new controls. For instance, he reviews every capital expenditure over $400,000. "Some people say that's micromanaging," Mead admits. "That's all right. When someone is watching, you get very good $400,000 projects and great $40 million ones. We've empowered people in the businesses, but we've given them a mission, we've given them goals, and we've given them guidelines. That doesn't stop action. It guides it."

But when he talks about cultural change, Mead focuses on the message he sends as often and as loudly as possible—the message about leadership. This, he says, has little to do with charisma and popularity, and everything to do with *leading change.*

Real leaders, Mead says, are often "recalcitrants, troublemakers, or gadflies." He offers as an example a Tenneco employee who was born in Asia and came to the United States as a boat person. Once in this country, the man worked to receive a college education, went on to Stanford Business School, and then became a White House Fellow. "He is the most aggressive, smartest guy you have ever seen," Mead says. "But, well, he can stir things up and step on toes. I've had to placate those in the chain of command. I tell the people in his company that he is exactly the mold we would like to see around here. He brings in some very exciting projects for us, and he delivers results."

To reward this brand of leadership at Tenneco, Mead now hands out awards each year in a widely publicized ceremony. But he communicates this value—the leading of change—in another way as well. All top-level bonuses are now based 50 percent on this measure alone. He himself makes the call, his decision based partly on the results of twice-yearly surveys of employees that ask directly, "Is your manager leading change? How?"

Finally, Mead spends a lot of time meeting people at Tenneco, recognizing the contributions employees are making and spreading the message about the systems and culture of change. He has another purpose, too: letting people know that the change process is never going to end.

"We make communication a priority and do as much of it as we possibly can. We have a quarterly video program called *Tenneco Journal*, in which I talk about change at Tenneco, and believe it or not, it's gotten to be very popular. And I'll go and talk to a hundred hourly workers at a quality rally, for instance. I've been going to Case and Pipeline picnics every year, and to the Farm Progress shows, the dealers' shows, and business reviews on site, with visits to mills, container plants, muffler plants, and the shipyard. And you may ask, 'Who needs another picnic that takes the whole day?' But I think it's a critical part of the job. We have to keep showing our employees the confidence we have in them, and we have to keep communicating what we're about."

Tenneco, he says, is now about change. It is the company's constant.

"People accuse us of being on red alert all the time," he reflects. "They keep asking me when things are going to get back to normal. We say that this *is* normal. You *are* on red alert. It's a serious point. We have to watch carefully our employees' ability to adjust. Unfortunately, some people wish the more comfortable old days would return. But we can't live that way and compete. Some don't like this pace and decide to leave."

For those who have remained, or those who have joined since Mead took charge, the battle has just begun.

AT GOLDMAN SACHS: FACING THE CHALLENGE OF CHANGE, IN GOOD TIMES AND BAD

In the high-stakes world of investment banking, few companies are more visible than the venerable firm of **Goldman, Sachs & Co.** So in 1993, when the company reported record-breaking profitability of $2.7 billion and every partner earned more than $5 million, it was the talk of the industry and beyond. And by the same token, when Goldman's earnings dropped to $500 million in 1994, and the company was forced to cut costs and lay off more than 1,000 employees, the news made front-page headlines.

But few on Wall Street thought the firm's troubles were permanent. The industry is cyclical; downturns happen, and Goldman was hardly alone in its underperformance. Moreover, Goldman still had its deep talent pool and expertise in investment banking, trading, and industry analysis; its $4.7 billion in capital; and its close relationships with many of the world's top companies.

It also had the key advantage of being a change-agent organization, owing in large part to the efforts of Stephen Friedman, one of the firm's leading partners from the mid-1980s through 1994. Friedman's tenure at the firm is one marked by transformation, and it is a story of just how challenging and controversial the change-agent approach can be. During Friedman's period of leadership, Goldman Sachs went from being perceived as a well-respected, U.S.-oriented firm, albeit somewhat uncreative and uneven in ability, to being known as global, highly innovative, and consistently competitive across the board. Its traditional relationship-driven focus was coupled with a newly emphasized idea-driven mentality—often first to market with products and client services. Of his last year at the helm, Friedman unhesitantly accepts responsibility, saying, "Certainly if I had done it perfectly, we wouldn't have had as disappointing earnings as we had." But he also notes that major change carries with it major risks.

"I have always said it's not a sin to overshoot the challenge, and it's not a sin to undershoot," Friedman says. "It is a sin not to face up to what has happened, analyze it, then move on, and keep changing in ways that are relevant."

Like the other business leaders in this chapter, Friedman believes he had no choice but to practice the change-agent approach at his company—the highly volatile world of global investment banking made the decision for him. But he also asserts that every CEO in today's marketplace must change his or her focus.

"Change for the sake of change makes no sense, of course," Friedman says, "but if you're not constantly working for constructive strategic change, then you are the steward of something which must erode. Competitors will leapfrog over you, and clients will find you less relevant. If that was your approach, why would you even want the job?"

To drive change through the organization at Goldman Sachs,

Friedman used a variety of tools, but his methodology was driven by one critical constraint: Goldman's partnership structure. CEOs may have to answer to a board of directors, but Goldman had an internal management committee and more than 100 partners, many of whom had CEO-like power in their areas. In other words, every significant change in the organization needed some form of consensus behind it.

For this reason, Friedman did his share of "preaching" throughout the organization, trying to generate excitement about his vision of Goldman's new direction. And yet, he notes that talk alone can't fundamentally alter the way people think and behave, a common conviction expressed by leaders who describe themselves as change agents.

"I don't know what happens to you when you go to your church or synagogue or place of worship, but I know what happens to me and I suspect with most of us: you kind of sit there and you paste an attentive look on your face and let the sermon wash over you," Friedman explains. "I mean, I have watched people sitting through my own sermonettes, and I can't help but wonder what is going through their heads. Are they thinking, 'Gee, this is restful elevator music,' or 'When is this guy going to be done so I can make some phone calls?' "

Which is why Friedman says he preferred action to talk to make change the focal point of value addition at Goldman—action like encouraging the promotion of people who shared the firm's new vision and shaking up the status quo with committees of "action-oriented, strategic Doberman pinschers, not poodles."

What he was working against, he says, was a complacency the firm had developed, and with it, attitudes that he calls, somewhat tongue-in-cheek, "the three change-resistant personalities of any successful organization.

"You have Barons, who perceive change as a risk to their fiefdoms and personal importance. You have Creationists, who feel comfortable with things as they are and distrust evolution. And you have Romantics, who hark back to some imagined Camelot, when every subject in the kingdom was happy and prosperous."

As Friedman saw it as he began his role running the firm, the strong parts of Goldman were carrying the weaker ones, but wouldn't be able to forever. "We were moving too slowly, or not at all, to face some serious competitive threats, with too little internal coordination between divisions and too much self-satisfaction. Too many crucial things were on autopilot and were not being reexamined. If we waited to fix them it might get to be too late. The challenge of my generation was to institutionalize a continuous process of reinvigoration."

One of Friedman's first steps in the early eighties was to form a strategic planning committee in the Investment Banking Division. "We composed the committee of bright, iconoclastic, younger people below the senior managerial levels, so they had no compulsion to defend the status quo," he says. Their meetings, he remembers, were "fantastic, informal, and fun." A number of ideas for Goldman's future were introduced, among them a suggestion from some of the younger members that the firm get into the junk bond business. "At first I was a skeptic: 'That's a terrible idea; we can assess a Baa but how are we going to assess a single B?'" Friedman recalls, referring to the different levels of quality assigned to bonds, single B being among the lowest. "And for the next meeting, they came back with good answers about quality controls and my other concerns and beat me up, and by the third meeting I was sold."

But Friedman knew his personal enthusiasm alone wouldn't carry the day within the firm—after all, it had taken a lot of persuasion to sell him. Nor would it help that the idea sprang from a committee of young mavericks. Moreover, the junk bond industry financed higher-risk, higher-return ventures, somewhat at odds with Goldman's reputation for conservatism. In any event, he wanted an unbiased sanity test on the new idea. For help—and to help build the consensus for change—he approached an experienced partner widely considered to be among the smartest and most cautious.

"We asked him to head a full-blown study as to whether and how we would enter the business," Friedman recalls. "Now, if he had some arguments about why we shouldn't do it, we wanted to know them, but we were confident he wasn't going to come to that conclusion, and he didn't. He came to the same conclusion we did, but with a lot more documentation and some useful refinements. And now he had bought in and was behind the plan. It had establishment blessing."

Another way he worked to build consensus for change, Friedman says, was to take many of his cues from deep within the organization. "The people who really know what's going on are the ones in the trenches. They know what competitors are doing, what clients want, what new pressures and opportunities are out there."

He also made it his role to protect other voices calling for change that didn't seem to be getting a hearing. He made himself, he says, a megaphone for ideas that sometimes even sounded a little off the wall.

"A lot of the good ideas start out, in different form, as 'off the wall,'" he says. "That's okay. I've always really valued the idea-driven missionary who grabs his seniors by the sleeve, tells us what we're doing wrong, and reasons us into changing our minds. That's real added value."

Like Dana Mead at Tenneco, Friedman acknowledges that these kinds of employees can step on toes, but he adds, "No firm can do without them. And I'll admit that over the years I made a few personnel mistakes in doing it, but all in all I believe it was very good for us."

Friedman also pushed change through Goldman via his people policies. "Obviously, any manager must give a lot of thought to the right people for key places," he says, "not only to help the organization run better day to day but because promotions and demotions send a message to the organization about what really matters to the leadership in the long run."

For example, Friedman says, "After we told someone who was a highly talented person that he did not become a partner because of a failure to adopt the firm's teamwork agenda and to work on it, the message began to percolate around the system, and it began to get people's attention."

The change vision of a global Goldman was spread similarly.

"People weren't particularly enthusiastic about going overseas," he recalls. "It just was not valued as an attractive career opportunity by most of our U.S. people, and their spouses didn't necessarily want to go, and their dog couldn't possibly endure living in Tokyo. . . .

"So we took an exceptionally talented young banker and promoted him to partner two years ahead of his class, because he went to Asia at great personal sacrifice. That story, too, got around quite quickly. People began to understand they could trust our urging that it would be good for their careers if they had international experience."

Finally, Friedman used performance reviews as a mechanism to effect change at Goldman. In the past, bankers would walk into these meetings thinking about one figure—the fees they felt they had generated. Although that number did not, in fact, control bonuses, the widespread perception was that it did. The fallout, Friedman believed, was that the values of teamwork and client service were not being supported by the incentive system. He and Robert Rubin, another senior partner who has since left Goldman to work as U.S. secretary of the treasury, hired an industrial psychologist to teach the partners and supervisors how to better assess employees and give candid, in-depth performance reviews—ones that would really address strengths and weaknesses—as well as reinforce the personal cultural traits the firm wanted to stress.

"With the exception of one area, today all professional employees' bonuses are subjective," Friedman says. "No one at a trading desk gets a share of the profits. No one in the merger area gets a share of a fee. We wanted everyone to think more about the firm's interests, as opposed to their own, personal interests. Dropping the formulas, or perceptions of formulas, helps a lot."

In short order, Friedman rattles off several other examples of systems he put in place to push change at Goldman. He speaks with a sense of accomplishment, but he also sounds weary. When we suggest that being a change agent is exhausting, he replies without hesitation, "Damn right—and it never ends because the environment keeps changing. Last year's approach is no longer good enough; if you're brutally frank with yourself, there are always some mistakes you need to face up to and then go back to the drawing board."

But he adds that there was one other part of his job that sapped more of his energy, to less avail—the role of ambassador, the "face" of the firm, meeting with clients or country officials, not to work on transactions but to shake hands and show the flag. It is a role that is crucial and also completely inescapable, he says, but it can take over your life if you let it, and it's hard not to.

"You could literally fill up every day and night of the week and also Sundays with these commitments, and each of them taken independently is useful and informative," Friedman says. "And you meet very impressive people, sometimes fascinating ones. But you have to admit to yourself that in many ceremonial cases, you're only adding value because you're physically there and you have an epaulet on your shoulder."

Friedman recalls a one-week trip to Europe in which he played the ambassador role in six countries, meeting with clients, finance ministers, and heads of state in a whirlwind of formal meetings, cocktail parties, and dinners. "The whole time I kept looking at the pilot of the chartered plane we were in, and I thought to myself, you know, he's a perfectly well-spoken guy, perfectly presentable. If I could just give this guy a nice blue serge suit, and teach him about eight lines, he could do the ceremonial part as well as I could at these big receptions."

The pilot might have managed, but the ruse would have been off when the plane landed in New York. Exchanging pleasantries with foreign dignitaries is one matter. Changing an organization like Goldman Sachs—for a long time known precisely for its tradition of staying the same—is quite another. And even though Friedman has retired, he is confident the commitment to continuous rethinking will not revert to what it was before. It must keep moving forward, perhaps toward different paradigms than the ones he sponsored, but forward in response to new needs.

His successor, Jon Corzine—known as "the bearded one" for being one of the few partners to sport facial hair—seems poised to do that. He is a nonconformist by nature, insiders say, just as eager to dispense with the status quo as Friedman was. Wall Street awaits his next move.

In the meantime, Friedman keeps busy with pro bono work and some investing, and a more family-centered life. (His yearly vestments as a partner in Goldman make him a millionaire many times over.) But he jokes that at his next job, if there is one, he would enjoy something extremely hierarchical, where employees click their heels at every command and bark "Check, chief!"

Turning serious, he disavows the notion. For anyone in business, he says, change has to be "the starting point, and the end point, all the while building consensus and helping the organization adapt." Otherwise, he notes, "you're trying to compete with obsolete software," and in today's challenging marketplace, that's as good as not competing at all.

AT MITSUI: TOUCHING THE SACRED

Change is hard—it's exhausting, it takes much longer than expected, it turns an organization inside out. These responses recurred in our interviews with top executives in the change-agent category. Each of them took on the daunting task of turning around companies not quite in crisis, designing systems and procedures to integrate new ideas and behaviors, revamping cultures, and invariably managing the resistance that went with these moves. But perhaps none of the CEOs we talked to faced a turnaround as massive as the one at the **Mitsui Group,** Japan's leading trading company and one of the ten largest companies in the world, with revenues in 1994 of more than $152 billion. Such was the challenge embraced by Naohiko Kumagai when he took over Mitsui in 1990. It was, he says, a challenge that required him to "touch the sacred"—that is, upend Mitsui traditions—and do so swiftly, without allowing a chorus of criticism to slow or stop him. Only now, with the change he initiated in full swing and reaping positive financial results, is Kumagai willing to reflect on how far the company has come under his stewardship. Once a rigid box built on stultifying rules and hierarchical relationships, Mitsui is approaching the paradigm of a more creative, flexible, human assets company. This is exactly what Kumagai intended; like many of the "people" CEOs described in chapter 3, he believes that if employees are motivated and empowered, financial success follows as a matter of course. In Mitsui's case, it has. In 1994, the company's unconsolidated after-tax profit rose to an all-time high of $15 billion.

Operating like an American holding company but markedly more complex, Mitsui comprises 742 member companies connected through cross-ownership, in businesses ranging from iron and steel to food and chemicals. Mitsui & Co. was founded in 1947 following the dissolution of the Mitsui *zaibatsu*—that is, a family-controlled industrial and financial combine. With government support, the new Mitsui quickly grew to include not just industrial concerns but also a lucrative trading function, and a banking arm as well. In fact, Mitsui grew so quickly and became so widely diversified that the corporate office soon abandoned any strategic role, leaving that job to the individual businesses. Corporate executives focused on installing and monitoring financial and organizational controls, such as setting up accounting systems, reporting relationships, and transfer pricing policies. If synergies were not being exploited and bureaucracies flourished, few objected. Japan's thirty-year economic boom helped build the Mitsui Group and others like it (Mitsubishi, for instance) into huge international powerhouses.

It was only when the bubble burst in the late 1980s that Mitsui felt the downside of its success. The company was overloaded with thousands of aging, high-cost employees, its dozens of divisions operated as isolated fiefdoms, manufacturing plants lagged in terms of technological breakthroughs, level upon level of management somehow left no one accountable for marketplace or investment decisions, and young employees lacked optimism since there was nowhere to move up in the organization. All of these factors impacted the bottom line: exports and imports declined steadily from 1990 onward, and sales and profits dipped or remained flat.

It was into this situation that Kumagai stepped in June 1990. By September, he had determined that the company's problem was, in a word, people. Not a few of Mitsui's 12,000 employees were unhappy, unmotivated, and unproductive—a potentially disastrous troika of effects, since people are a trading company's only levers for competitive advantage.

"People are the key assets of a trading company," Kumagai explains. "Unlike a manufacturing firm, our success isn't dependent on proprietary goods and technology, but rather on the experience and motivation of our staff. If I am not successful in tapping the full potential of Mitsui's human assets, then I have failed to fulfill my responsibilities as company president."

Kumagai quickly assembled a sixteen-person task force, and gave it six months to design a solution to Mitsui's "people problem." Under his guidance, the plan was ready by March 1991 and came in two parts. The first called for a complete restructuring of the company; the second involved overhauling the firm's human resource policies. The goal was to redefine Mitsui, to re-create it from the bottom up.

Kumagai's first task was almost the exact opposite of that undertaken by Ryuzaburo Kaku at Canon, who forced change into his organization by decentralizing operations. Mitsui had always been decentralized—too much so, by Kumagai's estimation. Each of its seventy-six departments had its own profit and loss statement, its own central staff, its own strategic goals; each acted as an entirely independent entity. "As Mitsui's business grew over the years, it turned toward specialization to answer market needs," Kumagai explains. "What was once the chemical division gave way to smaller divisions such as fertilizer, fine chemicals, petrochemicals, plastics, and others. And with this came more limited divisional responsibilities, a smaller business scope, and fewer opportunities to pursue." As an example, he points to Mitsui's grain business, which had grown so specialized and inward-focused that it never communicated with any other of the company's food operations. Says Kumagai: "That means we missed opportunities to identify cross-sectional synergies. So much could have been done, from exploring the potential for large food combine plants, to integrating wholesaler distribution functions, to streamlining delivery logistics, and finding new ways to enter the restaurant sector."

At the same time, the proliferation of divisions at Mitsui created a maze of management posts, and all those layers of authority meant no one actually had any.

"Managing directors were assigned control over several divisions and responsibility for overall management, but responsibility for the results of each division was with the divisional general manager, making organizational demarcation between the managing director and the divisional general manager unclear," Kumagai notes. "We had to make it simpler."

Kumagai's restructuring plan reorganized Mitsui into twenty-one groups, each with common products or services. He also abolished the system of managing directors overseeing and holding responsibility for divisions, thus eliminating twelve high-ranking posts. Both moves met immediate resistance, Kumagai says, not only from the managing directors but from unseated division heads as well, who saw their power eroded. "They questioned my intentions and attacked my decision as promoting an unnecessary sense of crisis," the president recalls, "or even destroying Mitsui's traditions.

"But that was hardly what I wanted. In fact, I felt the divisional structure had grown too fragmented and unwieldy. Although it seemed contradictory on the surface, my goal was to bring back *Hito no Mitsui*—'Mitsui's strength lies in the individual.' This could be done only by simplifying the hierarchy, clarifying responsibilities, and broadening the scope of divisional control." To accomplish this, Kumagai gave division managers and the new group heads full authority for decisions, "empowering individuals," as he says, "to become self-sufficient, innovative, and accountable.

"You can't ask people to be more responsible without giving them the freedom to make decisions," he notes. "We gave them that freedom, and decided we would not interfere and say, 'This is the right way,' or 'Don't do this.' We want to let them figure out the best way to run their companies now. After all, they are in the best position to do so. We are giving them a chance to perform. If they don't—well, then you can move them elsewhere or ask them to leave. But we will not interfere with them before giving them a real chance."

The restructuring also involved combining some business departments and eliminating others, and establishing new general investment and business promotion sections. These changes were aimed at attracting venture capital to the company, as well as reducing management layers.

Within six months, the restructuring at Mitsui was complete, and Kumagai moved on to the overhaul of human resource policies, attacking what he considered the company's most pressing problem: limited career options for talented young workers. It was a problem linked to Mitsui's large corps of workers over the age of fifty. "When I became president," Kumagai explains, "most management positions were filled, and because of the age of our workforce, few were opening up."

But the problem wasn't just how few openings existed. "A lack of new slots and higher postings also meant a growing number of 'window sitters'—people with senior titles but no work of substance," Kumagai goes on. "It's easy to imagine the thoughts racing through the minds of today's young employees—namely, the near impossibility of climbing the corporate ladder in the years ahead."

Kumagai responded by introducing an aggressive plan encouraging early retirement, and again he met resistance. "I was criticized for touching sacred ground, this time for attempting to tamper with Japan's much lauded lifetime employment system," Kumagai recalls. He was not deterred, but Mitsui did pay a steep price. The total cost of the program is hard to assess, but some observers have placed it at over $20 million a year.

These costs, however, are short term, Kumagai says. "The move helped us reduce the number of employees and eventually lowered personnel costs overall," he adds. "And the result is higher levels of satisfaction and motivation among our younger workers."

In a second radical change to human resource policies, Kumagai instituted a new program to rotate employees across divisions—not just managers but employees with anywhere from six to twenty-five years with the firm. (In the past, it was not unusual for an employee to stay with one business unit his entire career.) "We wanted to expand our employees' concept of what it means to work for our company, and to expose them to different operations," he says, again mentioning the problems created by Mitsui's previous tilt toward specialization. Rotating employees gives them new perspectives, helps them identify synergies, and encourages them to share information across divisional "borders," Kumagai says, ultimately strengthening Mitsui's organizational capabilities.

"The overall goal is to enrich the employees' experiences, and to make them into better entrepreneurs, more creative, flexible, and motivated to see opportunities for growth and innovation," he says. "There's really no mystery to it—motivated employees bring higher profits, and higher profits beget greater motivation."

As we noted earlier, Kumagai's change program has had a fast and positive impact on the bottom line. But like the other CEOs in this chapter, the Mitsui president acknowledges that the process was "fraught with difficulty," which is why he did not open his program to debate or respond to criticism in the first years of implementation. Doing so, he says, would have led to inaction.

"We want to give reform a chance to settle into our work flow, rather than to constantly argue and debate the merits of change," he says. "I know that nothing is perfect and mistakes are unavoidable, but I didn't want to hear opinions such as, 'Let's revert back to the old days,' or 'This will never work.' The key was to reach a broadly accepted decision and then to make it happen. And to make it happen, you need commitment and unity of purpose."

Not surprisingly, given Kumagai's subdued modesty, he is not ready to take the positive financial results as evidence that his change program has succeeded. "People policies bear fruit in the long run," he says. "Unlike the relatively short time frame in which structural changes can yield results, people policies take time. I expect the real results of our reform to begin surfacing in ten years or so."

In the meantime, he adds, he will push forward with additional changes to improve employee motivation. "After all is said and done, I want Mitsui to be a good company so that if your child tells you that he or she has taken a job here, your response would be, 'Yes, that is a good place to work.'

"It is along these lines that I measure my performance," Kumagai says, and then, echoing his brethren in this change-agent approach to management, he concludes, "I know I still have much to do."

AT NATIONAL AUSTRALIA BANK:
WHERE DEREGULATION MEANT INSTANT CHANGE

Nobby Clark, former CEO of **National Australia Bank,** became a change agent virtually overnight, owing to a singular event that caused major upheaval: deregulation.

The Australian government's decision in the early eighties to loosen controls on the banking industry unleashed a pricing war, plus new products, services, and competitors, at the same time as new information technologies were redefining the business.

"The financial services industry changed irrevocably once deregulation came," says Clark, sixty-six, who is now chairman of Foster's Brewing Group but who ran NAB, with its $93 billion in assets, for close to a decade. "The simultaneous changes in communication technology, explosive growth in credit markets, threats from foreign competition, and the unbundling of products all meant that the way people managed and behaved had to change fundamentally and forever. This triggered a remarkable transformation of the center's role."

By this, Clark means the corporate center went from being the organization's bean counter and guardian of its well-established bureaucracy to steward of continuous change. "We had to become very forward-looking and proactive," Clark says. "The environment was uncertain, the future was uncertain, but we had to lead the organization through this process by making sure it could adapt and thrive."

The tools Clark used are strikingly similar to those described by the other CEOs in this chapter. First, he hired the right people, those who embraced change and were flexible and creative enough to come up with ideas to keep the bank competitive in a fiercely competitive context. "We needed more intellectual horsepower across the board, from the very lowest levels up," Clark says, "we needed them to introduce products and services that fulfilled a wide range of customer needs while also taking out costs."

Next, Clark attacked the bank's centralized structure, tackling the most entrenched, change-resistant bureaucracies by having their senior managers report directly to him. During this same process, Clark redeployed the bank's "backroom" thinkers to the field, moving economists into the business units. He also refocused the institution's mathematicians and actuaries to the marketplace by having them develop plans to reduce the burden of interest rate increases on home owners. Similarly, Clark took the unusual step of replacing traditional loan officers and managers in NAB's rural branches with agriculture experts trained in banking skills. The change, Clark says, enabled NAB to get closer than ever to these farming customers during a tough economic period, when it was important for the bank to truly understand what was happening at each farm, with each crop and each type of livestock.

Then, with the right people in the right places, he began empowering them to make decisions, to "take risks, run pilot studies, initiate product prototypes."

Yet Clark also emphasizes that empowerment does not mean that the center abdicates its role. "Empowerment isn't about complete freedom," he says. "Even owners can't make unfettered decisions about their businesses. Empowerment is about working in an environment where you can make a major number of decisions about your business."

To build that environment, Clark quickly pushed many critical decisions out into the business units—among them the allocation of the center's overhead costs. In the past, the bank had dolloped out overheads according to a ratio involving the number of personnel and other factors, Clark recalls, "and the business units used to scream about it."

Shortly after deregulation set thoroughgoing change in motion at NAB, Clark reassessed the allocation procedure and decided to reinvent it. "I asked the business units, 'How would you like to manage overhead allocations?' And that's what we did." From that point on, business units assumed management and control of what were formerly centrally provided services, on a direct-cost basis. The result? The bank shed about 35 percent of its headquarters costs, and Clark notes, "I even think we could have done a bit better than that."

With decision making pushed into the field, the corporate staff had to reinvent its role, too, Clark says. Previously, "the staff people called all the shots on the way the field operated, what resources they received, and how they responded. I got pretty testy seeing these guys with such enormous power . . . and they exploited this power pretty effectively."

At the new NAB, Clark told the corporate staff it was there "to see that good decisions are made and that the implementation is effective—but that the line guy has to make the decision himself."

If the staff executive was unhappy with the line manager's performance, Clark wanted to know, with a caveat. "I said, 'You can come to me, but *with* the line guy, and we can all discuss it.' "

Interestingly, however, while Clark says he was spending much of his time managing National Australia Bank with the change-agent approach, he was also defining a box in the area of culture. Again, the reason was the volatile environment.

"When markets are moving or discontinuities occur, values and standards change, and usually for the worse," he notes. "Behavior becomes pretty sloppy and standards and morality decline. The center added value by developing some good, strong statements of what we believed was appropriate behavior in the markets. We developed a code of ethics and then communicated them relentlessly to the organization."

After ten years as a change agent, Clark expresses many of the same sentiments as the other CEOs in this category; like Steve Friedman of Goldman Sachs, he upbraids change for change's sake. And he sounds a similar theme, too, when he says that CEOs who define themselves as stewards of change must be constantly on the alert, as critical of the status quo as they are of their way of tackling it.

"As a CEO you must constantly be touching many pulses to let you know where the pulse is beating in a nice regular rhythm or at 100 miles an hour," Clark says. "You need a mechanism that makes you look at yourself, at the business, the customers and the marketplace, all the time."

That mechanism, he says, is the ultimate role of the center in an organization in the midst of change.

THE CHANGE-AGENT APPROACH: FAST, "VIOLENT," THRILLING, DAUNTING—AND POWERFUL

As the nineties opened, **American Express** was in trouble, despite its instantly recognized brand name, its seemingly ubiquitous charge cards, and its nearly 2,000 travel services offices worldwide. The charge card franchise, in particular, was under heavy assault; fewer people were acquiring American Express cards, as other cards with frequent flyer miles or merchandise discounts were stealing loyal customers. At the same time, merchants were challenging the company's fees. Its financial supermarket strategy, which had included acquisitions of Shearson and Lehman Brothers, was not working. The fallout? Institutional shareholders were clamoring for change.

There were dozens of small reasons for the downturn at American Express, says vice chairman Ken Chenault, and one big one. The company had become complacent in its success. It had neglected to keep current with what the customer wanted and what the competition was offering. It had stopped changing.

"We were blinded by our immediate profitability," says Chenault, head of the Travel Related Services division, which includes the charge card business. "We stopped looking for ways to continue the innovation that had made our company what it was."

Under new leadership, American Express has become an organization defined by change, in the same mold as the other companies in this chapter. Change-agent-approach CEOs, as we have seen, aren't necessarily trying to get their organizations from one predetermined competitive position to another. They are passionate about altering the *how* of how their companies do business. Many differ from strategists in that they don't articulate a point of arrival, but instead talk more generally about improving a company's capabilities and empowering employees to take active responsibility for creating extraordinary results. (Interestingly, American Express has also adopted the expertise approach, with the company's brand as its focal point.)

We won't outline here how American Express has incorporated its new approaches for powerful financial results, but rather to conclude with what Ken Chenault calls the "four patterns of change."

When an organization faces change of any significant magnitude, the first reaction, Chenault says, is denial—this can't possibly be happening. "Some people are constitutionally opposed to change," he notes. "They cling to the status quo." As J. P. Bolduc recalls of his wake-up call meetings with employees, "Employees were upset, employees were concerned." They didn't want to hear what he had to say, for it was sending their lives into upheaval. At Goldman Sachs, too, the first response to calls for global expansion were resisted,

Stephen Friedman remembers, with employees offering every excuse from fear of flying to worries about their pets surviving overseas travel. He is half-joking, of course, but this is the sentiment to which Chenault refers. Change gets a lot of lip service in business, but ask people to embrace it, and you'll hear them explain why they can't.

Chenault's second pattern occurs when organizations "accept change as a concept, but cope with it by trying harder." He expands this by saying, "People do more of the same, but do it faster. They increase productivity, but deliver more of the same." In other words, the organization avoids real change by not addressing *fundamental* change. Again, this is something the executives in this chapter encountered. At Tenneco, Dana Mead had to introduce the mantra of "results, not best efforts" to get his managers to understand that trying harder wasn't enough. If they had to completely change the way they did business to hit their numbers, so be it.

Pattern three is escape, in which very senior managers—the ones who should be leading change—decide to let someone else fix the problem. They retire early, says Chenault, or look around for a buyer, or negotiate a golden parachute, a comfortable exit package.

The fourth and final pattern of change, says Chenault, is when organizations adapt. "They learn the new rules and they develop the strategies they need to win. Those who don't go down with the old order. You have to embrace change, not just to succeed but to survive." Here again, Chenault describes what the other examples in this chapter illustrate. In every case, the organizations were remade through the change-agent approach. This doesn't just mean that they went from staid to flexible, but that they became places where change is a continuous process, a culture, *the* way of doing business. As Naohiko Kumagai at Mitsui says, he wanted to build an organization where employees felt free to speak out and make decisions, even if it meant "touching the sacred" to do so. Change has a way of breaking with the past that scares some and motivates others. At organizations embracing change, only the latter remain after the process gets going.

Chenault's four patterns capture an overarching message of this chapter: real change is hard. It is easy to redraw a company's organizational chart. It is easy to tell employees that they should feel and act in new ways. It is easy to fire and hire and shuffle chairs to create the appearance of change. But the CEOs who put themselves in this category say that effecting the real thing means fundamentally transforming values, behaviors, and actions. It means helping people accept risk, and helping them overcome their fear of the new. Such a challenge takes time, but more than that, it takes leadership.

7

PAST IMPERFECT:
APPROACHES THAT WEREN'T

We began this book talking about adding value, and how infrequently CEOs can honestly assert that they do. Our argument was that while virtually all CEOs (and their corporate staffs) claim to add value, from looking at the numbers—the numbers shareholders care most about—only 20 percent do so on a consistent basis.

In the chapters that followed, we looked at the different approaches that some of the world's leading CEOs say they use to include their companies in that 20 percent. This is not to imply that every example we used was culled from a company that has accomplished this task year after year, but to report how those ultimately responsible for a company's results approach what we have called maximum leadership—that is, to consistently deliver extraordinary results.

The five patterns of management that emerged from our interviews do, of course, raise the question of cause and effect. Does the "right" approach for a business situation, applied consistently, actually yield financial success? Conclusive quantitative analysis of this issue has yet to be done, but the anecdotal evidence amassed so far suggests there is a strong link. Given this connection, the emerging framework of the five approaches (and their permutations) raises other questions, too.

What if a company's center—its CEO and top staff—focus on the wrong approach for the business situation, or what if it practices no coherent approach at all? This chapter examines four once-successful companies that failed, or nearly did so, and considers what role their approach played. These stories are, not surprisingly, some of the most painful in this book, for companies slipping over the brink don't go alone. They take with them jobs, communities, and friendships, as well as fortunes small and large. But at the same time, these examples are some of the most encouraging because they indicate that a new approach—the correct one for the context, relentlessly applied—can help to reinvent a company given up as lost.

Of course, four companies don't provide enough data to draw definitive conclusions about why companies fail, but one theme did recur consistently enough to be quite provocative: these stories suggest that business failures can be interpreted in terms of failed *approaches*, wrongly selected for the situation, wrongly applied, or not applied at all.

In this section, we look at the case of **Wang Laboratories.** Once the bright star of personal computing, Wang fell into bankruptcy in 1992, having laid off 26,000 employees and lost billions of dollars in market value. Today, its three office towers stand empty along a Massachusetts highway. Built for $55 million at the pinnacle of the company's success in the mid-1980s, the complex recently sold for $525,000.

Much has been written about Wang's failure, some accounts laying blame on the insular leadership style of An Wang, the brilliant Chinese immigrant who founded the firm in 1951 and ran it until 1987; and some criticizing his son, Fred, who followed him as CEO. Others have suggested that Wang Labs was the victim, just like dozens of other computing firms, of the 1986–87 recession. Our hypothesis is that Wang's story can be seen as a case of a correct approach incorrectly implemented. For most of his career, An Wang managed his company as a strategist, with all the rigorous, systematic analysis and foresight described in chapter 2. But at some point that process ebbed. Wang's vision was not examined, not updated, not altered for the competitive environment—critical errors in a technology-driven industry. As Michael Dell of Dell Computer says, the computer industry's future is just six months off, a time horizon so tight there are only two kinds of players in it, the quick and the dead. By letting its strategy go stale, Wang Labs joined the latter.

Along with Wang, this chapter also examines **ITT,** formerly the world's largest conglomerate, and **British Leyland,** the once-formidable car manufacturer known worldwide as the maker of Jaguar and Triumph. And it will look at what happened at **Digital Equipment Corp.,** the computer giant whose meteoric rise gave way to $6 billion in losses over four years. Digital, we propose, is a case in point of senior management's selecting the right approach for one situation, but then not changing it to respond to a radically new situation —new customer needs, new competitors, new technology. Digital successfully built upon its expertise for many years, but fell off the technology superhighway when the markets were rewarding strategy and change organizations for what they offered. Today, with founder Ken Olsen gone and Digital undergoing a massive overhaul that has led to increasingly positive financial results, the company might just rise to the top of the industry again. But like the other companies in this chapter, the new Digital, a legacy of the old, is a thoroughly transformed organization, the survivor of an imperfect past.

AT ITT: LEARNING THAT ONE BOX DOES NOT FIT ALL

Although it never actually showed a loss on its books, one company frequently cited as an example of management failure is the international conglomerate **ITT,** under the stewardship of Harold Geneen.

Ironically, Geneen was once one of the most admired of America's corporate leaders, his management approach taught in business schools, his opinions sought after by the media and government officials. He had, after all, built a loose collection of telecommunication companies into one of the world's largest and most successful conglomerates, selling products from Twinkies to turbines, fire hydrants to hotel rooms, and radios to casualty insurance. By the end of Geneen's tenure in 1980, ITT employed more than 400,000 people in more than 250 companies with 2,000 units, and posted sales of $22 billion and earnings of $560 million.

But it took nearly a decade to repair the damage after his departure. For ITT, the eighties were a period of deflated sales and income, decreased stock value and slashed dividends, as well as the divestiture of sixty-nine companies, some at fire-sale prices. Some business observers have blamed Geneen's values or personality for the company's reversal of fortune: he was a tough, often harsh businessman who inspired fear in many of his employees. While this may be true, we assert that ITT's downfall can in large part be explained by Geneen's failed *approach*. He built a box, and for many years it was perfectly appropriate for the competitive situation. But ultimately Geneen's box was far too small to contain or control the business and economic change sweeping over ITT. Geneen built his box around too many situations where it did not belong.

ITT was founded in 1920 by Sosthenes Behn, an entrepreneur who entered the international telephone market at its inception. He guided the company's growth for the next four decades, turning the postwar period into one of enormous expansion for ITT in Western Europe, and one of enormous profitability for the entire corporation.

Geneen succeeded Behn in 1959, following a career as chief controller at several major corporations. At age fifty, Geneen was already a renowned numbers man, well known in American industry for his combative, hard-driving manner in implementing control systems and getting subordinates to hit budget goals. Within his first five years at ITT, Geneen replaced 30 percent of the company's executives and set ITT upon an acquisition campaign of unequaled magnitude in business history.

What drove Geneen? His strategy, he said himself, was simple. Wide diversification meant guaranteed profits with minimum risk. By owning hundreds of companies with different business cycles and margins, ITT shareholders were essentially owning an insurance policy. ITT's managers didn't need to know the fundamentals of the conglomerate's subsidiaries, Geneen maintained, they only needed to know how to manage.

How to manage—Geneen asserted that was clear, too. It meant operating within the box he had designed. Its walls were made of numbers—that is, of strict financial goals. As long as they were met, ITT was doing its job for shareholders.

Results seemed to bear Geneen out throughout the 1970s. The company's sales and income rose steadily, as did its stock price and dividends. ITT's conglomerate structure was heralded as the corporation of the future. At the same time, there was a personal cost to many of those managers executing Geneen's approach, because of its demanding nature and inflexibility. Ten months out of the year, every business unit head was required to write a detailed report outlining financial performance, including sales, profit, return on investment, and every existing and potential problem for the unit, and its solution. These reports would often run twenty pages, single spaced. As soon as they were done, Geneen collected them in a binder, sending copies to all ITT senior executives in preparation for the company's monthly meeting. These meetings were grueling, lasting up to fifteen hours a day, sometimes for days in a row. Geneen required everyone to participate, and particularly held the fire to feet of managers who had not hit their numbers. "You have to be prepared to have your balls screwed off in public," one such manager recalled at the time, "and then joke afterward as if nothing had happened."

Geneen also required every ITT business unit to develop, annually, a five-year business plan for his approval. If he disagreed with the plan, he let the managers know, often face-to-face. The pressure to avoid Geneen's wrath was so strong that managers did whatever it took to show a profit. Geneen, it is said, never asked what that "whatever" was. "ITT was an organization driven by fear," Martin L. Bowles writes in his book *The Organizational Shadow*. It was fear, it seems, of stepping outside the box.

But it was not Geneen's box that ended his career with ITT. Instead, two political incidents tarnished his reputation. The first occurred in the early seventies, when ITT was in the midst of acquiring Hartford Insurance. ITT was anxious for the deal to go through, since it wanted to use Hartford's asset base to pay down the billions in debt it had accumulated in its acquisition campaign. But ITT's plans to grab Hartford quickly were stymied when the government announced it was launching an investigation of six conglomerates for antitrust violations, among them ITT. The Hartford purchase was put on indefinite hold.

A few months later, however, the government unexpectedly approved the ITT-Hartford deal. Following a leaked company memo, the media reported that the approval was linked to a $400,000 ITT contribution to Richard Nixon's 1972 reelection campaign. Geneen strongly denied the allegations, and no charges were ever brought against him. His integrity was challenged again, however, a few years later, when newspapers reported allegations that Geneen had worked with the CIA to disrupt elections in Chile. (It was said that he wanted to prevent a new communist government from nationalizing ITT operations there.) Geneen was required to testify before the Senate in

1977, although he was never formally accused of wrongdoing. The Justice Department did, however, eventually file criminal charges against two ITT managers for perjuring themselves during these proceedings. Amid the turmoil, the board of directors asked for Geneen's resignation.

Another CEO followed Geneen, but his tenure was short. Then, in 1980, Rand Araskog took over ITT as chairman and CEO. In his book *The ITT Wars*, Araskog says little could have prepared him for the siege he was about to face. For the next several years, ITT was relentlessly pursued by several hostile raiders intent on buying the conglomerate, and then selling it off piece by piece. Management, Araskog recalls, was forced to devote all its energy to deflecting these attacks, draining its human and financial resources and nearly crippling the company.

What made ITT so attractive to the raiders? The answer lies in Harold Geneen's legacy. Believing that his box would correct any mistakes and could improve any business regardless of specific challenges, Geneen had bought too many companies too fast and paid too much. He left ITT with $5 billion in debt, with interest payments of $600 million annually.

These payments had been manageable during boom times, but they quickly became onerous in the eighties, with its recession, inflation, deregulation, and increasing interest rates. At the same time, the soaring dollar abroad severely impacted ITT's foreign income. Combined, economic forces crimped ITT's cash flow and limited its options.

Araskog found that his new job immediately required two things of him: fight off hostile raiders and completely restructure ITT. "It might have been easier if I had been a magician," he writes in his book. He describes the next few years as ones of "high anxiety," filled with "a whole constellation of problems that had to be faced down." The effect, he adds, was debilitating and distracting from the real business of operating ITT.

With the help of a close group of advisers and lawyers, Araskog did eventually fend off raiders, pay down a substantial portion of debt, and improve ITT's cash flow. Turning to the strategic approach the situation required, he sold off its telecommunications businesses and formed a protective European alliance called Alcatel to position ITT for the competitive pressures of the future. The hard lesson learned, Araskog says, was that "American corporations are treading on thin ice . . . if they think debt does not matter and that the good times will roll forever."

But there are other lessons, too, about the dangers of box management. First, boxes no longer relevant to the business situation can collapse in times of crisis. Too much happens too quickly for executives to rely on hard-and-fast rules to manage. Second, and perhaps more important, ITT is an example of what a box is not. Despite the security and predictability it can provide in some situations, the box is not a panacea to be installed at any company, at any time. At ITT, box management probably worked very well as an approach to some acquisitions—for instance, at ITT's heavily regulated communication companies. At others, such as its new technology and service firms, the context demanded greater flexibility and vision, and the people to make it happen. Harold Geenen acquired companies (and debt) with abandon because he assumed that one box—his box—would fit them all. That was a mistake, and ITT spent years paying the price.

AT WANG LABS: VISION THAT WAS NOT REVISITED

In some ways, the downfall of **Wang Laboratories** resembles the story of Digital—both companies were darlings of the computing industry, and both made technology and product decisions that turned them into outcasts. In Digital's case, as we'll see, senior management was so wedded to its expertise of powerful minicomputer systems that it did not heed the market's call for the flexibility of PCs.

Wang, too, was a company driven by a particular expertise—its specialty was desktop word processing—but while management chose the strategic approach, it executed it incorrectly. At the outset of his tenure, An Wang was a strategist, and strategic planning was (and is) one of the best approaches for the fast-changing computing industry. But as time passed, the very vision that drove Wang's success grew stale. Top management failed to constantly reexamine, reevaluate, and especially revamp it, based on the kind of systematic analysis discussed in chapter 2. This process is the imperative of the strategist, even at a company with as stable a product as Coca-Cola. As Coca-Cola's John Hunter says, "You can't sell today's consumers yesterday's product." Coke, he notes, "reinvents" its brand "for every new generation."

Wang management failed precisely on this count, holding fast to a vision that outlived its relevance to the consumer. While competitors responded to new and changing market demands, and in some cases anticipated them, Wang had neither the systems nor the culture to continuously challenge and reshape its strategy, thereby fortifying an organization built to support "yesterday's product." Today, one year after coming out of Chapter 11, the company resembles the original Wang Labs in name alone.

It is hardly the legacy anyone expected for the company An Wang, a Harvard-trained applied physics Ph.D., founded in 1951. Over the next two decades Wang and his team of R&D experts practically invented what today are called office communications systems, designing some of the earliest electronic keyboards and typewriters, as well as word-processing machines and software. By the late sixties, Wang Laboratories dominated the word-processing industry, building not just stand-alone products but the systems that linked them. By 1980, it employed 12,000 people; its revenues were $543 million and its profits $52 million, both increasing almost 30 percent a year.

But the industry was changing as fast as Wang was growing, and it was moving away from the organization's product strategy. More specifically, Wang produced word-processing software that would run only on its own hardware. In addition, it focused on one or two industries for customers, most prominently financial services. When the word-processing industry was new and expertise in this area was hard to come by, Wang's solution was perfect. But this situation was short-lived. New entrants came at Wang from every direction—some, like IBM, built better hardware, more powerful and more versatile, open to software by many vendors. Other competitors sold better software, with more applications, able to run any number of computer systems. Even shops that sold hardware and software, such as Leading Edge, made sure their products were compatible with competitive systems. With the notable exception of Apple, the industry was fast becoming a market of unbundled products, and customers showed their approval with their purchases.

Still, Wang stuck to a strategy of a closed hardware-software system and continued its focus on one end-user market. Why? Former employees and industry experts suggest that the organization's systems prevented the "challenge culture" that an effective strategic approach requires. For instance, because of a highly bureaucratic structure with many layers of managers, little leading-edge information about market trends reached the top levels of Corporate. In addition, An Wang had a somewhat insular management style, making major decisions with input mainly from a group nicknamed "the Chinese mafia," a small number of old friends who rarely disagreed with the CEO's perceptions. Finally, because of its rapid growth, the organization had apparently overpromoted people. The result, some say, was a large corps of inexperienced managers who had neither the knowledge nor the insight to question the company's strategy, let alone call for a new one. All of these factors allowed the company to hurtle forward with a vision that was no longer applicable.

Wang's slide began in earnest in 1985, when IBM introduced a PC that would fit on a desk, do more than Wang's equipment, and cost less. At the same time, Wang was gaining a reputation for being long on promises and short on delivery, as its products consistently hit the stores long after announced due dates.

To make matters worse, 1985 marked the beginning of an industry-wide slump, and Wang Labs posted its first-ever loss. The following year, Wang lost more than $100 million in one quarter, but managed to post year-end net income of $50.9 million. Again, the company was hurt by top management's analysis—or lack thereof—of future market trends. While other computer companies were consolidating their operations and reducing personnel, Wang assumed that the computer business would rebound and continued operations at full tilt. To contain costs, however, Wang determined the company would no longer aim for technological breakthroughs, but would concentrate on sales, marketing, and service. This, at last, was a change in vision, but it was too little, too late. And perhaps An Wang's heart was not in it at all. The next year, he handed the company over to his son, Fred.

Fred Wang, then thirty-seven, attempted a turnaround through cost cutting and major layoffs, but the organization had already acquired a has-been image that proved impossible to shake. In 1987, it brought out a dozen new products on schedule and bug free, but still profits sunk lower. In the fourth quarter of its 1988–89 year, Wang posted a staggering loss that included a massive restructuring charge, write-downs, and a one-time tax charge. The year ended with the announcement of a $424.3 million loss.

Three weeks later, Fred Wang resigned and was replaced by Richard Miller, the former director of General Electric's consumer electronics business, who had a reputation as a turnaround expert. He promised to overhaul the business from top to bottom, taking a hatchet to the headquarters staff. By December of 1989 employment at Wang had been slashed by one third from its peak of around 32,000 in the mid-eighties, and Miller had sold $600 million of the assets. It was to no avail. For two more years, Wang stumbled along, until finally, in August 1992, it filed for bankruptcy and its stock was pulled from the American exchange.

In the period that followed, Wang's senior management reinvented the organization as a "software and services company." Gone is its old approach, with its vision of a bundled Wang product line, and in its place is a new one: expertise in office productivity. The company makes software designed to make businesses more efficient, less costly, and more responsive to changing market conditions. In addition, the new Wang's 2,000 "technical support professionals" advise the government (and some companies) on office-automation systems, suggesting the best software and hardware solutions, among them Wang's products but including those of other manufacturers. (Wang's annual report now notes that Wang's software is compatible with virtually every hardware made, anywhere.) Finally, the company is also trying to position itself as an expert consultant to office-automation users, with services such as a seven-days-a-week software hot line and on-site repairs.

The success of this new approach is, of course, yet to be seen. The company had $855 million in sales and $22.5 million in income in 1994, for a return on equity of 8.5 percent. The old Wang may be gone forever, a relic of a failed approach, but perhaps its successor will be the chief beneficiary of the lessons management learned.

AT BRITISH LEYLAND:
THE WRONG APPROACH WAS NO APPROACH

In this chapter, we've seen management approaches wrongly selected for the situation, as in the case of ITT, or wrongly applied, as in the case of Wang. But the center fails most profoundly when it operates with no approach at all, or operates with a little bit of all of them simultaneously. Either way, the effect is the same: no direction, no consistency, no value added. Over the course of twenty-three years, Bain consultants have encountered this problem many times. Sometimes top management is unable to correctly assess its competitive context—it lacks the data, the personnel, or other resources—and so it briefly tries each approach on for size. Sometimes top management is mired in a political situation that seems to prevent the selection or application of the right approach. A CEO, for example, may believe the situation calls for a strategist, but he feels obliged to follow his predecessor's example in expertise management. He does so haphazardly, leaving a vacuum where the center should be. Or a new CEO may come into his job so uncertain of what role to play that he simply attends to the matters on his schedule, managing without any coherent program or objectives.

A company may survive for some time under these conditions, but not forever. No-approach companies all have one thing in common: they eventually self-destruct. Such was the case at **British Leyland Motor Company,** once the world's fifth-largest car manufacturer, maker of Jaguar, Triumph, and Rover. There, in the mid-1970s, a disengaged, unfocused center drove the company into failure, only to be saved at the last moment by the government and a CEO named Sir Michael Edwardes, who took over, picked the right approach, and stuck with it for five years under the most daunting of circumstances.

"It was chaos, complete chaos," recalls Edwardes of his first months at British Leyland in 1977. On his first day at work, he was greeted by 100 news reporters, shouting questions about how he planned to save a company that had become a painful symbol of that nation's industrial decline. Edwardes didn't answer; at that point, he didn't have answers. All he knew was that British Leyland, with 196,000 employees, was out of cash, that its factories had lost 33 million man-hours in strikes that year, that its quality didn't hold up to European standards, and that the company was filled with too many of the wrong managers in the wrong positions. Over the course of the previous years, Edwardes notes in his memoir *Back from the Brink,* his predecessors had "lost their will to manage." They had "simply lost control of the situation."

The "situation" began in 1968, when British Leyland was formed by a merger of British Motor Company, a behemoth that comprised several car makers, and the smaller Leyland, a truck manufacturer that also owned Triumph and Rover. The merger gave the new company 40 percent market share, but from the beginning it was a mess. Factories were not combined and remained unrationalized and uncontrolled. The new organization had about 30,000 extraneous employees, but none was laid off because of strong union opposition. At the same time, the company was gaining a reputation for poor quality and unattractive car designs. Its one successful model was the Austin Mini, which sold in large numbers across Europe, yet the company hadn't been able to show a profit from it. Cash was drying up, but instead of scaling back operations, management responded by diversifying, buying up companies in unrelated businesses such as printing and industrial refrigeration.

The CEO in the period leading up to British Leyland's demise was Donald Stokes, a highly respected businessman who had been head of the Leyland Truck and Bus Company. Years later, he was to comment, "I wasn't trained to run a company of 190,000 people." Stokes may not have been the best person to run a massive enterprise, but he was further hindered by his top management team. Edwardes describes the men who ran British Leyland's divisions as "barons," unwilling to accept that they were part of a larger organization that demanded coordination and cooperation—and sacrifice. Instead, each division operated as a separate entity, each with its own strategy, some of them turning out competing models that made the production of any one unprofitable. The center allowed the company to hurtle forward, without an overarching strategy to guide it through a marketplace that included fierce competition from Europe, the United States, and Japan.

But if British Leyland's top management wasn't focusing on strategy, it wasn't focusing its energies on much else, either. Human assets executives make it their focus to know who works where in their corporation, and they move people up, down, and out accordingly. When Edwardes arrived at British Leyland he had 2,000 senior-level managers evaluated for their capabilities, and found that at least 60 percent were in the wrong place, doing the wrong job. Previous management had let hundreds of people rise through the organization based on seniority alone, never testing, training, or talking to them about their performance or the company's objectives. The result was a company filled with unmotivated, underutilized managers. "They just put one foot in front of the other every day," comments a retired manager who worked at British Leyland at the time. "Every day, they attended to exactly what they had done the day before."

Given its situation, British Leyland may have very well benefited (in varying degrees) from the expertise or box approaches. Certainly the units had critical competitive information to share about quality, marketing, or design issues—virtually all of them were in the same business. This is precisely the reason Cable & Wireless's James Ross selected expertise management for his telecommunications firm. But at British Leyland, with the center's tacit approval, the "barons" kept their knowledge proprietary, to the organization's overall disadvantage. The center also failed to erect any kind of box to contain the company's sprawl. Any one of the crisis-management CEOs in chapter 8 would have made this his first order of business. Even with the successful Mini losing money, no modern reporting systems were installed, nor were other control programs that could have tracked and monitored the company's performance and assigned accountability where it belonged.

So if senior management was not focused on picking and implementing an appropriate approach to get British Leyland ahead, what was it doing? Mainly, it was battling with the unions. For years, labor had been at war with the company over wages and the length of the workweek. By the time Edwardes took over, a good day involved only a dozen work stoppages at British Leyland plants. In the first six months of 1977 alone, there were 357 walkouts in the main Longbridge plant, resulting in the loss of millions of dollars. The cash shortage that resulted was one of the main reasons why British Leyland had to persuade the banks to provide $175 million in emergency loans, which the government could not guarantee.

Edwardes, a South African who was then CEO of Chloride, an industrial battery manufacturer, landed amid this situation in 1977. Of his early days at British Leyland, he says there were only three people whom he trusted in the entire organization, and the feeling was probably mutual. He quickly set about changing that, not by making people like him but by picking two approaches—the box and human assets—and applying them relentlessly. If he wasn't popular, at least he was predictable, consistent in his goals, coherent in his values and objectives. He installed many tough reporting, accounting, and planning control systems, which led to factory closures and major layoffs, and at the same time conducted a massive housecleaning of management ranks. He fired people who underperformed, promoted those who showed promise, and brought in hundreds of new managers from the outside—some of whom he knew personally and who shared his vision. Still, progress was slow and painful. For years, there were repeated face-offs with the unions, both sides becoming more militant as time passed. Finally, three years after he took over, Edwardes got the concessions he believed were necessary to save the company. In 1982, workers were still striking, but on the order of 3 million lost man-hours in a year, not 33 million. And the company was again producing a winning model, the Mini Metro. This time, however, it was making money and the company knew how and why. Before he departed, Edwardes completed what he set out to do by selling off twelve divisions of British Leyland. Since then, twelve more have followed them. It is hardly the company that it once was, but it is more than it would have been had the center kept managing as it had—or not managing, as was more the case. British Leyland is a textbook example of a center without an approach, and thus a center without value. The company was lucky that the government saved it before it was too late, and perhaps even more fortunate to get a CEO who knew the importance of filling the void at the top with direction and purpose correctly suited to the situation.

Edwardes himself says leadership is all about "courage." This undoubtedly is true, but as the British Leyland case also proves, it is about the unwavering conviction to add value, when doing the opposite is the status quo.

AT DIGITAL EQUIPMENT CORP.: WHERE SUCCESS PLUS SUCCESS EQUALED FAILURE, SQUARED

Ask Bob Palmer what caused **Digital**'s downfall, and he'll reply, "It happens. Happens all the time."

He is not being glib: Palmer, Digital's chairman of the board, president, and CEO, recently researched the past fifteen years of American industry looking for examples of companies like Digital that had enjoyed spectacular success, then crashed. What he found, he says, indicates that, in business at least, there is something inherent about success that begets failure.

"When you are very successful, it leads you to believe you are very bright and you understand better. You must be smart--look how much money you're making," Palmer says. "Then the environment changes, and management goes into denial. It says, 'Let's keep doing what we did to make us successful, only more aggressively.' You're not allowed to talk about failure, as if it just can't happen. But because a certain arrogance and complacency have crept in all through the organization, that's what is going to happen. It's practically inevitable. It happened to us."

Digital's problems began, Palmer says, at the height of its glory days, in 1985. The company had been founded twenty-eight years earlier in an old mill building in Maynard, Massachusetts. There, Digital's world-renowned engineers invented the PDP-8, Digital's first minicomputer, a revolutionary system that changed the way scientists, mathematicians, and other engineers worked with massive amounts of data. In 1977, Digital introduced another breakthrough product, the VAX computer, a faster, even more powerful system that sparked enormous growth and profitability for the company. In four years, revenues tripled and with gross margins at 44 percent, profits did the same. By 1987, Digital stock was trading at close to $200 a share, and the company hired the *Queen Elizabeth II* ocean liner and docked it for use at a major product exposition. But cracks in the company's own hull were beginning to show.

The reason was as simple, and as complex, as the customer. For its entire history, Digital had been a technology-driven organization, letting its engineers tell the market what it needed. "The market wasn't mature enough to understand and articulate what was required, so people couldn't ask for what they wanted, because they didn't know what was possible," Palmer says. "As technologists, we decided for the customers, and we provided stuff, and they bought it.

"But at some point, of course, the market starts getting educated," Palmer continues. "And they start telling you what their needs are. We didn't listen."

Instead, Digital kept on producing proprietary closed systems, while the market was quickly shifting toward open systems, personal computers, and workstations.

"Customers would say, 'We want the flexibility, we want the openness' that PCs provide," Palmer says, "and we would answer, 'They're not powerful enough. They'll never be as good as this minicomputer or VAX computer.' And the customers would say again, 'But we really, *really* want a PC from you.' And we simply wouldn't hear it. There was an arrogance there."

Part of that arrogance came from fear, Palmer says. Managers were afraid to let go of the minicomputer because with it went their expertise, and quite possibly their jobs.

"The problem was that all of the threatened people were entrenched in the company. They had designed the old way, they liked it, and they were rewarded for it," Palmer reflects. "They liked the old model of Digital, in which we offered approximately everything, everywhere, all the time, for everybody. We had this huge product line in terms of breadth; we built customized systems in modest volumes, which we sold at a high price."

Unfortunately for Digital, the new model—the model the entire industry was turning toward—was standardized systems or stand-alone products, sold in high volumes for a low price.

How could Digital have missed this change? Palmer says some company insiders didn't. He says there were some managers who "jumped up and down," but the organization was not prepared to abandon its old strategy and focus on the minicomputer. In its early years Digital's approach had been to develop technology expertise—the company would make the best minicomputers in the world—then hire and reward those who shared this expertise. It worked only too well. But a technology-based industry like computing demands more attention to strategy and more openness to change, especially since customers' needs evolve as the technology does—and often lead it. This is the reason Michael Dell, at Dell Computer, has made listening to 50,000 customer phone calls a day an organizational priority—to keep the company's vision market focused and fresh. Digital's vision grew stale and lost its market focus, creating the kind of situation that Stephen Friedman, of Goldman Sachs, warns against. "If you're not moving forward, then you're moving backward," he said, "because everyone else will pass you by."

What happened at Digital, in fact, stands in marked contrast to several examples from the change organizations examined earlier. At Goldman, for instance, Friedman, along with his management team, put in place a number of systems that let change percolate to the top: he set up committees of "Doberman pinschers" to generate new ideas, he rewarded innovative employees with promotions, he championed mavericks who demanded radical breaks with the status quo. J. P. Bolduc of W.R. Grace had his own methods for shaking up his staid box organization and turning it into one that embraced change as a way of doing business: traveling around the world, meeting with employees through the night, answering E-mail, setting up a toll-free hot line for ideas and complaints. Another change executive, Naohiko Kumagai, president of Mitsui, used his people policies to create a flexible environment. He forced accountability into Mitsui's divisions, urging managers to get as close as possible to their customers and respond to their needs swiftly.

At Digital, senior management eschewed these methods, reinforcing an organization built around the technology that drove the minicomputer. The company's problems deepened. In 1990, sales of products began to slow while costs accelerated. A restructuring effort was launched at a cost of $550 million, without results. The next year, Digital posted a $1.1 billion restructuring charge, sparking the company's first-ever loss—of $617 million. Losses continued the following year, and by the middle of 1992, Ken Olsen, the company's founder and president, was forced to exit. After he departed, the company he had founded thirty-five years before was losing $3 million a day. Three years later, more than half of its factories around the world had been closed and its workforce slashed from 137,000 to 60,000.

The board quickly replaced Olsen with Palmer, a fifty-three-year-old Texan whose background is true grit. He was born in a peanut-farming community and separated from his family when he was fifteen. He worked to help put himself through Texas Tech, but was financially successful by the time he was forty, when a computer chip company he co-founded was bought out. He joined Digital in 1985, and was vice president of manufacturing and logistics when he was picked for the top job.

His goal was reinvention; the failed approach that preceded him left no other option. "I came into this office knowing I had to change this company, change everything about it," Palmer says.

Halfway through the process today, Palmer's efforts have begun to yield encouraging results—encouraging enough that some industry observers say that Digital may just become the turnaround story of the 1990s.

In the next chapter—on crisis management—we will examine the details of Palmer's recovery program, a case study in what it takes to get a company from past imperfect to future imperative.

PAST IMPERFECT:
NOT AN ENDING, BUT AN OPPORTUNITY

Asking why a company has failed is somewhat like asking why the *Titanic* sank. Was it the iceberg? The captain's navigational incompetence? The ship's faulty construction? The lookout crew's negligence? The arrogance of thinking the ship was unsinkable? Or was it all of them in some measure, combined?

Success, as Allen Sheppard, of GrandMet, says, is "dead easy." Failure is complicated. But these stories suggest that the center's management approach—and its match to the market—offers a way of understanding the roots of both. The examples in this chapter indicate that companies fail when approaches fail, most often because they are not married to the business situation. Approaches also appear to fail when they are incorrectly executed. At Wang, the very vision driving the strategy approach wasn't revisited to keep it relevant and fresh. At ITT, the box was so tight it stifled creativity, flexibility, and long-term thinking. At Digital, expertise-driven managers hung on to a competency that had lost significance to the customer. British Leyland was an example of the extreme: no approach, no added value.

But these four companies also suggest that although they are never the same in shape or scope, companies at the brink *can* be brought back. Our next chapter on firefighting CEOs hears six voices that describe how.

8

MANAGEMENT IN EXTREMIS:
THE APPROACHES IN CRISIS

One day in 1991, Kjell Nilsson walked into the corporate offices of **Trelleborg,** the major Swedish industrial group where he was CEO, called together his staff, and then hung his suit coat on the back of his chair.

"I'll put it back on when I return," he announced. He was forty-two at the time, his manner vigorous, even forceful. "Because right now we have to roll up our sleeves and get to work. We have companies that are in trouble."

In the year that followed, Nilsson and his staff doubled production in Trelleborg's metals and mining division while halving costs in another, the wholesale division. Together with its co-owner of Falconbridge Ltd. in Canada, jointly held by Trelleborg and a Canadian forestry and mining group, they installed systems to radically improve efficiency and reduce costs. And finally, they brought back from the brink Munksjö, Trelleborg's then-ailing pulp and paper company.

"What good was I if I could not save the company?" Nilsson asks now, once again behind his desk at Trelleborg headquarters. "We had companies that were dying, and that is our job here, to save them."

Nilsson is one of the six CEOs profiled in this chapter, and while he might personally be the most outspoken of the group, his story is not unique. All six took over companies on the precipice of disaster, and all six had to take drastic action to save them. Their voices sound different—Linn Macdonald of Canada's **Noranda Forest Inc.** is as subdued as Nilsson is forthright, but in several key ways these crisis CEOs are a breed apart, a breed united. Turning around a company is not an approach in the same way human assets and box management are. Crisis is a situation, and the CEOs we spoke to responded to it with strikingly similar approaches. First, all of the executives in this category began by erecting boxes to introduce control to out-of-control situations. Simultaneously, they all launched bold, often experimental initiatives, using many of the tools mentioned by change-agent CEOs. None of these firefighters could talk about his experience without mentioning the personal toll of fixing a broken company: the pain of layoffs, the sale of divisions, the struggle to rebuild morale. By the same token, none of them could deny the thrill of the challenge. (Some even say they would consider taking on another turnaround company.) But perhaps the most remarkable similarity among all these CEOs is what Jim Will of **Armco** calls the "legacy" of going into battle and winning. That legacy is that, as a manager, you never relax again. The war keeps raging inside you.

Now that the fire is out at Armco, Will, like the others in this chapter, describes his management style as what we have called the expertise approach. Yet, he adds: "People ask me, 'Jim, is it over now?' And I tell them, 'No, it's not over. It's never going to be over.' People have to realize that. We may have some divisions that are doing well now, but we can't forget what came before. We can never forget."

AT DIGITAL: STARING REALITY IN THE FACE AND NOT BLINKING

When **Digital** was at rock bottom in 1992, industry observers were busy writing its obituary. Bob Palmer, as noted in the previous chapter, is putting an end to that with several successive quarters of profitability, and in delivering those results, he offers an unfolding study in how to fight a fire of immense proportions.

Like many of his colleagues in crisis situations, Palmer's first action as CEO was to seize control of costs. In particular, he focused on Digital's research and engineering spending and its overhead, cutting the first by 36 percent and the latter by 27 percent. At the same time, the layoffs he began in his previous manufacturing role continued, ultimately reducing the company's head count by more than 50 percent.

But Palmer stresses that the Digital recovery story is not about financial gymnastics, a turnaround created by random cutbacks. It is instead, he remarks, a turnaround created by a new attitude that has everyone in the company focused on the reality of the marketplace, no matter how harsh or daunting its demands.

"One of the more difficult things we had to do, but it was one of the most important, was to get the organization through the denial phase about the marketplace and everything we had done here, and get it to accept the world as it is, not as we would prefer it to be," Palmer says, referring to the company's former focus on closed systems over open ones.

In large part, accepting the "world as it is" has meant getting Digital's business units to focus solely and relentlessly on what the customer wants, not on what its engineers can provide, Palmer says.

"We had to get people to understand that only the customer could guarantee their jobs. This is an *attitudinal* change, a cultural transformation, a very, very difficult one, but it's reality. Solving our problem here wasn't going to be just about holding down costs, or spending 20 percent less on some project or another, or living within the budget. You have to have a totally different model for doing business."

Digital's new model, a customer-driven organization, means that every employee must "separate what needs to be done from how difficult it is," Palmer says. Responding to the marketplace *is* hard— that's a given, Palmer asserts. It is also no excuse for inaction.

It is to these two key messages about attitude and focus that Palmer devoted most of his time during the first phase of Digital's recovery. In part, he communicated them through those he hired, fired, and promoted. He also changed the company's compensation and bonus system to recognize employees who embodied the right attitude and focused their attention on the market. Likewise, he canceled projects that didn't jibe with Digital's new direction.

At the same time, Palmer met frequently with employees around the world. "Question and answer sessions, 'town meetings,' one-on-one conversations, videos—a CEO doesn't have many other tools as effective as these to spread the message," he says, a comment echoed by several other crisis managers. "And unless the CEO hammers the message and hammers it and hammers it, it doesn't stick, especially when it's an unpleasant message," he adds. "I mean, we're going from a culture that was very paternalistic and said it would take care of everyone forever, to a culture that says every individual had better make sure he or she adds value to the customer or they're history. That's the kind of message that has to be said over and over again, every way and every time I can."

Since Digital registered several profitable quarters and its stock price began its upward surge, Palmer says he finally has the freedom to look to the future, tackling the kind of questions and analysis of a strategic CEO. He continued to push the company into 64-bit technology ahead of the rest of the industry, he says, in order to be there first for customers, and is currently critically examining companies with which to pursue partnerships. Palmer says he and his management team are also focusing on how Digital designs and introduces new products.

Discussing these initiatives, Palmer sounds energized—but he strikes another common chord of crisis managers when he speaks to the endurance required by a turnaround and the personal toll it takes.

"This is a marathon, and we might be at the halfway point," he says, "and part of what we have to say to our people is, 'By the way, your reward for winning is you get to run next week.' I mean, you never stop."

Have Digital's recent results made the marathon any easier or more enjoyable? Palmer is forceful with his answer. "It's been so painful. It's hard to find anything satisfying about this experience. We've reduced our population in half on a worldwide basis. Most of those decisions, I'm directly responsible for. I didn't personally discharge each person, but there's no question I'm responsible."

He says it will be the year 2000 before he knows if those layoffs were for naught, or for the cause of truly rescuing Digital.

"If I still have the privilege of having this position at the end of this century, and I can see that 80 or 90 percent of our decisions were right, then that would be very satisfying," he reflects. "I'm looking forward to that, but we won't know until then."

In the meantime, Palmer says one of his chief roles will remain never letting Digital fall into the complacency that nearly destroyed it. Success, as he noted in the previous chapter, has an insidious way of begetting failure.

"We can't forget the lessons that we've learned very painfully in this company," he says. "It will be quite some time before we're successful enough to feel complacent again, but the possibility exists, and I'm accountable for that. That's the CEO's job. That's my job."

ARMCO: TO THE BRINK AND BACK

The story of **Armco**'s demise actually starts with its extraordinary success in the heyday of American steel in the 1960s and 1970s. Bolstered by the cash flowing in from its core steel-rolling technologies, Armco expanded into six other businesses, few of them directly related to the company's expertise. But then the recession of 1982–84 hit, and Armco took it harder than most; the company veered close to bankruptcy on several occasions. Management quickly pulled the conglomerate out of its diversified businesses and reduced the size of the ones that remained. It wasn't enough. Even in its steel divisions, Armco was incorrectly positioned strategically to compete with other American, as well as Japanese and Third World, producers, and it continued to hemorrhage money throughout the decade. A massive restructuring program was put into place, but thirteen years later it still was not producing results. (In 1991, for instance, Armco lost $336 million on $1.2 billion in sales.)

In 1992, Armco acquired Cyclops Industries, a company in the stainless steel industry. Jim Will came along with the purchase, and after acting as COO for two years, was named Armco's CEO. Under his direction, the restructuring has continued, but Will has introduced other, perhaps more fundamental changes as part of his campaign to save the company. In 1994, Armco finally showed a profit—$77 million against $1.4 billion in sales—and several Wall Street analysts upgraded the stock from "hold" to "buy" status.

But Will hardly broke out the Champagne. If anything, the results made him even more of the roadside preacher he had become since joining Armco. His gospel is about winning; he is looking for converts.

"I've got to get everybody into this war, I really, truly believe that," he says about Armco's turnaround, his expression turning from affable to adamant as his momentum increases. "This is an all-out war, from a world standpoint. Everybody is trying to take our company away from us. We are trying to win it back and become a very successful company. I cannot do that by myself. I've got to have every man, woman, and child in this company fighting for it with me."

That said, it is no surprise that Will describes his role at Armco as the person responsible for getting the message about radical change to his employees. He sees himself as the company's chief communicator, its commander-in-chief as it marches into battle after battle. A bit of hyperbole? Undoubtedly. But on a day-to-day basis, it means Will spends much of his time talking to groups of employees at every level of the corporation about joining his army. It means he travels to plants in Butler, Coshocton, and Zanesville, Pennsylvania, and walks among the machine workers, spreading his own version of the "good news." It means he attends strategy sessions, company picnics, training classes, and performance reviews.

But Will's activities, in reality, extend far beyond rallying the troops with inspirational speeches. In describing his schedule, it becomes clear that his job involves creating and implementing the systems that make change possible, and most of these systems come down to people—how they are hired, why they are fired, where they are trained, and how they are paid. Moreover, Will devotes his time to setting an explicit example for his managers of how they should organize their time. "They've got to see me doing it right," he says. "That's how a culture gets reborn."

At the core of Will's passionate push for change is his conviction that Armco has to, as he puts it, "get next to the customer." This notion of being market driven is fundamental in most retail businesses, but in the monolithic, volume-driven world of steel making, it can sound like heresy. In fact, until recently, it even made Will uncomfortable.

"It's hard to put people first, to put the customer first, because of our engineering," he says. "I'm an engineer. That's my background, where I came from. I think equipment. I think volume. I think capacity. I think long runs. I don't think customer.

"But you *have* to think customer. It's a matter of survival. It sounds simple, right? It sounds so simple to say we're going to focus on the customer now. But it's so hard to put into practice."

Still, that is what Will wants Armco to do. That's what he is de-manding. And he is making it happen, he says, by converting—or clearing out—the people who work for him.

"You need to have systems in place, systems that tie you to the customer electronically, for instance, or systems that let you keep your customer's inventory," Will explains. "But that alone won't do it, because there is the people side of the equation, where you need people who are looking at the customer and saying, 'How can I help him do better?' You need people who say, 'How can I get Armco into the equation of helping that customer do better?' Now, imagine if you have everyone saying that. That is really a success story. The whole culture has changed."

But how to get there? Will says he has started by figuring out what kind of employees were likely to be customer focused. "And to do that, I'll be honest with you, we had to get inside people's heads and we had to start talking about the competencies of people needed to do these jobs." This has involved bringing psychologists into Armco, sending them into the best plants, and asking them to determine which people were responsible for the successful operations. In one case, Will recalls, he asked the psychologists to identify a successful plant's *real* leader.

"They came back and said there were no leaders in that plant—in our most successful plant, in terms of customer service, and our most profitable plant. I said, 'What? There's no leader down there?' And they said, 'No, you have the best single *team* we have ever seen in our lifetime. Everybody works together. Everybody gives the credit to everyone else. But nothing gets done without the team.' Well, that opened my eyes."

After that experience, Will says, he reshaped his notion of what kind of person belonged at Armco, and he decided to put in place a training system to encourage team behavior. Today, Armco operates one of its plants as a "school," where promising managers attend yearlong stints.

"We are trying to create a different kind of boss at Armco now," Will explains. "A boss who is a team player, who gives credit to the people down below, who sees a person down there who needs some help and who picks him out and says, 'I'm going to get you that help you need,' who is in constant communication with that employee about how he is doing. That is the kind of boss we are talking about today. He's almost like a parapsychologist, this guy. And when we find a guy like that, we've got to get him out on the front lines.

"In the past," Will adds with a laugh, "when we found someone good, we moved him right into Corporate, took him right out of the mainstream. Not very effective, but that's what we did."

But if Will sounds anxious to hire, train, and promote the right kind of people—people eager to put the customer first—he also says that many times he has had to fire those who don't get with his new program.

"It's tough," he says, "because finally you have to say, 'Joe is not the right guy. He used to be a good salesman, but he's not a good salesman under this new scheme. We've got to get rid of Joe.' That's tough, but you have to be willing to change the organization in order to make this work."

Firing employees "is the hardest thing for me to do," Will reflects, "because I thought we could train all people to be different, but I've found that's not so. There's something inside a person who wants to have that servantlike attitude to the customer that we can't find in everybody. And if someone at Armco doesn't have it, you have to do it. You have to let them go."

Along with managing people for change, Will manages himself to set the example for change. He says he spends 25 percent of his time with customers, to learn their needs but also to develop a model of how to talk and listen to them. He offers to send his people into the customers' plants to discuss solutions to manufacturing or other problems, and he sometimes asks if they will send their people into Armco plants. "That's when the bonding starts to happen. That's how relationships get formed. I get ideas from customers you wouldn't believe," Will says. Those ideas, he adds, are quickly passed down to the managers and the plants, both to share information and also to spread the message that the CEO is, as he says, "walking the talk" of being market driven.

Finally, Will says he is working on changing the company's incentive and compensation package to turn his preaching into dollars and cents for his employees. The details of the changes are not yet finalized, but Will says that bonuses, benefits, and salary, once determined by an employee's tenure, will be more variable, linked closely to company and individual performance.

The goal, Will says, is for Armco to build on success stories like the one he loves to tell about a company called Arvin Industries, a customer based in Columbus, Indiana, that makes automotive exhaust systems.

"We were supplying 20 percent of their material, and they *hated* us," Will recalls with a smile. "And we decided to use them as a test case of everything Armco could do differently if we had a winning strategy going. And we decided we were really going to make this happen.

"First, we changed the people who talked to them because they weren't the right people. We changed the systems we used to integrate with them. We sent our research people in to talk about their business—what their problems were and who their customers were and what they wanted. And we made them like they were a division of our own.

"I will tell you," Will says, "that in June of next year, we will be a 100 percent sole supplier to them. They will deal with nobody else."

Again, no cause for Champagne. "You know, you can do anything once with one customer, we know that," Will says. "The trick of this game is to do it for all customers, all the time, day after day. I don't think we can do that today. . . .

"It's the long haul that wins, you know," he adds. "At any given time, one army is going to beat another army. But in the long haul, who is going to win the day? It's the guy who has the fundamentals in place. And I've got to constantly get those fundamentals out there. Everybody has got to."

Will shakes his head. "You know, there are people out there who tell me all this 'war' stuff is malarkey. They say we can relax now. And I understand that. It's part of human nature to want the change to stop."

But here Will talks about the legacy of his job. "Change is going to be there every day, from now on. It's never going to stop, because our competitors are out there innovating, and our customers are out there with their needs changing," he says. For a moment, he sounds daunted, but then he continues and clearly he is not.

"Part of my job is to show people that it is possible to have an organization constantly in crisis and still have a good time," he says. Asked if he is having one himself, he smiles.

"Well, I never thought it would occur to me, or that I would feel this way, but I am really having a lot of fun, a lot of fun going out and finding ideas, and looking at things and bringing those ideas back and trying to understand how they match up with our organization. I see the gleam in the eyes of a lot of people," he says. "Some of them are working until eight or ten at night on projects, and I seeing there's a little spirit picking up here.

"You know," Will admits, "this is kind of a neat thing happening."

NORANDA FOREST:
SEEING THE FOREST FOR THE TREES

Linn Macdonald knew **Noranda Forest Inc.** was in trouble when he took over in 1991. "The whole industry was in distress," he notes, he just didn't realize how much.

"The company I came into wasn't running successfully," Macdonald explains. "So there were quite a few changes to make." He is soft-spoken, and chooses his words carefully, as if not to aggrandize his actions. But there is no getting around the fact that the changes Macdonald made were sweeping in their scope, the first to stop the bleeding, the remainder to rebuild Noranda Forest's strategy, culture, and operating procedures.

When Macdonald came to Noranda Forest from Abitibi-Price Inc. —another company in the forest products industry but not a direct competitor—the firm was about to lose $200 million that year. A lot of money, certainly, but it was not alone. The entire pulp and paper products industry was in a down cycle at that time, burdened with the worldwide decrease in demand and the recent installation of several $500-million machines that led to overcapacity, and the resultant crippling price cut in commodity products. Noranda Forest was further hurt by the fact that its other businesses, pulp and building-material products, were also in downturns, creating a three-pronged assault that put the firm's performance at the lowest in its history.

Macdonald walked into this situation hoping for an upturn in the economy to aid him. But he soon discovered that Noranda Forest's problems were deeper and wider than a bad down cycle. It had to do with the company's former strategy—or lack thereof—and with attitudes and operating styles.

"The fellow who was here before me had a very hands-off style. He took the role of industry spokesman, which was something he liked and enjoyed and did very well. He didn't spend as much time on the businesses themselves," Macdonald says. "The company operated in a very decentralized fashion, with individual units able to spend the cash that they generated. Capital expenditures in general didn't follow any clear long-term plan or allocation procedure." As a result, Noranda had no explicit road map for managing the industry's cycles, save to ride them out.

If that wasn't enough, Macdonald also soon learned that Noranda had $300 million in debt in the form of demand loans from Canadian chartered banks. "We were afraid, quite quickly, that some bank might look at our negative cash flows and come to the conclusion it was smart to say, 'Time's up, time to pay,'" Macdonald recalls. "And as soon as that happened, we fully expected the other banks to be on their heels.

"So I wouldn't say we were better or worse than other firms in the industry in terms of management," he adds, "but we were certainly financed more precariously."

Macdonald acted swiftly. Strategy could wait. The first thing to do was to get the banks off Noranda's back.

"We went into a hand-holding mode with the banks," he said, although if pressed, he will admit that for the first year, it was mainly he who dealt with the loan officers assigned to Noranda Forest's case. (The company was without a CFO until early 1992.) "Our communications with the banks became much more frequent and more honest," Macdonald says. "We would say, 'Look, here are our results for the quarter. Here's our explanation. Here's where we've made progress. Here's what we're going to do in the next quarter.' All we had to do," Macdonald says, "was paint a picture that we were doing at least as well as the other companies in the industry. We were selling the hope that we were going to get better and we were going to get out of this."

At the same time, Macdonald was concentrating on working capital, cutting all but necessary capital expenditures, and selling businesses that were cash drains, such as three small sawmills. He was also curtailing the free flow of money to the company's units. All cash generated came to the center and was reallocated from there.

Asked if the business units objected to the change in procedure, Macdonald says with a laugh, "I'm six-foot-four so it didn't hurt me too much." More seriously, he adds, "No, really . . . people understood that something had to be done. They [the business unit CEOs] realized we had to make the changes, or someone else was going to come in and do it for us. They cooperated."

For more than a year and a half, Macdonald kept Noranda Forest in this holding pattern—talking frequently with the banks and clamping down on company spending—but he ultimately knew it was not enough to get the company out from under its huge debt.

"It became clear the only option, really, was to sell our holding in MacMillan Bloedel," Macdonald says. This was no small decision; MacMillan Bloedel was considered by many to be Noranda Forest's crown jewel, the largest forest products company in Canada. Noranda Forest owned 49 percent of the firm and each year received about $15 million in dividends, but at the same time it was paying $100 million a year in interest on $1 billion of debt to finance the holding. "MacMillan Bloedel was a good company with good prospects, but it had no plans to share its cash flow with us," Macdonald says. "We had to do something about it, or else sell off the other divisions."

Macdonald's next task was to convince Noranda's board of directors that divesting MacMillan Bloedel made sense. He recalls that it wasn't difficult, once he presented the other options. Soon after, a group of underwriters purchased all of Noranda Forest's shares in MacMillan Bloedel in a "bought deal," infusing the firm with $930 million over the course of two years.

"It did take the pressure off," Macdonald says, and you can hear the relief in his voice even in remembering the sale. "It eliminated the drain immediately. We were able to start paying down debt immediately, and we went to Moody's and had our credit rating upgraded to Triple B-minus—which isn't great, but it wasn't junk—and we were able to issue some convertible debentures and get two chunks of long-term debt, totaling $400 million in all. And so the shareholders started feeling much more confident. We were out from under the banks.

"I can't tell you," Macdonald says almost buoyantly, "for an engineer who had spent his career building things, only to find himself spending much of his time fending off banks, what a treat it was to be out of that situation."

With this new freedom Macdonald himself felt the confidence to move forward with other radical changes in the way Noranda was run, from an operational standpoint.

His first step was to create a clear, common understanding of the role of the corporate office, and to make sure everyone in management shared it. He explicitly communicated what he had said in his first months—that all cash from the units came to the center, and then was allocated from there according to Corporate needs. Each business unit was self-contained in terms of marketing and manufacturing and able to control its own results, but its strategic plans had to jibe with Noranda Forest's overall strategic vision. And speaking of plans, that process was to change, also. Gone were the days when they were presented for Corporate's perfunctory review. Macdonald scrutinized business plans closely, questioning them, refining them, and expecting them to be met. He set a corporate goal of profitability in the top quartile of the industry, and he told managers he didn't want excuses, he wanted performance.

As results improved and cash started coming in, Macdonald sought to bring top managers into the turnaround process. And to that end, he asked them to develop plans for growth through acquisition, marketing, or new products. He expected, he says, ten times as many proposals as could be supported. He got none.

It was this disappointing experience that pushed Macdonald toward other approaches. First, he hired a strategic consulting firm. "When we went to the divisions to ask for strategic plans, no one was able to get beyond their own facilities. They wanted to spend money on what they already had," Macdonald says. "We decided we had to have a top-down approach to decide which products had opportunities, which production facilities had capacity, and what looked good for the future, and at that point it made sense to bring in some perspective from the outside. To get the big picture."

Simultaneously, Macdonald changed the incentive structure of his top managers, rewarding them not only for how their units performed but also in equal parts for the individual performance and overall corporate results. He then initiated an annual two-day off-site session with divisional CEOs to drive home the interrelatedness of Noranda Forest's businesses. Finally, Macdonald replaced two of four division CEOs, plus others in the top management ranks.

In a cyclical industry, of course, it is hard to tell exactly how well management efforts such as Macdonald's have paid off. In 1994,

Noranda had a good year: revenue was $1.3 billion and income was $106 million. But Macdonald is the first to tell you that the economy has picked up, the cycle is on the upswing.

Still, you believe him when he tells you Noranda Forest will never return to the days when an engineer had to concentrate on the financials of the business rather than on its fundamentals.

"The first year, we were really just running fast enough to keep away from the people snapping at our heels," he says. "But there's been a tremendous change. Today I came to a meeting where we were talking about acquisitions. It's very exciting.

"We have goals now," Macdonald remarks. "We are planning ways to see the cycles coming so we don't get caught in the middle of capital projects when money is scarce. We're moving aggressively into some value-added products." He names thermal paper, the rolled kind used in facsimile machines, and oriented strand board, a competitor of plywood, as two.

"You know, the money is going to start rolling in again," Macdonald acknowledges, "the markets are going to be good for the next few years. But the challenge will be—can we keep people focused on making improvements?

"I keep getting accused of moving the bar up in terms of standards," Macdonald says with a self-deprecating laugh. "Everyone accepts the center setting pretty outrageous standards when the company is in trouble. In good times, we have to keep pushing up the bar. That's my role."

He pauses for a long moment, and then adds, "The real test is to see how we come through the next downturn."

UNITED DOMINION:
"IT SHAPES YOU . . . IT TRANSFORMS YOU"

Before the turn of the century, a Canadian company called Dominion Bridge left its mark in steel and concrete by constructing the massive bridges that spanned Canada, and for decades afterward, that company thrived in the heavy-duty business of building North America's infrastructure, erecting train stations, government buildings, and hotels. During World War II, the company moved into the fabrication of steel, ships, marine engines, boilers, and condensers. Afterward, it expanded even further into products not seen on any store shelves but that touch people's lives constantly, such as the steel systems inside low- and medium-rise buildings; the equipment that processes food, drinks, and drugs; and the machinery that builds roads and airports. In the 1960s, the company broke into the oil refinery and petrochemical businesses, designing processes and plants. All this growth meant success in equal measure. By the 1970s, Dominion Bridge, renamed AMCA International after a number of acquisitions and mergers and relocation to the United States, was awash in cash.

What followed was a fifteen-year diversification binge, during which AMCA grew to fifty-one businesses in five segments. (The acquisition campaign was based on senior management's belief that the United States was about to experience a boom in manufacturing.) Suddenly, the company that had started by building bridges owned a jewelry firm, a construction equipment manufacturer, and a machine tool maker—and now it was practically drowning in debt. In a *Forbes* magazine article published in 1986, aptly headlined "Shop Until You Drop," it was estimated that AMCA's debt, at $570 million, was twice its equity. The company lost $120 million in that year alone, and its stock, down from a high of 24, languished near 8, slightly above its book value. In fact, *Forbes* suggested, the only reason why AMCA's stock was trading at 8 at all was because 51 percent of the company was owned by Canadian Pacific, which was thought to be a sympathetic parent.

Bill Holland stepped into this situation when he took over as CEO in 1986. Reared in a small Oklahoma town, Holland was an attorney in Arkansas before joining AMCA's legal department in 1973. He worked in various executive positions, including chief administrative officer, before he was appointed to the top job of a company he himself describes as "out of control."

"Let me hasten to say I was certainly not a so-called turnaround expert," Holland recalls of the time, "but we were faced with the exigencies of the moment." In other words, he became one—fast.

Like Linn Macdonald at Noranda, the first thing Holland did was declare that cash was king. Strategy was not relevant. Stock price was not relevant. Long-term planning was not relevant. Only cash flow mattered.

To that end, Holland started selling off all divisions that were not related to the company's three core competencies. In two years, the company's fifty-one businesses became twenty-one; five segments became three—industrial products, engineering services, and construction products and services. The balance sheet told the story: in 1985, AMCA's net worth totaled $1.4 billion; in 1991, it was $873 million.

"In those first three or four years after I took over the company and was working through this restructuring, I spent no time on outside activities. I wasn't on any boards. I spent my time either with my family or on the company," Holland recalls. "And I spent almost no time in the strategic area, because it was survival mode. It was survival and redressment. Whatever it takes to pay down the debt, redress the balance sheet, and obtain a positive cash flow, that was the order of the day."

At the same time, Holland was sending a new message to all business unit heads: improve performance by a set date or else face liquidation or divestment. He made good on his word, and many executives left during this period.

"It was extremely stressful. I could not overemphasize that," says Holland, speaking in his office on the twenty-fourth floor of **United Dominion**'s Charlotte, North Carolina, headquarters. (The firm was renamed United Dominion in 1990.) "And it shapes you. It transforms you as an individual and a manager. It inculcates values and principles, and it makes you see things in a way you would never see them if you had not gone through a trying period of some kind in your life."

Holland is thoughtful as he continues, gazing occasionally at the panoramic view of the North Carolina countryside beyond his windows. "I don't necessarily recommend it as a way to shape a manager," he reflects, "but I think it has a tremendous benefit once you've gone through it."

For Holland, that benefit has translated into the way he now runs the company. He has put in place a system that he believes creates "controlled entrepreneurship" among the business units. That is, he gives the divisions as much responsibility for their actions as possible, and he leaves them alone, by and large, as long as these actions produce profits. The business units can consider and pursue acquisitions. They define their own strategies, devise their own marketing plans, design their own product lines. The corporate office acts as a place for advice and suggestions; it gives the units financial support to make moves they could not make alone. "We just bought a small company in Mexico for one of our businesses," Holland offers as an example. "They're not going to make big bucks out of that for a while. But it gives us a beachhead in Mexico, and it gives us more of an opportunity to take product there. It was an opportunity that one division standing alone, just based on the numbers, might find it difficult to do." As another example, he mentions a recent conversation in which he suggested to a business unit that it explore the Chinese market. "We have three joint ventures going in China that they didn't know about, but we in Corporate can see across the lines, so that's the kind of counsel they get from us, rather than anything having to do with the mundane day-to-day decisions."

Except, that is, when performance is not acceptable. Then Holland moves in, quickly and with great purpose—it's the turnaround legacy at work.

"Even right now, when we're doing very well, we're saying to units that are not performing, 'We'll have this action by a certain date. Otherwise, we'll sell it, close it down, change management, or some other form of action that will stop the drain.' Basically we have an ironclad rule . . . that you will not survive in this company very long if you lose money, period. Period." There is no theater in Holland's voice. His words are plainspoken.

"I mean, I started here when we were doing so well, it was inconceivable that we would ever get into the trouble we were in," Holland goes on. "And I don't look upon myself as a cynical person, but I'll say that I am much more questioning now about things that you hear that are sort of trite excuses. You'll hear, 'Well, the market is in bad shape.' And what that manager is really saying is, 'We're doing everything right, but the market is not rewarding us.'

"And these trite statements just sort of perpetuate themselves," Holland says. "But I don't believe them. Really, there can be no reason for underperformance."

Which is why Holland spends a good percentage of his time traveling to United Dominion's operations, spreading this exact message; even if the crisis is over, cash flow is still king and always will be. He often travels with just one or two other members of the corporate staff, and asks for no "dog and pony shows," as he calls them. "We'll tour a plant, meet with employees in a nonpressurized way. The point is to tell them the United Dominion story, what we're trying to do." Holland also started a company newspaper, and has begun to send out a video of himself twice a year, talking about the company's goals and guidelines. "We spend a lot of time commending people, patting them on the back," Holland says, "but also being upfront with them. If you're not performing, you'll be told that. You'll be told relatively soon what our attitude is about it, and what you must do to correct it."

That said, Holland does point out that his job these days is a lot more fun than it used to be. He describes it, in fact, as a "tremendous joy after suffering the travail of the turmoil." But he returns just as quickly to the lessons of that turmoil. It humbled him, he says, probably forever. In 1994, United Dominion brought in more than $2 billion in revenues and $62 million in net income, and it expects an even better year in 1995. (By mid-1995, the company's stock price had gone as high as 25$^{1}/_{8}$; apparently the market expected markedly improved results, too.) But Holland, like the others in this chapter, says you never forget what you've been through.

"I've seen far too many CEOs who have, frankly, what I'll call pride, insufferable ego, or whatever. There are people who say it goes with the territory. I don't think that it does," he says quietly. "I also see a lot who don't have that and are filled with humility and a sense of appreciation. And those are the ones who I like and respect, and I really believe are great leaders."

Holland doesn't explicitly put himself in that category—that's not his style—but United Dominion's shareholders might.

FUJI BANK—FIGHTING THE FIRE AT THE "BEST BANK"

Just as Tolstoy said that every unhappy family is unhappy in its own way, every unhappy company, it seems, is likewise unique. Armco fell into disarray when it lost touch with its customers. Noranda's beleaguered era was ushered in by an economic downturn and a disengaged chief executive. United Dominion's problems arose from a nonsensical diversification binge. But even with these differences, one constant remains. The turnaround began *after* profits collapsed.

By the time the CEOs at each company technically became firefighters, the flames had reached the sky.

Then what to make of **Fuji Bank,** where the president went into emergency mode when there was only a lit match in the forest? The year was 1991, and not only was Fuji the largest bank in the world in terms of assets—nearly $595 billion—but earnings were up to nearly $1.2 billion. Was *this* a turnaround situation?

To hear Toru Hashimoto tell it, the answer is yes. At fifty-nine, he is soft-spoken, unpretentious, and remarkably down-to-earth for a man running a company with the power and prestige of Fuji Bank. "The business was in danger," he says of his decision to reinvent the company under his command. "If we went along as we were, without any changes, the organization, the customer base, and any human feeling that existed in either group, would all be destroyed."

Since he took over, Hashimoto has put into motion radical reform at the gigantic institution, a program unusual in Japan for its pace, its range, and its details. A popular three-year strategic plan was abandoned and high-level managers were transferred. The president himself broke with the tradition of the unapproachable chief executive and met informally with bank clerks over coffee or beer, not once, but more than eighty times. Employees were urged to raise "harsh and discordant voices" in the name of change, and were rewarded for doing so.

As a result, profits dropped by nearly 50 percent, but Hashimoto appears unfazed. Like the other business leaders in this chapter, he sees Fuji Bank's turnaround as a do-or-die proposition. "I feel that this year, or next year, or the year after, we will begin to see the benefits of this process," he says in a quiet voice. In contrast to many Japanese CEOs, Hashimoto is relaxed and frank, putting visitors immediately at ease. "We will see our way through the problems," he says.

It's not hard to put a date on the beginnings of Fuji Bank's problems, as Hashimoto defines them. The crisis began in 1990, when the bubble burst—that is, when many of the huge Japanese companies were hit by a recession, and in turn sapped the banking industry of its strength. Like many other financial giants, Fuji Bank saw major commercial loans go bad. Then, in 1991, the organization took another, extremely public hit in what was called the Akasaka incident. It involved fraudulent loans granted by Fuji Bank totaling $2.5 billion, many of them masterminded by a manager at the Akasaka branch. At the same time, information about other similar schemes at Fuji emerged—information about forged certificates of deposit that had been used to raise other fraudulent loans for four years running. As a result of both scandals, Chairman Taizo Hashida resigned, and several top managers followed him. Shortly afterward, a former Fuji employee published his memoirs, which described the Fuji culture as inhumane and obsessed with profits. "We want you all urinating blood," the employee recounted a manager telling one business unit. Other managers reportedly physically assaulted unproductive employees or publicly humiliated them. The book's allegations were reported widely.

In the midst of this, Hashimoto was named president.

"My term began with a lot of crises," he states matter-of-factly. But even with the scandals, these crises were not financial. At the time, Fuji Bank was marching forward under a three-year strategic plan named the Ever-Pioneering Best Bank, which had as its core one goal: increased profits. The plan was working. Fuji stood as one of the top banks in the Japanese financial sector.

But from Hashimoto's new vantage point from his office in Fuji's Tokyo headquarters, the bank's monetary success disguised the fact that "the organization was dilapidated and the spirit of the employees was frayed." The scandals had taken a severe toll on the bank's most valuable asset of all, trust—trust between the bank and its customers, between the bank and its employees. "Emergency improvements to the foundation had to be made to restore trust," he says. "People place their savings in a bank because they trust it. Recovery of that all-important trust, therefore, had to become the highest priority, and we had to put all our effort into it. That's why we did all the things we did."

Hashimoto's first step was to overhaul administrative controls. In addition, new systems were installed "to prevent improprieties," he says. In other words, using massive new reporting requirements, the company rebuilt its box, this time with higher walls.

But it was Hashimoto's second step that set the real turnaround in motion. He decided the Ever-Pioneering Best Bank strategic plan had to go, and with it, the focus on profits. Fuji Bank's new focus was to be the customer. To that end, everything would change: employee hiring, training, evaluations, and compensation. New managers who supported the program were installed. Branch offices would be required to alter their daily practices and procedures, with customer response cards and new customer service units driving the process. In fact, the entire bank would leave behind business as usual and embark upon a journey toward "new useful services," Hashimoto announced. "This radical reform was about long-range vision, about leading us into a new financial age as an integrated financial services group, aiming to become the customer's first choice," he recalls.

A corporate directive to focus on customers—the same pronouncement in a Western company, especially in the late eighties, would have provoked yawns. But at Fuji Bank, Hashimoto's calls for change were greeted with support—a radical departure from just a few years earlier, when his predecessor's calls for a new program had difficulty in gaining acceptance. Instead, Hashimoto found employees responding much as did Linn Macdonald's when he informed the organization that MacMillan Bloedel had to be sold. Many were unhappy, but everyone understood the dire consequences of refusing to accept drastic change. If firefighters have little else in their favor, they do often have an organization's siege mentality to help them move forward quickly and forcefully.

"People knew something had to be done about the danger the bank was in," Hashimoto recalls. "It was relatively easy to bring people around to the idea that the bank would prosper if things were done differently."

Acceptance was one thing, but Hashimoto still had to educate the organization about what the new strategy meant in operational terms. To that end, he and his top executives held more meetings, traveling around the country to nearly 300 branches. They went from Hokkaido in the north to Kyushu in the south, holding discussions with groups of thirty to fifty employees at a time, often over beer or coffee. Employees were encouraged to be open and honest. Some meetings were productive, Hashimoto says, others were more difficult, as employees struggled with the details of what the new strategy would entail.

Particularly sensitive was the issue of employee evaluations. In the past, managers were rated on the profitability of their units; in fact, that was the only measure of their performance. That system, Hashimoto decided, was to be replaced with a "subjective" system that rated managers 50 percent on profitability, 50 percent on their responsiveness to the customer. Many employees also questioned Hashimoto's call for prominently displayed response cards at every branch, cards that prompted customers to rate several dimensions of service. Still others felt uneasy about the establishment of "customer service units," teams of employees charged with developing and implementing services customers wanted. In the past, the services offered at each branch had come down from the corner office, not up from the line at the teller's window.

"The branch bank heads had a rather antagonistic view of this," Hashimoto remembers. "Some of them were afflicted with a kind of defeatism." The task of change ahead of them, he reckons, seemed too overwhelming.

At the same time, Hashimoto announced that hiring and training programs were to be revamped, to draw in and create a new breed of Fuji employee—one Hashimoto describes as strong-minded, spirited, even outspoken. Education programs for new hires, with an emphasis on customer relations and communication skills, were extended from six to twelve months. "We want to hear bad news very quickly," Hashimoto says. Traditionally, Japanese employees are rewarded for loyalty to the corporation, which often means *not* coming forward with "bad news." But in calling for new behaviors, Hashimoto was rejecting tradition, and he said so. "It is impossible to know when anything is wrong if harsh and discordant voices, which carry good information, are stopped," he told Fuji employees in meeting after meeting. In other words, speak up; you will be rewarded.

Hashimoto also replaced some of the key staff at headquarters with new personnel. A more typical or traditional Japanese CEO might have tried to change direction with the same personnel in place, but Hashimoto decided against that method. "It is always difficult for people to change themselves," he reflects. "And so we had to have new staff members, and we had to have new officers. It went far below the top level. In order for there to be reform, the people in charge have to be different. People find it very difficult to change something they themselves have made. And so the people who would have prolonged the old policies were moved out. A substantial number were replaced. That was how we brought about the reform."

That, and the fact that, slowly but surely, Fuji employees began to adjust to the idea of a new customer-focused bank and all it involved. Part of this acceptance came about because Hashimoto's new systems basically forced such a conversion; faced with "subjective" performance evaluations, for instance, employees had to pay more attention to customers. But another part of it was Hashimoto's campaign of persuasion—all those meetings, all those cups of coffee (and beer), all that listening, all that talking softly.

"The president doesn't use fancy words. There isn't a more earnest person to be found," says Kazuhiko Kasai, deputy president of Fuji and a longtime associate of Hashimoto. "He is genuine, with no hidden sides.

"Sometimes things that are said softly," submits Kasai, "are easier to hear, as well as being more effective."

AT TRELLEBORG:
THE CRISIS MANAGEMENT CEO AS A SURGEON

The anguish of laying off longtime employees. The awkwardness of "hand-holding" with bankers. The challenge of controlling cash. Every CEO in this chapter has described the turnaround process as tough, draining, even brutal.

But Kjell Nilsson, the CEO and president of **Trelleborg,** who has turned around more than a dozen of his industrial conglomerate's companies in the past ten years, has a different take on crisis management. "Yes, sometimes it can be painful, but I love my work," he says. "I think if I were offered the job as CEO at some successful insurance company or a bank, for example, I would most certainly turn it down. It just isn't my cup of tea. In that type of business you never find the same kind of challenge. I love a fight, frankly."

That's a good thing for Trelleborg. The concern, with $3 billion in sales and approximately $125 million in net income in 1994, consists of a large portfolio of cyclical businesses such as metals and mining, rubber, and paper products. At fairly regular intervals, at least one of them is in trouble. Because of this situation, Trelleborg is unique in that it is a company in which the center's main, recurrent role is crisis management. Nilsson and his senior executives serve as turnaround "specialists" who move in, sometimes even physically, and take over when divisions start to founder. Once in charge, they use the same tool kit as every CEO in this chapter: they sell off businesses, reduce head count, rein in capital expenditures, and stem the flow of cash. As soon as operations are profitable again, Nilsson and his team exit.

The setup works, in part, because Nilsson runs Trelleborg with an approach that is as hard box as any we've seen. Divisions are managed through strict, scrupulously monitored financial targets and goals. If they are met, Corporate needn't look twice. "I sometimes joke that you can get away even with murder in this company if you make your numbers," Nilsson says. "But it is true that you can create your independence if you deliver. Tell me, why should I fiddle around with those who are having good performance?"

At the first sign of bad performance, however, Nilsson acts swiftly. Such was the case described at the opening of this chapter. Trelleborg's Munksjö division was severely hit by the recession in the pulp and paper industry—the same recession, incidentally, that damaged operations at Noranda Forest. Soon after taking control of Munksjö, Nilsson ordered the divestment of the company's diversified acquisitions, in businesses such as caviar and biscuits, furniture, and parking garages. He narrowed the core company's product line, laid off hundreds of employees, and ultimately introduced the company to the Stockholm stock exchange in a successful initial public offering. When Munksjö showed a small profit, Nilsson left for another ailing division.

"It's practical, in many situations, to let me do the 'dirty work,' " Nilsson explains. "First, I have done it before. Second, I know a great deal about these companies, therefore I can act right away; there is no lead time for decisions, which I have the authority to make, by the way, because I am president. And third, sometimes the current management like it this way, simply because it's hard for them to fire someone who has been with the company for twenty-five years."

Moreover, Nilsson says, there is little point in demonizing the division's management in the eyes of those employees who are staying. "People have long memories," he says. "Even when the company is doing well again, they will remember who did the firing, who sold off this division or that, who destroyed all the values they had spent years developing. It is better for me and my colleagues to take the heat, because we leave." In his wake, he says, he often appoints a new leader for the turned-around division. "He can be the nice guy," Nilsson notes, "who doesn't have the historical burden of being the one who fired a lot of people. He can be the one to come in and do the optimistic work, to build market share and start the growth again—the gardener, instead of the surgeon."

Finally, Nilsson says, his method is based on the simple fact that saving a division from failure is, ultimately, his responsibility. "I am responsible for the group's development to the board and to the shareholders, so it is my job," he says. "And if I have the responsibility, I might as well do the work."

If the other CEOs in this chapter are relieved to be out of the firefighting business, Nilsson instead seems to accept without regret that it is his primary role—his main way of adding value to Trelleborg, along with the maintenance of a hard box. There is, he says, no other way to run a cyclical business like his.

CRISIS MANAGEMENT: USING APPROACHES TO FIGHT THE FIRE

Perhaps the best thing that can be said about crisis management is that it is usually temporary. The stories in this chapter are evidence that a bad year, or bad cycle, can be fought and defeated. These stories also suggest that firefighting CEOs can and do use several similar approaches to dousing the flames. The first step is to regain control: control of cash, control of capital expenditures, control of costs, control of who is making decisions and why. Control, even, of control systems. All other matters, from customers to new products, are put on hold. Given the circumstances and their urgency, there is little time to think about long-term planning or the hiring and career development of employees. Instead, divisions are sold off, employees let go, product lines narrowed. Crisis management first builds a box, a rather small one, with new rules, regulations, and policies completely focused on financial survival.

But the examples in this chapter also show that once that box is working effectively, crisis management CEOs turn swiftly to selecting and implementing the approach that will create a sustainable competitive advantage. United Dominion became a human assets company, Fuji Bank an expertise one, and Armco opted for strategy. Linn Macdonald of Noranda Forest notes with great relief that he, too, can now devote his energies to analyzing markets and technologies in the cyclical pulp and paper products industry—picking the company's point of arrival, as it were—and systematically mapping how to get there.

Yet even with their new approaches in place, the legacy of the firefighting CEOs is consistent: after the crisis is over, a culture of "no excuses" begins—and remains. All the CEOs in this chapter assert that they will never let their organizations go to the brink again, meaning they will never let their box of controls shrink too much, nor will they lose their focus on relentlessly applying the right approach for managing through good times and bad. Crisis management may be temporary, but its message about survival is not.

9

NOT FOR CEOs ONLY:
THE APPROACHES OUTSIDE
THE TRADITIONAL CORPORATION

In the preceding pages, we have discussed the use of the five approaches at large businesses—most of them diversified, global, and publicly held. But leadership is hardly a concept unique to profit-making enterprises, or even to standard-issue companies with a traditional CEO center. In this chapter we suggest that the approaches laid out by the business leaders in this book can and do add value in virtually *any* organizational setting, be it a school, church, museum, law firm, or library. We might even go so far as to hypothesize that the approaches describe how families function: one partner is the box, setting the rules and values for all members to follow, for instance, while the other is the strategist, imagining where the family will live, what it will earn, and so forth, a decade hence. But this is not a topic we will examine here.

Instead, we profile four organizations—not standard-issue companies—in which the center adds value with one or two of the five approaches. In two cases, **Harvard Business School** and **Partners HealthCare,** the latter of which includes two of the finest hospitals in the world, the "center" has dramatically different objectives than the other institutions in this book. Dean John McArthur isn't thinking primarily about revenue, for instance, and Dr. H. Richard Nesson isn't concerned about dividends. Yet both leaders are focused on empowering the people who work for them. Both have assessed their situations and responded with a coherent management approach, not unlike the CEOs at Coca-Cola, Hewlett-Packard, or any number of companies that happen to have "tickers" on Wall Street. Another example from our interviews with nonprofit organizations is England's **National Health Service,** which provides medical care, free at the point of delivery, for the nation's population of 46 million, operating with an annual budget of close to $54 billion. Chief executive Alan Langlands describes the results expected of his organization not in financial terms but as "efficiency, responsiveness, equity, and compassion," and notes that his most demanding constituents are the sick, the elderly, and government politicians. Yet he approaches his role as head of NHS just as do many of the strategists described in chapter 2, spending a large part of his time "looking upwards and outwards" of the organization.

"This week, for example, I have been in Liverpool working with a group of doctors, nurses, and managers about the development of a clinical audit and its linkages with our R&D program," he says. "Last night I was at the Royal College of Physicians, talking with a number of statutory and voluntary agencies about the development of services for the elderly. Demographic change, scientific and technological developments which are now occurring at breathtaking speed, will have a fundamental impact on health and social services over the next few years." Echoing a common theme of many of the strategic approach leaders we talked to at for-profit companies, Langlands says his management style involves collecting and critically analyzing large amounts of information so as to understand his organization's point of arrival—where it must go and what it must be in the future in order to succeed. "I do not believe in 'vision' as in inspired thoughts from a board or a few people at the top," Langlands says, "but I believe in the foresight capacity that gives you insight into all the different trends and all the different pressures, analyzed creatively and harnessed for their good."

In addition to Partners HealthCare and Harvard Business School, this chapter will profile two venture capital firms that act as, or oversee, the CEO of the companies they acquire. What makes these companies unique is how they use the approaches to fill that role. They are decidedly not in the mold of the plethora of LBO and venture capital firms that dominated the financial scene of the eighties. The eighties were characterized by easy money—financing, by debt, equity, and a variety of other new instruments, was abundant. By the nineties, easy money was history. Too many enterprises had failed, too many investors had failed with them.

AEA Investors and **Bain Capital** not only survived but thrived. Both of them have outperformed other firms in the industry by carefully selecting acquisitions with a rigorous "discovery" process and unleashing their full potential afterward. The methods they use are an illuminating combination of the strategic and human assets approaches. Their stories raise a question mentioned by many of the fund managers themselves—why can't CEOs act more like we do?

Given returns that range from 30 to an extraordinary 200 percent, it is a question some shareholders may find themselves asking as well.

AT PARTNERS HEALTHCARE:
THE RX IS HUMAN ASSETS MANAGEMENT

In 1991, when *U.S. News & World Report* published its annual list of the "Best of the Best" hospitals in the United States, most of the institutions so honored already had long-standing reputations for excellence in medicine and scientific research. Among them were Johns Hopkins in Baltimore; the Mayo Clinic of Rochester, Minnesota; and Massachusetts General Hospital, where on a given day, both kings and homeless people receive leading-edge treatment from Harvard-trained physicians.

But the list also contained a newcomer, **Brigham and Women's Hospital,** which was created only twelve years before out of the merger of four small, relatively unknown Boston hospitals. And even that merger was shaky at first; three years into the process, it looked as if the whole was still less than the sum of its parts.

That changed radically when Dr. H. Richard Nesson was named CEO of the combined institutions in 1982. A soft-spoken nephrologist who had spent most of his career in the field of medical administration, Nesson determined that to survive, Brigham and Women's Hospital had to be able to compete for patients with the city's other powerhouse medical institutions, such as Massachusetts General and Children's Hospital, and receive its full share of respect and staff from Harvard Medical School, with which it was technically associated as a teaching hospital.

In short, Nesson had to reinvent Brigham and Women's, and when we asked him to describe the methods and means of that process, his response bolstered our sense that the approaches as we have delineated them apply in organizations outside the for-profit business sector. Nesson, in fact, clearly defines himself as a human assets CEO, using many of the same techniques and expressing many of the same convictions as corporate executives such as Al Zeien at Gillette and Wayne Calloway of PepsiCo. He speaks of taking personal interest in many of his employees, helping improve their skills, planning their career paths, challenging and guiding them. He speaks also of the importance of teams and consensus. And he speaks of setting and championing institutional values, such as those of integrity, excellence, empowerment, and cooperation.

In fact, Nesson begins the discussion of his management philosophy with the story of Laura Spitler, a pregnant woman with such severe heart disease that she had been warned by doctors never to bear children. The daring, extremely complex operation that saved her life, and the life of her baby, involved three of Brigham and Women's medical teams working in moment-to-moment coordination through one near-death crisis after another. Laura Spitler's successful operation, Nesson says, is a testament to the power of the human assets approach, evidence that it can create an environment where people rise to their full, and often extraordinary, potential.

"Many people believed Laura Spitler could not live, and that her baby had only a small chance of survival," Nesson recalls. "But the team we were building really rallied to save them both. They saw if they worked together, the sum could be greater than the parts. They saw there was a greater benefit for everyone."

Laura Spitler's ordeal occurred in May 1982, when the woman, thirty-two years old at the time and seven months pregnant, was admitted to Brigham and Women's for an emergency cesarean section. Doctors were expecting a complicated and delicate procedure because of Ms. Spitler's heart condition, but it was far worse than that. Ms. Spitler went into cardiac arrest on the operating table, forcing doctors to perform heart massage for fifteen minutes to keep her alive while her son was delivered and rushed to the neonatal unit. Seconds afterward, doctors began extensive open-heart surgery on Ms. Spitler that would last another six hours. She recovered fully, along with her baby boy.

In the media reports that followed, Brigham and Women's was lauded for achieving a medical feat that few other hospitals in the world could have. But to Nesson, Laura Spitler's operation wasn't just a medical feat but an organizational one as well.

"It's all about people—hiring the right ones, coaching them, mentoring them, teaching them the values and behaviors that are acceptable and appropriate," he explains. "The people you work with are like your children in one sense," he adds. "You have to set the example yourself, and set guidelines about how they should act. You have to steer them into areas where they excel. You have to discipline them when they do something wrong. That's the only way to make sure we can achieve our ultimate goal, which of course is making sure we serve our patients."

Like many of the CEOs in chapter 3, Nesson spends much of his time one on-one with his senior managers—in his case, the physicians who serve as directors of the various medical areas. His objective, he says, is to know them well enough to determine their capabilities and weaknesses, and then assign them responsibility accordingly. He notes that one of his "chiefs" has a remarkable aptitude for long-term strategic thinking, and so he has focused him on long-term issues, while others excel at thinking about medical ethics issues and managed care, both key areas of concern for hospitals in today's changing health-care marketplace.

It has been, in fact, this environment of change that has characterized Nesson's tenure since he was named CEO. Taking over in the midst of the merger, Nesson decided that the hospitals' quality had to dramatically improve and their costs dramatically decrease. The situation was further complicated by politics: two of the three hospitals had been run by a chief of service who saw himself as CEO, and his high-level staff, which was accustomed to communicating directly with the board of directors. Some of these managers were openly hostile to Nesson, "as they discovered they were no longer in charge," he recalls. Finally, there was a widespread sense of gloom among many employees, from the highest to the lowest ranks. Many believed the hospitals were fated to close, Nesson says, and had lost their pride in the services they provided.

Nesson tackled all of these issues—quality, costs, chain of command, and culture—through his approach to personnel management.

First, he co-opted the opposition, meeting every other week with the eight chiefs of service, some of whom most doubted his leadership. "I brought them inside to help make the decisions," he says, "and I started the process of gaining consensus." At the same time, Nesson was hiring new senior managers whom he describes as "intelligent, with a sense of humor, the right attitude about teams, willing to work hard and to fix things without being told." Like so many other human assets CEOs, Nesson says he proactively seeks out managers who embrace his goals for the institution and empowers them to make significant decisions.

"I don't believe in job descriptions," Nesson says. "I ask people to come do something interesting with us, but not to be boxed in by certain tasks. If they see something bigger they can do, something new and important for us, I'm very flexible. I want them to grow." Nesson also practices another hallmark of human assets management: he identifies "special people," as he calls managers with particularly strong promise, and carefully monitors and advances their careers. "I know them well," he remarks, "and I make sure I keep them in my sights." What does this mean specifically? Nesson describes frequent coaching sessions, in equal parts critical listening and instruction. "I listen very carefully. I'm not a big talker," Nesson says, "but I do tell people when I know they can do better. Sometimes it is the first time that has been said to them."

As further evidence of his self-assessment as a human assets manager, Nesson notes that he lets go those who do not fit the mold he has designed for the organization or aggressively work toward its objectives. In his first eighteen months, he says, he fired twenty-two senior administrators. "It was awful," he recalls, "but it had to be done. The right people were key to getting what we wanted, which was better care for the patients, and getting our financial house in order for the future."

Nesson also used some familiar human assets devices to rebuild the hospitals' culture in his new image. He explicitly communicated the values and behaviors he wanted, rewarded those who demonstrated them, and punished those who didn't.

"We had a senior surgeon really act abusive and yell at a nurse in an operating room," he says as an example, "and she was doing the right thing, but he didn't like it. That wasn't acceptable behavior. He lost his privileges for two weeks," meaning the doctor could not see or treat patients at the hospital. "I never told anyone, but that story," notes Nesson, "got around."

Nesson also made his values clear by showing up at many hospital functions, such as grand rounds, as well as lectures and social gatherings. "In those early days, sometimes we would hold parties just to celebrate that we had made it," he recalls.

By the mid-eighties, Nesson's efforts began to show up in performance and reputation—the Laura Spitler operation is a case in point. The momentum continued: respected doctors began to join the staff, and admissions rose, as did the level of federal research money.

In 1993, Brigham and Women's ascendancy was so secure that Nesson began talks with the senior management at Massachusetts General. Combining the two academic medical centers, he suggested, might create powerful benefits for both patients and the institutions themselves, in care, research, and cost improvements. The merger, he said, would enable the hospitals to eliminate many redundancies. Massachusetts General's leadership agreed, and the merger process is now under way. The new organization is a $2-billion-a-year (nonprofit) business, admitting 78,000 patients a year and handling more than 1 million ambulatory visits. The hospitals have a research budget totaling $300 million a year, making them possibly the largest nonpharmaceutical medical research operation in the world.

But Nesson, who is now CEO of Partners HealthCare, which oversees the merged institutions, dismisses the idea that the merger is evidence of his role as a strategist such as those discussed in chapter 2.

"I'm not a visionary or a great producer of ideas, nothing like that," he says simply. "I don't know what the future holds. I saw the merger, frankly, as a legitimate experiment. I knew we had to make the system better, and this was one way of getting at that."

Sounding strikingly like Jan Timmer of the electronics giant Philips, who described his human assets management philosophy with the words "I always get back to the people," Nesson describes his in these terms: "I don't think there is anything more important than people." Profit or not, these leaders' beliefs about the means to success are one and the same.

AT HARVARD BUSINESS SCHOOL:
MANAGEMENT BY BEING THERE AT 2 A.M.

When John H. McArthur stepped down as dean of the **Harvard Business School** in 1995, the university's magazine noted that his was a legacy of "Babe Ruthian" proportions. It was an apt description. During McArthur's fifteen-year tenure, endowed professorships increased from fifty to eighty-six; the market value of the school's endowment rose to $600 million, a sixfold increase; and annual spending on research and course development quintupled, to more than $50 million. The campus, an ivy-covered enclave across the Charles River from Harvard College, underwent massive new construction and renovation. At the same time, McArthur directed the expansion of the business school's prestigious publishing enterprise and its executive education programs, which now generate $100 million a year. Under his leadership, the school's faculty became known for its leading-edge research, while the organization also maintained its reputation as the world's foremost creator of case-study teaching materials. And finally, McArthur spearheaded a wide-ranging transformation of the school's core—the M.B.A. program—to include a new focus on leadership, field studies, internships, and team projects, as well as the study of ethics, entrepreneurship, international business, and the role of private enterprise in society.

But if McArthur hit these grand slams during his tenure, he's too unassuming by nature to tell you himself. "I'm not going to give the speech at Agincourt because I'm not able to do it," he says, referring to the grandiloquent oration about victory delivered by King Henry V in Shakespeare's play of the same name. "I'm inept at that."

Instead, McArthur brought renewal to HBS the same way Dr. Nesson transformed his hospital organization—one employee at a time, with the human assets approach. His long-term goal, McArthur says, was to build enough trust, loyalty, and goodwill between himself and the school's constituents, from the faculty to the groundskeepers, that his major change goals for the school would be reached, even when vast in magnitude, difficult, or unpopular.

"I wanted to have lots of people who would feel that I had helped them or I would help them when something happened at two in the morning, so that I would, over time, have their support on some things that I wanted to do that they really didn't want to do," he explains.

McArthur's management philosophy translated into the kind of responsiveness and personalized, one-to-one relationships that were typical of many of the CEOs in chapter 3. The dean's office during his tenure, for instance, received 200 phone calls and fifty letters a day. McArthur insisted they be responded to, either by him or by an assistant. He met with members of the HBS community constantly, and not just heavy hitters such as tenured faculty members or other university administrators, but "with the gardeners, and the secretaries, or with a student who is in the hospital, having just lost an organ." Over the years, McArthur handled faculty assignments personally, and took an active role in mentoring the careers of many young professors. He also was known to show up in the middle of the night for family emergencies of HBS staff members, and more than once offered extended paid vacations to employees who were sick or had children, spouses, or parents in need of supervised care.

"I didn't want it to be me just sitting there in my office, renowned bastard, looking foreboding," McArthur says. "I wanted to have the kind of organization where I knew people and they knew me, and I wanted to deal with them in a way that in the end there's almost nothing I could ask people to do that they wouldn't do."

Several times in this book we've noted that a leader's management approach doesn't seem to be solely a function of personality, but is more a function of the situation he or she faces. McArthur's is a case in point. At first analysis, his shy, almost introverted character makes him an unlikely candidate for the human assets approach, but the school and its character and needs made the choice an effective one.

"There are only two thousand people in this community, and really only a core of several hundred that endure year after year," he says of the campus, which has 1,600 students in the two-year M.B.A. program and hundreds more every year in shorter-term executive programs. "My thought was that by starting at six every day and working until nine, I could see enough people and work with enough people on their own agendas, and still have time to run the school. I mean, I can follow everybody, know what they are doing, and thinking. I can do it directly."

His colleagues at Harvard's larger schools can't. Speaking of another dean, McArthur notes, "He has 284 buildings. That's three times as many full professors as I have, just in buildings!"

At the same time, McArthur stresses that he didn't choose the human assets approach simply because of the business school's size, but because of the kind of changes he wanted to make—major in scope and in their potential for sparking an insurrection. He also recalls that when he was named dean in 1979, the school was in the midst of an identity crisis. Many professors were demoralized by the competition between HBS and Stanford Business School being played out in the media, and by what some considered the school's diminishing reputation for cutting-edge business thinking. Other faculty members were confused and upset by the school's inconsistent assignment and hiring practices.

McArthur knew of this unhappiness personally; HBS had been his home since he came to the school as a student in 1957. His route there, however, was hardly typical. Raised in a small, rural town in British Columbia, McArthur started working nights and weekends at the local sawmill while in ninth grade. The company's owners, Czech refugees, sensed his promise, called him to the main office one day, and offered to send him to college. "These were people who came to our tiny house every Christmas with a can of Crisco and a jar of English candies," he says of the sawmill's owners. "They just really wanted me to get an education," he recalls, "which was something we never talked about in my family. It just wasn't the milieu that we lived in." The sawmill's owners persisted, and McArthur eventually accepted their offer, studying forestry for five years. Uncertain what to do next, he took the advice of the school's dean and applied to Harvard Business School.

"I'd never heard of the place," he remembers.

After receiving his M.B.A., McArthur worked as a researcher for the school and went on to earn his doctorate in business administration. All along, he and his wife intended to return to Canada, but when HBS asked McArthur to fill in as a finance professor, the future dean's career path was sealed. "I loved it," he says of teaching, "it was instant gratification."

McArthur continued as a professor and was assigned additional administrative duties until Derek Bok, Harvard University's president at the time, offered him the job running the business school. Despite his commitment to HBS, McArthur says he pondered the decision for several weeks before he said yes, for he knew his vision of the school would require the slow, relentless, and all-consuming processes of changing an institution steeped in tradition and populated with strong personalities.

Even his earliest executive decisions bore him out; he sparked controversy with his efforts to change the kind of junior faculty members hired by HBS and with his program to bring in business executives (in addition to academics) as full professors. Another decision—to make the HBS grounds safer, quieter, and more of a traditional campus, closed to car traffic—also engendered resistance from professors who had parked in front of their offices for years. To head off a revolt, McArthur took the unusual step of calling five student leaders, who were home on vacation at the time, and sending them tickets to fly to Boston immediately. "I told them I had an important problem and I simply had to have their help," McArthur recalls. "We walked around the campus, and I told them, 'You see, there are no cars here, and next Tuesday morning, when school is back in session, they're going to throw me out because of this.' "

That Tuesday, the student newspaper ran a front-page article strongly supporting McArthur's plan to close the campus to traffic, saying it would make the school a better place for people to live.

"No one ever mentioned it to me after that," McArthur recalls. "I mean, I knew they were all seething in the trenches, but no one ever said a thing to me about it, and in the meantime people came to realize it was the right idea. It transformed our community."

As time passed, McArthur says his relationships with members of the community grew in number and deepened in meaning to the point that making changes of much larger importance than traffic patterns engendered less resistance. The total redesign of the M.B.A. program is an apropos example. Interestingly, in a two-hour interview, McArthur himself never mentions his own role in this, one of the defining achievements of his career. Instead, sounding like many other human assets managers, he describes and lauds the role of the many individuals, committees, corporations, and alumni who were involved in the three-year process. It began in 1991, when McArthur launched an exhaustive review of the HBS curriculum. Four task forces studied the history of HBS, benchmarked it against other business schools and training programs, conducted extensive market research of alumni and employers, and critically evaluated the current program by interviewing students and faculty. When all the data were in, the message was clear: the Harvard M.B.A. program, while strong in many areas, nevertheless had to undergo significant changes in its curriculum to stay competitive and relevant in a business world increasingly driven by technology and globalization. In addition, the school needed to devote more attention to topics such as teamwork, cross-functional cooperation, social responsibility, leadership skills, diversity, local communities, and international issues. It needed to offer courses on the challenges faced by small and medium-size businesses and nonprofit organizations; it needed to emphasize business skills such as public speaking and interpersonal relations—plus more.

The road from these broad recommendations to the massive changes that are now under way at the school was winding, and heavily trafficked by students, professors, alumni, employers of HBS graduates, and many of the corporations that support the school financially and otherwise. At times, it seemed each constituency wanted the program to take a different direction. But McArthur diverted crashes, pileups, and jams by managing the process slowly and carefully, building consensus through committees, team reports, and countless sessions of dialogue between and with opposing groups and individuals. He was often the mediator and the facilitator, roles he could effectively assume because of his close and long-term relationships with so many of the individuals involved— the human assets approach in action, at its essence.

McArthur himself says the power of the approach lies in its ability to make an organization with many disparate members function as a family or a team—a winning team.

"I think you've got to create a community that people feel is supportive and cares, and will be there when they need it," he says. "And not just *professionally* need it. But for all matters, whether personal or professional."

The transformation of the M.B.A. program will probably be complete by the end of 1996, but McArthur, true to form, will not be on campus to witness it firsthand. His plans after he steps down from the dean's office are not yet definite, but one thing is certain: he is leaving HBS outright instead of returning to teaching. "It is not right for those in leadership roles to stay on in organizations after their work is done," he explained in a letter to the faculty.

His successor will inherit a school vastly different from the one where McArthur landed, almost accidentally, nearly forty years earlier—a school transformed person by person, through the human assets approach.

AT AEA—FUNDAMENTALS FROM THE MANAGERS, ADVICE FROM THE MASTERS

John Heine, CEO of Sola International, the world's largest maker of plastic eyeglass lenses, remembers what it used to be like to work for his old employer: not much fun and not enough money. Today, he has lots of both.

The reason, he says, is the secretive, highly successful LBO firm named **AEA Investors,** which acquired Sola from the British conglomerate Pilkington in 1993. Sola's top 100 managers, including Heine, participated in the $335 million deal, all of them becoming shareholders, and 40 of them getting additional stock options.

"They're a great outfit, AEA is," Heine says in a thick Australian accent at Sola's Menlo Park, California, headquarters. He is fifty, friendly but blunt in manner, a straight-shooter. "They do things very well. The interesting thing is, I didn't set out to do a buyout. It just worked out that way. I'm glad it did."

For good reason. Since the buyout, Heine reports that the company's earnings, on $340 million in sales, have increased more than 30 percent, and the company has just completed an initial public offering (IPO) of stock netting the shareholders a gain of more than $150 million. Heine attributes the success largely to the fact that he and his managers have, by his estimation, 35 percent more time to attend to the company's fundamental operations. It's time they used to spend, he says, attending to irrelevant bureaucracy and politics when they were a part of Pilkington, a manufacturer of a variety of consumer and industrial products, from plastic foam to contact lens solution. Moreover, he says he and his staff, as equity owners, now have powerful incentives to perform to their maximum potential. And, finally, he says that if any problems do arise, all he has to do is pick up the phone and call a member of his new board of directors. The person at the other end of the line is likely to be one of the world's most prominent business leaders.

The Sola buyout is a case study of how AEA functions. Unlike the financial engineers made famous in the 1980s, AEA has been quietly doing deals since 1968. On average, its compound annual return on investment has been greater than 30 percent.

Yet despite this notable statistic, one almost feels compelled to talk about the firm in a hushed voice, and that's the way AEA wants it. The company was founded over lunch one day by J. Richardson Dilworth, the Rockefeller family's financial adviser; George Love, then chairman of Chrysler Corporation; and Sir Siegmund Warburg, of the European financial dynasty. Their idea was to assemble a group of successful, wealthy retired chief executives and use their money and experience to act as principals to buy and grow middle-market companies. There were to be no overleveraged balance sheets, hostile takeovers, management layoffs, phony paper profits, or asset dumping—simply well-researched investments, intelligent strategies, carefully coached and properly motivated employees, and timely divestments.

The idea worked. At last count, the company consisted of 100 shareholders. Some of them are the world's most renowned retired CEOs, including Frank Cary of IBM, Irving Shapiro of Du Pont, John Smale of Procter & Gamble, Hamish Maxwell of Philip Morris, and Walter Wriston of Citicorp. In recent years, the shareholder list has expanded to include a few institutions such as Princeton University, MIT, and the Carnegie Foundation, as well as some international families prominent in the finance business, such as the Wallenbergs of Sweden and the Lees of Hong Kong. But the core of AEA investors bring not just money but profound business acumen to the table, acumen used in the acquisition, management, and ultimate sale of AEA properties.

"The reason AEA works so well is because we rarely try to do anything but improve a company's fundamentals—its strategy, its operations, its people, its incentive system. We've never played a paper game," explains Chip Baird, one of AEA's managing directors. "Even before we go in, we understand a company and its industry, and its potential. We work closely with management to help develop insights about how the company can be managed differently and performance can be taken to the next level."

Baird says AEA's approach may seem old-fashioned compared to the debt-heavy deals executed by the LBO firms of the eighties, but then again it has outlasted many of the firms that cut them.

"Two things drove those deals in the eighties, and it had nothing to do with improved operating performance. The math is inexorable," Baird goes on. "The first was just leverage, going from 40 percent debt to 80 percent, for instance. And the second was the expansion of multiples for the S&P during that period, where PE ratios went from less than 10 to more than 20.

"So put those things on a computer, and suddenly you get 60 or 80 percent internal rates of return, never thinking about the operations of the business."

In the nineties, Baird says, all that easy debt has dried up and banks have become smarter; he notes, "The rules of the game have definitely changed." Meanwhile, AEA keeps doing what it has always done, employing a two-pronged approach to add value.

The first part of the AEA system is to focus management on the most leveraged areas for improved performance. These are often the "tough decisions that it was easier or safer not to make under the prior ownership," Baird says. With this focus in place, AEA then installs a board of directors to serve as the acquisition's on-call team of experts and advisers to help them execute the new operating plan. "The idea is that if the manager of the firm has a marketing question, he can pick up the phone and call John Smale of Procter & Gamble or Hamish Maxwell of Philip Morris, and ask them what they think.

"Or say it's an expansion issue, and they need to know whether to go into Mexico or Latin America," Baird adds. "Then they can call Chuck Pilliod, who is the former CEO of Goodyear and the former U.S. ambassador to Mexico, and get his insights. Or maybe call Doug Danforth, the former CEO of Westinghouse, who opened something like twenty-five plants in South America during his tenure there."

At the same time, AEA professionals such as Baird himself help management with more day-to-day strategic decisions, on both the offense and the defense. "Sometimes we'll talk to them about opportunities to grow into different product lines or make acquisitions," he says. "Other times, it's about closing a plant or changing a marketing strategy that's failing. The value comes in the frequent informal interaction among people who are significant shareholders, whose primary objective is increasing shareholder value. This is often not what drives decisions in large corporations."

That, says Heine, was exactly the problem when Sola was part of Pilkington.

"They were a huge bureaucracy that demanded huge amounts of information and time from the people who ran their businesses," he recalls. "The objective of the top managers was to make themselves look good in front of their bosses in the corporate office. They had no real understanding of what was required to actually run the business. And to tell you the truth, I'm not sure they were all that interested in knowing."

Since the AEA buyout, Heine says he has spent the time he didn't have before designing a system that encourages his company's fourteen manufacturing plants around the world to share production expertise. The project includes a new information system and other "exchange mechanisms," and has been complicated—but worth the effort. Heine estimates that it has improved Sola's gross margin by five percentage points. "That's found money that was lost while we were part of Pilkington and I didn't have the time or the incentives to focus on my business," Heine says. "It's about independence and empowerment."

Heine says he also spends a portion of his time doing exactly what AEA hopes he will do—talking to his board of directors. "Irving Shapiro is our chairman," he says. "He's a fantastic guy, the kind of guy you can just pick up the phone and ask, 'Look, I've got this problem that is really bothering me. Did you ever come across it when you were running Du Pont?' And he'll say, 'Actually, I did.' And he'll chat away and give you lots of really good advice."

The second part of the AEA approach is to realign an acquisition's incentive program with the identified performance improvement opportunities, then reward managers for superlative performance and punish them for less than that. In short, AEA puts the risk of running a company on its top managers by making them owners through stock options for 10 percent of the company, as well as other cash incentive plans that are directly linked to earnings and cash flow. "In big corporations, managers are rewarded for meeting budget," Baird says. "We give them an incentive to blow away the budget.

"In other words, if they beat the budget by 20 percent, they can make 100 percent or more of salary in an annual cash bonus," Baird adds. "Incentives are just a huge opportunity to change the performance of the company." At the same time, stock options remind managers that what they do to beat the budget must be for the best of the company in the long term. It is, Baird says, a simple and remarkably effective system.

"AEA has helped us enormously, to say the least," Heine says. "Performance is what AEA is after. That's what they do right."

Heine's assessment is echoed by another CEO of an AEA-acquired company, Jim Rogers of Specialty Coatings International, a former division of the James River Corporation, a consumer products–oriented paper company with $5 billion in revenues. (Rogers, it should be noted, is a *former* CEO, since Specialty Coatings was resold less than two years after AEA bought it. The quick turnaround was an unusual move for AEA.)

"Those guys were great and they were helpful," Rogers recalls of AEA's involvement with Specialty Coatings. "First, we designed and put in an incentive system that reflected both the upside and the downside; they let us own that risk. But beyond that, the board of directors they gave us allowed us to become a reputable firm overnight. That opened a lot of doors, and we took full advantage of it."

The AEA buyout of Specialty Coatings took place in April 1991. At that time, Specialty Coatings posted $700 million in sales within James River, but that number wasn't big enough, Rogers says, to earn it the attention it wanted and needed from its parent.

"I think James River was like a lot of huge corporations," he reflects. "It had systems in place that tended to override the systems and needs of smaller business units. They forgot what to measure about our performance; they didn't really appreciate the inner workings of our business. They didn't measure what data were relevant to our performance. We became a different kind of operation for them. We had very close, customer-driven relationships and different technology from their other units, but this didn't seem to get the attention it deserved. . . .

"And I think this happens a lot," Rogers says, "because in large corporations senior management is getting pressure heavily related to corporate performance. They tend to focus upward instead of downward."

In this environment, Rogers says, joining AEA held enormous appeal. He and ten other top managers bought into the $350 million deal.

"After that, we had to start thinking like business owners," he recalls. "I mean, I went out and borrowed more money than I've ever borrowed in my life to buy stock. I had all my assets secured against that loan had it gone south."

Next, Rogers and the other new owners agreed to AEA's new incentive system. Bonuses were based not only on the company's earnings but also on the performance of cash flow and working capital. And at the same time, AEA installed a board of directors that Rogers refers to as "mentors."

"They monitored major strategic decisions, acquisitions, capital, expenditures of large amounts, compensation," he says. "Reg Jones [former CEO of GE] was my chairman, probably the most respected CEO in the last twenty or thirty years. And on the board, we had Frank Cary, former CEO of IBM, Phil Caldwell of Ford, Howard Clark of American Express, Bob Hatfield of Continental Can, Charlie Brown of ATT, and Irving Shapiro of Du Pont.

"We were able," Rogers recalls, "to quickly start addressing long-term needs, all through our seven operating businesses."

The process was cut short in 1993, however, when in the process of taking the company public, Specialty Coatings was sold to a British concern. Rogers says now that he wishes the sale had occurred later, when returns might have been even larger.

Still, in the eighteen months under AEA's stewardship, Specialty Coatings created an additional $150 million in value. Part of that was from debt pay-down, and fully half was from improved operations.

"AEA came in and did two things that got us focused on the fundamentals," Rogers says, referring to the LBO's two-pronged approach. "Big corporations don't do that for their business units," he adds, "but they should."

AT BAIN CAPITAL:
SAYING NO TO "PLAIN VANILLA SOLUTIONS"

On the wall of Mitt Romney's office at **Bain Capital** in Boston is a framed letter that begins, "Dear Mitt, I thank you, my wife thanks you, my children thank you, my parents thank you."

It is from a man, Romney says, "whom we made very rich." It could be from hundreds of people. In the past ten years, Bain Capital has bought, repaired, and sold about sixty companies, posting an annual rate of return of more than 50 percent during the same period that the stock market was averaging annual increases of 15 percent. In other words, an investor who put $10,000 into the fund in 1984 would have made almost $600,000 over the course of a decade, all for believing Romney's assertion that Bain Capital is dramatically different from other LBO firms in the way it does business. Specifically, that means investing significantly more time, people, and money than do its competitors in deciding what companies to buy, and then fixing them with bold-stroke solutions that substantially alter operations. Instead of limiting itself solely to "blocking and tackling issues" such as pricing and distribution, for instance, Bain Capital gets its companies to integrate backward or forward, or go from a hundred products to two. In one case, it fundamentally changed the way the elderly received cataract treatment, moving the surgery out of hospitals into more affordable doctor-run clinics.

"We aren't interested in companies where we can improve matters by a few percent with plain vanilla solutions," Romney says. "We only invest in businesses where we think we can create more value in them than virtually anyone else, or we don't invest. We go for the brass ring, or not at all."

It's a hard strategy to argue with, given Bain Capital's track record. The list of its success stories includes Staples, the office superstore featured in chapter 2, Specialty Retailers Inc., the southwestern department store chain, and Sports Authority, which was sold to Kmart. But Bain Capital isn't just in the business of retailing or start-ups. It most often buys mid-market firms or divisions of corporations, such as Accuride, the steel wheel maker; Masland, an automotive component manufacturer; and Vetco Gray, a Texas-based manufacturer of equipment for the oil industry. In Masland's three years under Bain ownership, the company's sales went from $220 million to more than $380 million, with a 125 percent increase in the bottom line.

"We've helped make a lot of people rich—not just investors but also managers and employees—and we've helped create 16,000 jobs," Romney says, "and I'm proud to say that." These are, in some sense, fighting words from the forty-seven-year-old senior partner who, in 1994, lost his bid to unseat Massachusetts senator Edward Kennedy. Many political observers attributed Romney's defeat to Bain Capital's success, noting that the opposition focused on his personal wealth and the complex financial workings of his venture capital company. In TV and print advertisements, many of Romney's experiences and accomplishments were used as evidence of his insularity from the dilemmas of ordinary working people. They noted that he grew up in the governor's mansion while his father ran the state of Michigan, that he holds business and law degrees from Harvard, that he lives in a wealthy Boston suburb with his wife, who does not work, and five sons. But perhaps what surprised and angered Romney the most were claims that Bain Capital had hurt the economy with layoffs and plant closings. The media also gave heavy coverage to a group of striking factory workers from a Bain Capital–owned company in Indiana who traveled to Massachusetts to lobby against Romney. Romney fought back, saying Bain Capital had, in fact, created thousands of jobs over the past ten years. "Perhaps I was naive," he notes now, "but I never thought my business track record would be held against me in the way it was. I thought it was one of my best assets."

After the campaign, Romney returned full time to Bain Capital. Officially, he has not ruled out another try for political office, but he now spends his time as he did before the campaign, overseeing the company's twelve partners and thirty staffers as they sort through and pick out deals. The first fund, which started at $36 million, was followed by two others, the most recent holding at about $350 million. Romney is in no hurry to spend it; that's part of the Bain Capital strategy.

"We *study* these businesses," he explains. "I mean, a lot of people in this business will read a prospectus from an investment bank and then call someone in the industry and say, 'I've got this shipping company I'm looking at; tell me about the shipping industry.'

"I couldn't care less about that kind of analysis," Romney goes on. "Because that's telling me the conventional wisdom, and the only way we're going to buy something is if we come up with something un-conventional. What we're looking for is something no one else has seen. Sure, we'll read the prospectus, but then we'll sit around the room and ask, what kind of things might we be able to do in the shipping industry that no one else is doing—no one?"

Bain Capital's involvement with Staples is an example of this phi-losophy at work. As we described in chapter 2, Staples was launched after Tom Stemberg, then a grocery chain executive, came up with the idea to offer low-cost office supplies to small businesses, which usually paid a premium for pens, paper, stationery, and the like be-cause they bought in such small volume. He approached several ven-ture capital firms with his concept, telling them his own research showed that a typical small business spent about $1,000 per em-ployee per year on office supplies. Almost every time, his request for backing was refused. "They told me no one spends one thousand dollars a year on office supplies, and beyond that, no one cares how much they spent," Stemberg recalls.

He got a different reception at Bain Capital. The firm took Stemberg's contention and checked it, interviewing more than 100 small businesses about their office supply costs and then examining their invoices for a more systematic analysis.

"They did an enormous, thorough amount of homework," Stemberg recalls. "They looked at the whole concept in a very funda-mental way. They started by looking at the demand function and asking, 'How big is the demand?' and went from there."

After Bain Capital made its investment, "they stayed right with us with a couple of very important suggestions," Stemberg adds. The most important was Romney's assertion that Staples should use di-rect marketing to reach its customers. "I didn't know what marketing was," Stemberg laughs, but today he points to Romney's insight as one of the reasons the company succeeded.

Another example of Bain Capital's strategy at work is the firm's experience with Accuride, the steel wheel maker. When Bain ac-quired it in 1986 for $190 million, Accuride was a division of Fire-stone Tire and Rubber. For years, it had shown good performance, with managers routinely hitting their budget numbers, and little else. But Bain Capital's partners, in analyzing the market, the competition, the production system, and the company's incentive system, saw potential for explosive growth and profitability.

"We had a real strong product, a real strong team, and the competition was relatively weak," Romney recalls. "And even though this company had a very large market share, 50 percent for the particular type of truck wheels it was making—and this was perhaps our biggest insight—our team said, 'We could get to substantially greater market share.'"

Bain Capital came to that conclusion after interviews with dozens of Accuride customers, discovering that rock-bottom price mattered more than any product feature or service the company could offer. Accuride's costs were inflated by the fact that its factories made so many types of steel wheels—nearly 100.

"Our analysis showed that if we could get a lot more volume from a much smaller number of wheel types, rationalize production between our two plants, and lengthen machine run lengths, then we could give our customers a lot lower price," Romney says. "We calculated what would happen to cost and price if we doubled volume, and that really opened some eyes. We could lower prices dramatically, lower costs, and retain very good margins."

At the same time, Bain Capital scrutinized Accuride's two plants, one in Canada and the other in the United States, and assessed that it could reengineer the process by which Accuride's wheels were made for even greater savings in costs. Soon after, a decision was made to buy the division and immediately execute the needed changes.

Bain Capital's next step was to overhaul Accuride's incentive system.

"Back when Accuride was part of Firestone, the management team had an incentive to average earnings, not to put too much in any one year," Romney recalls. "That's not unusual in a large corporation that has its compensation structure based on the total income of the company as opposed to the performance of that particular business unit. People say, 'Let's sandbag the numbers a bit this year to make sure we can always hit budget.'

"When we went in, we saw the opportunity to align incentives for the performance of Accuride alone. We had a strong team, so there was no need to change horses, just the way they were rewarded." Bain Capital did that by making the top Accuride managers owners of the company with grants of stock and stock options, as well as linking their cash bonuses to "brass ring" budget and sales goals.

The effect was swift. Within a year, Accuride became the sole steel wheel supplier to the leading four players in the truck industry. Sales and profits surged more than 50 percent in eighteen months.

Yet for all Bain Capital's success with Accuride, Romney doesn't fault Firestone for not enacting the same changes. "Public corporations have their constraints," he says, chief among them the fact that they must answer to stockholders who may not approve of risk taking. "Going after the big win and saying, 'Let's take a shot on that' isn't always in their best interest, and so they play a very conservative game, with goals that are believable, goals they know they can achieve." This phenomenon is compounded, Romney says, by managers who want to keep their jobs, not risk everything to look like heroes.

"If they do a good enough job, they're still going to be employed in two or three years; they'll even be promoted to the next division," Romney says. "And we understand that thinking, but we're not looking for that. We're looking for someone who says, 'I got a way here to make this thing really sing. If we take this big gamble, we can make this thing go through the roof.'"

In 1988, Bain Capital decided to sell Accuride. "We had done what we set out to do," Romney says. "And we decided we should no longer own the asset because we weren't adding value anymore. You should only be the steward of a company while you're making it better. Somebody else might have a new vision or synergies that could make it worth more to them than it is to you." That company was Phelps Dodge, a Phoenix-based company that wanted to own a business that was countercyclical to their copper business. When it bought Accuride, Bain Capital's $2.9-million equity investment yielded over $60 million.

Another recent example of Bain Capital's approach is ABRY Communications, a company started by Andrew Banks and Royce Yudkoff, both former consultants with Bain & Company. The two had worked extensively in the entertainment industry and knew that many independent TV stations across the country were unprofitable because of the excessive price of programming. (Prices had quadrupled after President Reagan deregulated the broadcasting industry in the mid-eighties, dramatically increasing the number of independent stations and thus the demand for programs.)

"Andrew and Royce saw that this could only mean one thing," Romney says. "It meant the programming industry was going to be beefing up to meet the burgeoning demand. It was going to assume that growth and high prices were going to continue forever, and it was going to spend gazillions of dollars producing new programming."

Banks and Yudkoff interviewed dozens of programming and television executives, which led them to believe that with supply increasing, programming prices would eventually collapse. Independent TV stations, back in the driver's seat and properly managed, could become very successful.

"That was the insight," Romney says, "that no one else had."

Banks and Yudkoff approached Bain Capital, which put up $10 million to buy five independent TV stations in midsize markets such as Kansas City, Baltimore, and Cincinnati. (They borrowed another $70 million of capital, and received $20 million more from two other investors.) They then negotiated new contracts with programming suppliers at prices one-third to one-quarter the historic rates.

The strategy was a home run. By 1993, audience share for the five ABRY stations had doubled and revenues had soared to $90 million, while cash flow, which was a combined $100,000 at the time of acquisition, grew to $20 million. The stations are now worth $200 million, making the deal's annual rate of return 44 percent.

"This wasn't our idea," Romney is quick to point out. "Royce and Andrew had the insight and they brought it to us. We took it and did our own analysis, and only then were we able to say, 'This looks like a very good prospect.'" ABRY offered what Bain Capital looks for—an unconventional spin on conventional wisdom and the chance for Bain Capital's own staff to scrutinize the numbers, the people, the assumptions, and the details. If it isn't original and doesn't involve a lot of analytical work, Romney says, a deal usually isn't worth the investment it requires.

But even in telling the Staples, Accuride, and ABRY success stories, Romney admits that Bain Capital's approach is not without its risks. He cites the failure of Handbag Holdings, which cost the company $4 million, and Mothercare stores, which lost Bain Capital $1 million, both in 1991. "There are always things that are out of our control," he says. "Rarely do we find riskless investments. We're willing to live with those risks."

One reason is that there is a safety valve at Bain Capital. Every deal is voted upon by all twelve partners, and a single vote can block it. "That's a big pair of brakes," Romney notes. In addition, Bain Capital partners are paid relatively low base salaries, but are compensated on the overall returns of the fund, encouraging teamwork instead of volume. Finally, each Bain Capital partner invests substantial personal money in each investment, "so each of us cares enormously whether the investment is going to be successful or not," Romney says. In turn, that means that after Bain Capital sinks its money in a prospect, sets new strategy in motion, and aligns management incentives, its partners watch, and watch closely.

"We do not get involved in day-to-day decisions," Romney reiterates, "that's management's job, not ours. But because we want major changes and major results, we stay close to the big picture.

"We don't let management lose sight of that—of the bold, really extraordinary strokes that have to be made. But because we've done the analysis, we know the risk is worth taking, that's the essence of what we do."

THE APPROACHES: NOT JUST A BUSINESS CONCEPT

This chapter has posed the question, Do the five management approaches belong only to global, publicly traded, diversified businesses with one CEO at the top? The answer seems to be that they don't.

The leaders in this chapter described how they add value in much the same way as the leaders in every other chapter. Dick Nesson of Partners HealthCare identifies "special people" and monitors their careers over the long term, just like many of the human assets managers in chapter 3. John McArthur of Harvard Business School likewise has transformed his institution by managing one individual at a time. And in the two examples of LBO "centers," Chip Baird of AEA Investors and Mitt Romney of Bain Capital speak, just as do the "traditional" strategic approach CEOs in chapter 2, of their rigorous and systematic focus on an acquisition's point of departure and its point of arrival.

The reason for these similarities is that the approaches that emerged in our interviews with business executives are not about *business* management but about *organizational* management. Every organization has its own version of the bottom line, of what constitutes extraordinary results—from an increasing stock price to a world-class faculty—but the *how* of delivering them can be understood within the same framework, the framework of the five approaches.

CONCLUSION

More Than Stories—Responses to the

Challenge of Maximum Leadership

Helmut Maucher demands the removal of a "cluttered" billboard advertising **Nestlé** products along a French highway. Haruo Naito deploys **Eisai** managers into hospitals and rest homes to witness life-and-death situations. Stephen Friedman assembles a team of "Doberman pinschers" to chase new ideas at **Goldman Sachs.** Stories like these—some of them dramatic, others amusing, a few poignant, many of them entertaining—are instructional for what they say about how some of the world's leading business executives tackle the challenge of maximum leadership in today's competitive marketplace.

Maximum leadership is, simply put, *the ability to consistently deliver extraordinary results.* But as the stories in this book illustrate, many effective and experienced top executives believe there is nothing simple in achieving that. Their many voices speak to how difficult and daunting it is to sustain competitive advantage, for as Charlotte Beers of **Ogilvy & Mather** says, "the CEO must do those things that simply no one else can do, make those decisions. And you come to them in dark and lonely hallways because they're never very fun. But making them is the difference between a manager and a leader."

But even in acknowledging this difficult exigency of the job, as many CEOs do, the voices in this book also begin to suggest that there *are* distinct and comprehensive ways to navigate effectively through complexity, competition, and rapid-fire change.

Those methods—sometimes used alone, sometimes overlapping, and other times used in combination—are the five approaches we have discerned.

THE STRATEGIC APPROACH—The province of chief executives who describe their main role as long-term thinking, strategy formulation, and marketplace analysis as a means to competitive advantage. The CEOs in this category told us they spend most of their time focusing on their organization's point of departure and point of arrival, and drawing the map between the two, designing the Holy Grail of the business, as it is put by Dr. Georg Obermeier, CEO of the German energy, chemicals, and metals conglomerate **VIAG.** "There is no use of the corporate center mixing too much with the daily business," he says, echoing a common chord sounded by the strategic executives we interviewed. "The business units are stuck in the daily routine. Their view is shorter, they are more tactically motivated. We see the scheme of things from the perspective of above that, and beyond that." Like the teams running **Staples, Dell Computer,** and **Coca-Cola,** Obermeier says he and his corporate staff devote the majority of their time and energy to assessing the competitive dynamics of the markets of today and tomorrow, and then using that analysis as the linchpin of their management activities and decisions.

THE HUMAN ASSETS APPROACH—The province of chief executives who describe their main role as proactively managing individuals and the relationships between them as a means to achieving competitive advantage. Human assets CEOs like Al Zeien of **Gillette** and Wayne Calloway of **PepsiCo** are the quintessential representatives of this category: they personally interview hundreds of job applicants, become deeply involved in career planning, and are in the loop on every high-level dismissal or demotion. At the heart of this approach is their belief that a certain code of behavior and set of values, inculcated in each employee, are the best ways to manage risk while encouraging creativity and flexibility. The approach's hallmark is often embodied by a top executive who seems to be everywhere, all the time. As John Devaney, chief executive and managing director of the United Kingdom's **Eastern Group,** says, "A big part of my job is coaching, helping people do more by themselves. The only way to do that is by talking with them. I'm rarely by myself." This sentiment is echoed by George Paul, chairman of both the United Kingdom's **Harrisons & Crosfield** and **Norwich Union,** the former in diversified businesses from chemicals to animal feeds, and the latter one of the nation's largest financial services companies. He, too, says he spends much of his most valuable time with employees. "I think the most important thing I do is try to ensure we have the best available people in the top jobs, and an absolutely key characteristic of that role is to spend very little time talking about yourself, but to get out there asking questions and then listening very closely to the answers. That's how you get to know people well."

THE EXPERTISE APPROACH—The province of chief executives who describe their main role as developing and disseminating critical expertise throughout the organization. Many of the CEOs in this category defined themselves as champions of a key competitive advantage, from processes, such as mining technologies at **Anglo American,** to information, such as insight into the customer's experience at the Japanese pharmaceutical company **Eisai.** These executives told us they put the expertise approach into action through a remarkably similar set of "pollination" programs, such as **Cooper Industries'** SWAT team of manufacturing experts that travel from division to division and **Motorola'**s quality specialists who grade each unit. Their stories were also similar on another count: the concern these CEOs express about the importance of keeping their expertise both fresh and proprietary.

THE BOX APPROACH—The province of chief executives who describe their main role as designing and implementing an explicit control system—financial, cultural, or both. All companies have boxes, but the CEOs who fell into this category were those who said they focused on controls as their primary way to manage toward success. At the international insurance and financial services giant **Fortis AG,** for example, chairman Maurice Lippens says he believes the previous three approaches largely belong to the business units, where they can be applied with the knowledge of individual markets and employees. The corporate center's role, he asserts, is to apply "the pressure of orthodoxy," a term which aptly describes the box at its essence. Fortis uses hundreds of auditors and frequent internal benchmarking between units to oversee the results of its many businesses, not so much to make sure their strategies are correct, Lippens says, but "to assure they are being carried out in a way that shows they are in control of the situation."

THE CHANGE-AGENT APPROACH—The province of chief executives who describe their main role as creating systems, policies, and cultures that embrace and encourage continuous transformation. The CEOs and presidents we spoke with often said their approach was a reaction to box management gone wrong, boxes built too small for the exigencies of the marketplace or simply that no longer work. Such was the case at **Mitsubishi Corp.,** one of the world's largest trading companies. For years, says president Minoru Makihara, Mitsubishi flourished like a flower in a greenhouse, nurtured by government regulations that protected Japanese industry. When the economic bubble burst in 1990, Mitsubishi had to face the elements of the outside world, and to do so successfully, the center had to create an organization that responded quickly and effectively to customers and competitors. That involved transforming the company's culture, its hiring and promotion practices, its views about expertise, its very organizational structure. "Our first and main goal is to make everyone aware of the need for change," Makihara says, speaking for many change-agent chief executives. "And although it may bring a lot of pain, if we don't change, our company isn't going anywhere."

■ ■ ■

Like many of the executives we interviewed, Makihara didn't adhere solely to the change-agent approach. (He also spoke of his role as a strategist.) But he did, like so many others, say his role was primarily focused on one approach—*centered* on it. Virtually every CEO we spoke with said he or she applied all of the approaches in some measure, but the examples in this book strongly suggest that the most senior executives select the one best suited for their situation and focus intently upon it. Their goal, many said, is to add extraordinary value, to transcend the seemingly inescapable demands that dog nearly every top executive: the administrative tasks, tax and legal matters, luncheons with stock and bond analysts. These responsibilities cannot be ignored, the CEOs agreed, but they can't be allowed to take over your schedule. "And it's hard not to" let them, as Goldman Sachs's Stephen Friedman commented.

Perhaps Sir Christopher Hogg, chairman of **Courtaulds** and **Reuters Holdings** and considered one of the deans of British business, spoke of this dilemma best when he said, "Organizations are like an internal combustion engine. They are 30 percent efficient and 70 percent of their time is wasted. It seems to happen naturally.

"The more I go on," Hogg added, "the more I think that it is fantastically demanding to be effective at the center. I mean, anyone can be all-singing and all-dancing, and plenty of people can do one or two things well, but to do more well than badly over a long period of time is very, very difficult because it requires so much focus and energy and self-restraint, too."

THE FIVE APPROACHES, FROM PRACTICE TO THEORY

The purpose of this book is not to offer a silver bullet for business success, because we don't believe that one exists. Instead, it is to introduce a new way of talking and thinking about that much-coveted goal, based on the voices and insights of those ultimately held responsible for it: the CEOs themselves.

Does the "right" approach lead to organizational effectiveness—to success? Many of the stories in this book seem to suggest so, but it is also important to recognize that the reflections are the view from the top of the organization. They are the opinions in most cases of one senior manager at each corporation about how and why the organization functions as it does. More work needs to be done to relate these opinions to the organization's *understanding* of the CEO's approach, and beyond that, to financial results. We are committed to more study on this topic of management approach and its link to financial and operational outcomes, and we will share this knowledge as it develops. At the same time, we believe the stories in these pages are valuable on their own because they remove some of the mystery of what goes on in the inner sanctum of business. The stories take us from the practice to the theory of maximum leadership, a theory that can begin to be applied and tested in any organization.

Every day, senior managers in every kind of business and every country face this leadership challenge. Some are already using one or more of the approaches. Others are at the opposite pole: they are starting anew, deciding which kind of path they will forge in the hard journey to results.

One such chief executive is Martin Taylor, who recently took over as chief executive at **Barclays,** one of the leading banks in the United Kingdom, with upward of $262 billion in assets and more than 65,000 employees.

Taylor, boyish-looking and soft-spoken at age forty-two, holds a degree in Chinese from Oxford, and spent four years as a columnist with the *Financial Times* of London. After switching to industry, at thirty-eight he was running Courtaulds Textiles, a major multi-national fabric manufacturer. He is credited with overhauling the structure and culture at Courtaulds Textiles, much to the benefit of the company and its stockholders. It was a process, he has said, akin to "teaching an elephant to dance ballet."

In 1994, Barclays asked Taylor to try the same at the conservative bank, or at least to lead it into the twenty-first century as a both strong and nimble competitor. With no banking experience, Taylor himself was surprised by the job offer, but intrigued by the fact that Barclays was, as he says, "at a crossroads."

Taylor arrived at Barclays recognizing that its situation was radically different from the one he had managed at Courtaulds Textiles. His response would have to be as well.

"The temptation is not to change, of course," Taylor notes. "I mean, the temptation is to keep on doing what had been done here, or to do what other banks are doing at the moment. But the herd instinct is paralyzing, and I don't want any part of it."

This intention—to pick a new, appropriate, and unique course for Barclays—defines Taylor's challenge. It is a challenge to focus both on *what* needs to be accomplished and *how* to get it done. In analyzing these issues, Taylor may begin with several basic questions often asked by CEOs:

1. What are the most serious risks faced by the company on a regular basis, and are there policies, procedures, and people in place to manage those risks?
2. What are the current sources of the company's success—in

other words, what drives current profitability and how sustainable is current performance?

3. What are the greatest opportunities for growth and increased profitability?
4. What are my competitors doing, and how does that affect me?
5. What is the company's full potential—that is, what are the company's outermost levels of growth, efficiency, creativity, and market share?
6. How will the company achieve this full potential?

As Martin Taylor sorts through these questions, his challenge is to make sure what has to be done is clear to employees at every level of the organization, that its implementation is consistent throughout the corporation, and that commitment is being created around it. How these things happen may lead him to choose an approach, be it the change-agent approach as selected by Nobby Clark at **National Australia Bank,** the traditional box we saw at **BankAmerica** and **HSBC Group,** or the strategic approach championed by Hilmar Kopper at **Deutsche Bank.** In a recent interview, Taylor said he was leaning toward transforming his organization through the human assets approach, noting, "I don't build boxes; I want to change the way people think about things. But Barclays is an enormous machine. You can't take it head on. You have to go around the back, get inside, and persuade people to change themselves."

Whatever his ultimate decision, it is at this juncture that Martin Taylor can draw upon the interviews in this book, and in particular the following six observations that recurred frequently, across industries, cultures, national borders, and even the approaches themselves:

An approach appears to be most effective only if it is correctly matched to the business situation.

By dint of personality, some CEOs seem drawn to certain approaches. Herb Kelleher, CEO of **Southwest Airlines,** is one example. His relaxed, humorous, down-home character seems to make him a natural human assets manager. Stephen Friedman of **Goldman Sachs** is another. Assertive and demanding, he would likely gravitate toward championing change at any organization.

Both cases, it seems to us, are fortunate but coincidental dovetailings of personality and approach. More often, CEOs must—and do—transcend their personal inclinations to match the approach they use to the business context—that is, the company's marketplace dynamics and internal capabilities. "There's not a God-given role for the corporate center," says Sir Geoffrey Mulcahy, chief executive of the British retailer **Kingfisher,** owner of the Woolworth and B&Q chains. The role of the CEO, he notes, "varies by company to company, and even within one company can change and evolve over time given the circumstances." Dana Mead, CEO of **Tenneco,** for instance, says he had to reinvent himself as a change agent after years of managing through the human assets approach at International Paper.

Stories like his suggest that for any of the approaches to work as the CEOs intend them, they must be a carefully considered response, not a gut reaction. They must spring from a thorough and systematic assessment of the business situation and all it entails—not just for today but for five and ten years from now. And that information must then drive the decision about which approach, given the behaviors and outcomes it delivers, makes the most sense.

Installing an approach requires explicit commitment and action from the very top of the organization.

The case studies in this book indicate that it is not enough for a CEO to say, "I am devoting myself to being an agent of radical change." He must say it over and over, to as many people as will hear it, and then he himself must consistently "walk the talk," through decisions and deeds. Dozens of executives we interviewed noted that managing an effective organization—focused on results and coordinated in implementation—means being explicit about what you do all day and why you do it. In that way, every action, from hiring to firing to product-line decisions, is a message to the company about the center's priorities, values, and goals—and its commitment to them.

Even if the center itself is committed to an approach in action and deed, it needs the organization's gut-level approval and cooperation to make it happen.

Many CEOs noted that part of being a CEO is that employees tend to automatically nod at every directive. They appear to agree, they say they agree, but for real forward motion to occur, they have to *feel* that they do. Some of this happens when the center demonstrates its own commitment, but it also happens through consensus building and dialogue.

One executive who spoke to this point was Ken Chenault, vice chairman of **American Express,** who asserted that the connection between the center and the front lines, in fact, must be "a very personal one."

"I have found it very important to have meetings at different levels throughout the company, both scheduled and informal, where I can talk to employees face to face," Chenault says of Corporate's change campaign to reinvent American Express as a company intensely focused on the customer and on its brand. "You really need to have a two-way dialogue to get the message across. If employees just hear you give a speech, they may be inspired for the moment, but at the end of the day, they might wonder, 'Is this just a speech?' But if they can experience a dialogue and see how you think and act with respect to the customer's needs, they're going to take more ownership."

Sometimes it takes two steps, or three, to get to where you want to be.

The stories of a significant number of CEOs we interviewed seemed to indicate that an executive sometimes has to travel through one approach to reach another. In 1990, Naohiko Kumagai was appointed president of the enormous trading company **Mitsui** and quickly determined that, for strategic reasons, people were its most valuable asset. In the past, the company had grown to be governed as a box, and as a result many of its managers needed to be remotivated and their skill base broadened. Still, as Kumagai told us, he was determined to manage the company with the human assets approach. He knew, however, it couldn't be done, at least not immediately. First he had to create a change organization, and with it in place, he could move toward his desired objective. He has spent the last five years doing that, and predicts that by 1998 he will be able to manage Mitsui the way he believes is best. In other words, it appears some approaches are at such cross-purposes they cannot be connected by a straight line. And it also appears that change—that is, a company managed by a change agent—is often the passage between them.

Some approaches seem to be harder than others.

A revealing comment came up in several of our interviews. About a dozen CEOs said they actually envied the firefighters, since their mandate was so urgent they could take drastic action without the usual process and resistance. It seemed odd at first, since we had talked to these firefighters—the turnaround CEOs featured in chapter 8—and heard them speak about the pain of their actions, the layoffs, the selling of assets, the closing of plants. But they all described a certain freedom in their movement. "Did anyone object?" we asked Linn Macdonald, CEO of **Noranda Forest Inc.,** about his decision to sell off the company's crown jewel, MacMillan Bloedel. "No," he replied simply, "they knew the alternatives all too well."

Making drastic changes in less drastic situations is more complex, and often engenders more resistance. Yet it seems clear from our interviews that running a company as its chief strategist, for instance, engenders less resistance than running it as a change agent. (Many CEOs noted that organizations seem to have a natural and immediate negative reaction to an executive who announces he is going to shake up the status quo.) The examples in this book also suggest that managing through expertise requires a CEO to be on constant alert to threats to the company's proprietary knowledge about products or processes. Perhaps no approach is as physically daunting as the human assets approach for the sheer legwork it requires, and yet our interviews indicate that the travel and personal contacts this approach demands are balanced by the pleasure—the "fun"—many of its proponents describe as part of the job.

In other words, some approaches do seem to be harder to implement than others. This shouldn't be an excuse for inaction—rather it's the stimulus to plan, prepare, and persevere. It is as Allen Sheppard of **GrandMet** noted at the outset of this book: the CEO's ultimate responsibility, no matter what approach he or she uses, is to "add value, or get out of the way for someone who will."

And, finally, putting an effective approach into place takes time and the self-knowledge that a CEO can achieve only as much as his organization will allow him.

Many of the executives in this book, and many others we interviewed, spoke of how much time and energy it takes to create a coherent and comprehensive approach to management. Their organizations, they said, are like orchestras, with dozens of instruments to tune—the instruments being promotion policies, for instance, or the way people are trained, or even the entire corporate culture. Sometimes getting through the process of installing an approach can take years.

By the same token, many CEOs also said the hardest thing they have to do every day is accept that they cannot do everything every day. A CEO, despite his or her vaunted position, has too many constituents and too many constraints to act as a free agent. The organization "owns" them and CEOs are most effective when they recognize and accept that reality.

One executive who spoke to this point was Brian Loton, chairman of **Broken Hill Proprietary,** Australia's largest company, with major operations in mining, petroleum, and steel. "We want to make every one of our businesses successful, and we try very hard to do that," he said.

But, he added, "a CEO is only effective when he or she works well within what is possible. Now you can want the moon and the stars and the sun, but it's not going to happen. An effective chief executive knows what his board will go along with, knows his corporation's capabilities, knows the businesses' abilities, has that feel for where more can be achieved, where less can be achieved. I don't think you can ever get away from the gifted, talented CEO who gets more out of the business in whatever way, versus the pedestrian CEO who with all the best systems in the world can't make it work."

AT THE END OF THE DAY, THE LEADERSHIP CHALLENGE IS TO ADD VALUE

Six questions, six observations, and perhaps dozens of other factors to consider, even for a single company like Barclays—such is the nature of the "infinite job" at the top of an organization. But in facing these issues, chief executives such as Martin Taylor are accepting the challenge of what their position demands: results.

We concluded many of our interviews with the question, "What do you like best about your job as CEO?" Some chief executives said they most enjoyed meeting new employees, others said they loved the days they got to spend on the factory floor or in far-flung branch offices, and one even spoke (with a broad smile) about the pleasure of "green-lighting" a plan that he knew would put the brakes on a perennial competitor. But almost invariably, the chief executives answered our query with some mixed emotions. "Greatest job in the world," said one executive who spoke for many, "but the hardest thing I've done, and it's getting harder."

This is a comment, perhaps, to which all working people today can relate. As companies grow larger, markets go more global (and simultaneously demand more local knowledge and commitment), technologies advance at a dizzying rate, and customers expect more, faster, and better, competition gets ever more fierce. Success today requires intelligence and speed, plus human, operational, and financial capabilities. The burden for success falls on every member of an organization, but at the end of the day, it falls on the man or woman at the top.

The voices in this book are varied, and at times contradictory, but they all address this complex struggle, day to day, of meeting the objective: to consistently deliver extraordinary results.

To do any less is to fail the challenge of maximum leadership.

INDEX